英語リーディングの王道

The Royal Road to
Current English Reading

Jim Knudsen 著
日本大学准教授 小中秀彦 解説

南雲堂

はしがき

　「どうしたら英語のリーディング力が伸びますか？」という質問を学生からよくされます。「多読だ！」と即答される先生方も数多くいます。もちろん多読は必要ですが，私は「動詞を中心とした構文を意識すると，英語のリーディング力が飛躍的に伸びるよ」と答えることにしています。英語はきわめて構造的な言語です。文の構造が意味に大きく影響するのです。例えば，give という基本動詞ですが，< give+A >「A を与える」という目的語が 1 つだけの構文だけを意識して英文を読んでいると，自分で和訳したのに何を言っているかわからない難解な(?)日本文を生み出すことになりかねません。実際に英文をたくさん読んでいると，< give+A+B >「A に B を与える」という目的語が 2 つ並ぶ構文の方によく出会います。本書に登場する give the world what it most urgently needs right now（今すぐ最も差し迫って必要なものを世界に与える）は，the world が A，what it most urgently needs right now が B になる < give+A+B > の構文です。このように動詞の後ろにどんな形がくるかを予想しながら英文を読むことができれば，英語のリーディング力は必ず伸びます。

　動詞中心の構文を意識することとともに，長い呼吸で英文を読むクセをつけることも大切です。先ほどの < give+A+B > の例も 10 語前後先を読まなければ，目的語の < A+B > が見えてきませんでしたよね。もう 1 つ本書から例を挙げると，He underscored the importance of not letting nations that are emerging from conflict relapse into bloodshed.（彼は紛争から抜け出しかけている国々を流血にまた逆戻りさせないことの重要性を強調した）にある < let+A+ 動詞の原形 > の「動詞の原形」は relapse（逆戻りする）で，関係代名詞 that から始まる節 that are emerging from conflict が A を修飾しているということがわかるには 10 語前後まで一気に先を読まなければなりません。< let+A+ 動詞の原形 > という構文を知っていても，実際の英文では，A のすぐ後ろに「動詞の原形」がきているとは限らないのです。このように実際の英文では，目的語にいろいろな修飾語句がつき長くなったり，主語と動詞が離れていたりすることが多いのです。ですから，動詞の先を予測しながら長い呼吸で読むように心がけましょう。そうすれば，少しずつ先に目が届き，読解の正確さとともにリーディング速度も大幅に向上します。

　もう 1 つ厄介なのが句動詞です。句動詞は動詞が副詞や前置詞などと結合して，1 つの動詞の働きをするものです。die out のように「死ぬ＋完全に」から「絶滅する」と動詞からすぐに推測できる句動詞はあまり問題ありませんが，get by（なんとか暮らしていく）のように推測が難しい句動詞はきちんと自分のものにしておかなくてはなりません。

　このように動詞中心の構文や句動詞を意識して，長い呼吸で英文を読むことを心がければ，リーディングの正確さやスピードがぐんと上がるのです。

　本書には，語彙問題，イディオム問題，内容把握問題，リスニング問題などバラエティーに富んだ練習問題がついており，英語力を総合的に伸ばす手助けができるように編集されています。本書が皆さんのリーディング力を中心とした英語力を飛躍的に伸ばすきっかけとなれば幸いです。皆さんのご健闘を心よりお祈りいたします。

　最後になりましたが，編集・出版にあたり，いろいろお世話になった南雲堂・編集部の加藤敦氏に深く感謝いたします。

小中 秀彦

Contents

はしがき		3
Lesson 1	What the World Needs Now	6
Lesson 2	The Horns of a Dilemma	16
Lesson 3	Of Nukes and Minefields	26
Lesson 4	Languages Lost and Found	36
Lesson 5	It's About Time	46
Lesson 6	Where Would We Be Without It?	56
Lesson 7	Virtually Better	66
Lesson 8	It's Never Too Late	76
Lesson 9	Global Concepts 1: People	86
Lesson 10	Global Concepts 2: Trends	96
Lesson 11	Psychology	106
Lesson 12	The Environment	114
Lesson 13	History	122
Lesson 14	Space	130
Lesson 15	Education	138
Vocabulary		146
Verbal Constructions and Phrases		153

The Royal Road
to Current English Reading

英語リーディングの王道

Lesson 1
What the World Needs Now

● ● ● **GETTING READY TO READ** ● ● ●

Key Concepts:

Match these key words or phrases from Today's Reading with the definitions/explanations below. Write the letters of the definitions on the lines.

1. ___ poverty
2. ___ gender equality
3. ___ child mortality rate
4. ___ create a sustainable environment
5. ___ bankruptcy
6. ___ tribal and civil war
7. ___ aid
8. ___ antiretroviral treatment

a. men and women having the same rights and opportunities
b. serious economic or financial difficulty
c. violence within a country between different ethnic groups
d. gifts of money or loans from rich countries to poor countries
e. protect and preserve the natural world
f. a combination of drugs for AIDS patients
g. the percentage of children who die very young
h. the state of being very poor

Active Reading:

As you read through Today's Reading, look for answers to these questions. Mark the sentences in the reading where the answers are found.

1. In the year 2000, the United Nations set some goals for the world. What was the general aim or purpose of the goals?
2. What did some people think about these goals?
3. Why did they think that way, especially about Africa?
4. Who is Jeffrey Sachs and what does he say about the situation today?
5. What did a UN conference held in 2010 conclude?

Words in Context:

Choose the word or phrase that is closest in meaning to the underlined word in each sentence fragment below.

1. ... the target date for <u>achieving</u> these goals ...
   (A) keeping   (B) reaching   (C) deciding

2. ... to <u>ameliorate</u> social and economic conditions ...
   (A) make worse   (B) make better   (C) make happen

3. <u>Specifically</u>, the goals included ...
   (A) In fact   (B) In detail   (C) Indeed

4. ... and <u>promote</u> gender equality ...
   (A) demand   (B) request   (C) foster

5. <u>Initially</u>, these goals ...
   (A) At last   (B) At most   (C) At first

6. ... and overly <u>optimistic</u> ...
   (A) hopeful   (B) foolish   (C) dangerous

7. ... the situation has changed <u>dramatically</u> ...
   (A) very little   (B) very much   (C) very often

8. ... <u>cynicism</u> has been replaced by hope ...
   (A) anger   (B) pride   (C) doubt

9. ... poverty and hunger are <u>declining</u> ...
   (A) improving   (B) going down   (C) increasing

10. Wider <u>distribution</u> of bed nets ...
    (A) production in factories
    (B) making available or supplying
    (C) understanding

11. ... to <u>assess</u> how much progress ...
    (A) criticize   (B) judge   (C) report

12. ... what it most <u>urgently</u> needs right now ...
    (A) essentially   (B) positively   (C) calmly

Lesson 1   What the World Needs Now   7

● ● ● TODAY'S READING ● ● ●

Read this essay carefully. Then do the exercises that follow.   2

Back in 2000, the United Nations (UN) held a special summit at its headquarters in New York City. Some 192 nations and 23 international organizations took part. The purpose of the conference was to set up what the UN called the Millennium Development
5 Goals, or MDGs for short. The summit's participants named 2015 as the target date for achieving these goals.

Generally, the MDGs aimed to ameliorate social and economic conditions in the world's poorest countries. Specifically, the goals included:

10   Get rid of poverty and extreme hunger;
       Give children everywhere at least a primary-school education;
       Empower women and promote gender equality;
       Reduce the child mortality rate;
       Fight AIDS, malaria, and other diseases;
15   Create a sustainable environment.

Initially, these goals were met with cynicism. Many critics looked upon them as unrealistic and overly optimistic—impossible, in fact. After all, the situation at the time, particularly in Africa, seemed hopeless. Most African countries were on the brink of bankruptcy.
20 Most Africans got by on less than one dollar a day. AIDS, malaria, tuberculosis, and measles were out of control. Tribal and civil wars were being fought in a dozen places.

But today the situation has changed dramatically, says Jeffrey Sachs. Sachs is the director of the Earth Institute of Columbia
25 University and a long-time fighter in the war against world poverty. Sachs believes that now, cynicism has been replaced by hope. Thanks to stepped-up efforts by African governments and increased aid from rich countries, real progress has been made, he says. Economic

conditions are improving throughout the continent. Extreme poverty and hunger are declining. AIDS is in decline, too, because millions of Africans are receiving antiretroviral treatment. And wider distribution of bed nets has cut deaths from malaria "decisively."

In September 2010, a follow-up summit was held at the UN. This time, the purpose was to assess how much progress had been made towards realizing these goals. Although there is still a long way to go, the summit concluded, the Millennium Development Goals are now "within reach." And they still represent, says Jeffrey Sachs, our most "realistic path" to giving the world what it most urgently needs right now.

● ● ● EXERCISES 1: COMPREHENSION ● ● ●

Reading for Information:
Fill in the blank(s) in each sentence.

1. The target date for reaching the MDGs was set for _____ years in the future.

2. One MDG is to make sure people have enough _____ to eat.

3. The UN says that all children should receive at least _____ years of education.

4. The _____ summit aimed to give _____ the same rights and opportunities as _____.

5. Another MDG was to keep the natural _____ from becoming _____.

6. In 2000, most _____ had to live on _____ dollars a year.

7. In addition to teaching at _____ University, Jeffrey Sachs tries to help the world's _____ people.

8. African _____ have been taking steps to solve their countries' problems.

9. AIDS is in decline thanks to _____ drugs.

10. The second UN summit was held _____ years after the first.

Listening for Ideas:

 3

Listen and fill in the blanks in each sentence. Then circle T if the sentence is true, F if it is false.

1. T F One _____ of the 2000 _____ was to reduce childhood _____.

2. T F In 2000, _____ and _____ conditions in Africa seemed _____.

3. T F _____ Sachs says that civil _____ in Africa are no longer being _____.

4. T F Money given to Africa by rich _____ has done _____ to _____ the _____ there.

5. T F The _____ summit _____ that most MDGs had already been _____.

6. T F Sachs seems to believe that the best _____ to solve the world's most _____ problems is to increase our _____ to achieve the MDGs.

EXERCISES 2: COMPOSITION

Making Questions:

4

Write the question you would need to ask to get each answer below. Use the hints. Listen to check your questions.

1. Question: Where were _____ ?
   Answer: In New York City.

2. Question: How did _____ ?
   Answer: As overly optimistic and unrealistic.

3. Question: _____ replaced with?
   Answer: With hope.

4. Question: How have _____ ?
   Answer: Through wider distribution of bed nets and medicines.

Writing with Idioms:

5

Rewrite each sentence below by substituting one of these phrases for the underlined part. Make the necessary changes. Listen to check your answers.

on the brink of   get rid of   look upon   thanks to

1. I wish I could <u>recover from</u> this stubborn cold.

   _____

2. <u>With</u> your advice, I was able to choose the best career for me.

   _____

12

3. She <u>is seen</u> by many as a possible candidate for president.

   _____

4. Many species are <u>about to</u> die out.

   _____

Word Forms:

Fill in the blank in each sentence with the correct form of the word on the left.

1. *cynicism*   The critic is known for his _____ worldview.

2. *achieve*   The award recognizes his many great _____.

3. *promote*   My boss said I will get a _____ next year.

4. *distribution*   Please _____ these test papers to the class.

5. *specifically*   Do you have a _____ restaurant in mind?

6. *assess*   I disagree with your _____ of the movie.

7. *optimistic*   _____ speaking, economic recovery will take at least a year.

8. *urgently*   I cannot overemphasize the _____ of the situation.

● ● ● EXERCISES 3: CHALLENGE ● ● ●

Using Key Concepts:

Fill in the blanks in each sentence B below so that it is similar in meaning to sentence A. Use the Key Concepts on page 6.

1. A: Today, many companies are failing.
   B: Today, many companies are filing for _____.

2. A: We need to keep the natural world healthy.
   B: We need to _____.

3. A: The new law gives men and women the same rights.
   B: The new law guarantees _____.

4. A: Better nutrition means fewer children are dying.
   B: Better nutrition has reduced the _____.

Vocabulary Expansion:

Look at these dictionary definitions of "poor." Then read the sentences that follow. Decide what "poor" means in each sentence. Write the numbers of the definitions on the lines.

1. (adj.) having little or no money or possessions
2. (adj.) lacking in a specific resource or quality
3. (adj.) not excellent; inferior
4. (adj.) lacking in value; not good enough
5. (adj.) lacking in quantity or number
6. (adj.) deserving pity; pitiable
7. (n.) people with little or no money or possessions

a. _____ Because of poor attendance, the course was cancelled.
b. _____ She quit the job because of the poor wages.
c. _____ The poor man lost his entire family in the accident.
d. _____ Children from poor families don't do as well in school.
e. _____ The new program aims to help the city's poor.
f. _____ Poor in oil, Japan has to import its supply from abroad.
g. _____ The actress gave a poor, uninspired performance.

Listening Activity: 6

Listen to the short talk about malaria. Then read the sentences below. Circle T if the sentence is true, F if it is false.

1. T F   Malaria is caused by the bite of a monkey.

2. T F   Malaria means "bad luck" in Latin.

3. T F   Malaria occurs mostly in hot, humid places.

4. T F   Malaria is especially dangerous for children.

5. T F   One symptom of malaria is severe hunger.

6. T F   All types of malaria are equally serious.

7. T F   Though treatable, malaria still kills many people.

Lesson 2
The Horns of a Dilemma

● ● ● **GETTING READY TO READ** ● ● ●

Key Concepts:

Match these key words or phrases from Today's Reading with the definitions/ explanations below. Write the letters of the definitions on the lines.

1. ___ mammal
2. ___ endangered species
3. ___ international ban
4. ___ poaching
5. ___ law enforcement official
6. ___ extinction
7. ___ GPS transmitter
8. ___ tranquilizer dart
9. ___ the dodo

a. the hunting of animals or taking of crops that is against the law
b. a signal-sending, global-positioning device placed on objects so that the objects can be followed or found
c. a tiny arrow used to shoot nerve-calming drugs into an animal so that the animal can be examined or treated
d. plants or animals that may soon disappear from the earth
e. making something illegal [against the law] all over the world
f. a warm-blooded vertebrate [animal with a backbone]
g. an Australian bird hunted out of existence in the 17th century
h. a person hired to make sure laws are obeyed; policeman
i. dying out; total disappearance from the earth

Active Reading:

As you read through Today's Reading, look for answers to these questions. Mark the sentences in the reading where the answers are found.

1. What are the horns of the rhinoceros used for in Asia?
2. What happened after rhinoceros hunting was made illegal around the world?
3. Who "poaches" rhinos today?
4. What is the WWF and how is it trying to save rhinos?
5. How does a unique new save-the-rhino program work?

Words in Context:

Choose the word or phrase that is closest in meaning to the underlined word in each sentence fragment below.

1. ... these <u>massive</u> African animals ...
   (A) ugly   (B) huge   (C) dangerous

2. ... tradition has <u>coveted</u> the horns ...
   (A) used   (B) desired   (C) captured

3. ... medical and sexual <u>ailments</u> ...
   (A) treatments   (B) mysteries   (C) illnesses

4. ... are <u>carved</u> to make various decorative items ...
   (A) sewn with a needle
   (B) painted with a brush
   (C) shaped with a knife

5. But <u>predictably</u>, this gave rise to ...
   (A) normally   (B) as expected   (C) in time

6. ... where thousands of rhinos once <u>roamed</u>, only ...
   (A) wandered   (B) died   (C) fed

7. ... will <u>slaughter</u> a rhino ...
   (A) hunt   (B) capture   (C) kill

8. ... that's how <u>lucrative</u> the business is ...
   (A) profitable   (B) illegal   (C) evil

9. ... have become increasingly <u>aggressive</u> ...
   (A) mean   (B) bold   (C) skillful

10. ... has <u>embarked</u> on an aggressive campaign ...
    (A) invented   (B) endeavored   (C) started

11. ... less <u>vulnerable</u> to poaching ...
    (A) weak   (B) valuable   (C) capable

12. ... the <u>scheme</u> is expensive ...
    (A) product   (B) program   (C) tool

● ● ● TODAY'S READING ● ● ●

Read this essay carefully. Then do the exercises that follow.   7

With its thick, wrinkled skin and horned snout, the rhinoceros has to be the ugliest of mammals. But that doesn't mean these massive African beasts aren't highly prized. For centuries, Asian tradition has coveted the horns of the "rhino," believing they can heal a variety
5 of medical and sexual ailments. In many other cultures, the horns are carved to make various decorative items such as Middle Eastern dagger handles. And for nearly two centuries, so-called big-game hunters, rich Europeans and Americans on safaris, have been killing rhinos for the sport of it, later hanging their stuffed "trophies" on
10 the walls of their dens. As a result, all five remaining rhino species are now endangered.

By 1976, the rhino's situation had become so dire that an international ban was placed on rhino hunting and the trading of rhino parts. But predictably, this gave rise to widespread illegal
15 hunting, or poaching. Over the next 20 to 30 years, 90% of Africa's rhinoceros population was wiped out. In 2010, rhino poaching reached an all-time high. As a case in point, in Zimbabwe, where thousands of rhinos once roamed in the wild, only 700 remain.

Rhino horns can fetch up to $20,000 per kilogram, surpassing
20 the price of gold. Poachers will slaughter a rhino to get only an inch or two of horn; that's how lucrative the business is. In the old days, poachers were mainly poor locals trying to earn a living. But according to the World Wildlife Fund (WWF), rhino poaching today is highly organized. Gangs of professional poachers, armed with
25 powerful rifles, have become increasingly aggressive and will "shoot on sight" anyone who tries to get in their way and prevent them from getting what they want. Gunfights between poachers and law enforcement officials are frequent, with deaths reported on both sides. It's the stuff movies are made of.

30 Now, to save the rhino from extinction, Yahoo News reports that

18

the WWF has embarked on an aggressive campaign of its own. Game officials are fitting rhinos with GPS transmitters to make it easier to keep track of them. Foot soldiers, themselves heavily armed, are on duty 24 hours a day, seven days a week, patrolling for poachers. And in a unique new program, wildlife "police" are finding rhinos, shooting them with tranquilizer darts from helicopters and then, when the animal is down, removing its horns with chainsaws. This may sound extreme, but experts say it is wholly necessary: the painless process makes the animal less "tempting" and vulnerable to poaching—"disfigured, but alive," as one WWF official put it. Although the scheme is expensive and time-consuming, it is helping to keep the rhino from going the way of the dodo.

● ● ● EXERCISES 1: COMPREHENSION ● ● ●

Reading for Information:

Briefly answer each question below. Write your answers on the lines.

1. What is another word for a rhino's nose? _____

2. What do some Middle Easterners make with rhino horns? _____

3. Where do big-game hunters like to hang the heads of the rhinos they have killed? _____

4. How many of the five rhino species are now endangered? _____

5. In what year were rhino hunting and parts trading made illegal? _____

6. In what year were a record number of rhinos poached? _____

7. Which is often more valuable, rhino horn or gold? _____

8. How much rhino horn will poachers kill a rhino for? _____

9. What is making it easier to track rhinos these days? _____

10. Where are the tranquilizer darts shot from? _____

11. How do wildlife "police" remove the rhino horns? _____

12. Does the process of removing the horns hurt the animals? _____

13. How does one official describe a rhino that has had its horns removed? _____

Listening for Ideas: 8

Listen to the "or" questions. Then complete the answers below.

1. They have been used for _____.

2. They have killed them _____.

3. It made _____.

4. They are _____.

5. _____ have been killed as well.

6. They _____.

7. They say _____.

8. It costs _____.

EXERCISES 2: COMPOSITION

Making Questions:

9

Write the question you would need to ask to get each answer below. Use the hints. Listen to check your questions.

1. Question: How long _____?
   Answer: For nearly two centuries.

2. Question: What happened _____?
   Answer: Some 90% of Africa's rhino population was killed off.

3. Question: How much _____?
   Answer: Up to $20,000 per kilogram.

4. Question: _____, seven days a week?
   Answer: They patrol for poachers.

Writing with Idioms:

10

Rewrite each sentence below by substituting one of these phrases for the underlined part. Make the necessary changes. Listen to check your answers.

> give rise to   a case in point
> keep track of   get in someone's way

1. As <u>an example</u>, let me tell you about my own experience.

   _____

2. Don't <u>bother me</u>! I'm doing what I have to do!

   _____

3. Raising university tuition <u>resulted in</u> student demonstrations.

   _____

4. Make sure you <u>don't forget</u> where you've filed these papers.

___

Word Forms:

Write the correct form of the word in brackets.

1. I [predict → _____] the Rams would win, and I was correct.

2. The ship will be [embark → _____] at 6:00 a.m. tomorrow.

3. Mr. Jones was [covet → _____] of everything his rich, handsome neighbor possessed.

4. With several of its best players injured, the team was in a position of [vulnerable → _____].

5. The candidate [aggressive → _____] campaigned to attract female voters.

● ● ● **EXERCISES 3: CHALLENGE** ● ● ●

Using Key Concepts:

Rewrite each sentence B below so that it is similar in meaning to sentence A. Use a word or phrase from the Key Concepts list on page 16.

1. A: Slavery should be made illegal around the world.
   B: There should be an _____ on slavery.

2. A: Police quickly arrived on the scene.
   B: It wasn't long before _____ showed up.

3. A: The law protects disappearing plants and animals.
   B: The law protects _____.

4. A: The suspect's car has a signaling device.
   B: We installed a _____ in the suspect's car.

Vocabulary Expansion:

Read these dictionary definitions of verbs that describe different kinds of "killing." Then rewrite the sentences below by substituting one of the verbs for the underlined word in each sentence. Use the correct word forms.

murder: to illegally kill, usually out of anger or malice

execute: to kill to carry out a capital punishment

assassinate: to kill a famous or important person by surprise attack

massacre: to kill completely, as an entire army or population

euthanize: to kill a dying person to end his or her suffering

1. Police stopped the planned <u>killing</u> of the Pope.

   _____

2. Raskolnikov <u>killed</u> the old woman and stole her money.

   _____

3. The <u>killing</u> of the condemned man was carried out at dawn.

   _____

4. Hundreds of "mad cows" had to be <u>killed</u>.

   _____

5. During Rwanda's civil war, thousands of people were <u>killed</u>.

   _____

Listening Activity:

Listen to the short talk and the questions that follow. Complete the answer to each question below.

1. The WWF is described as _____.

2. It was launched by _____.

3. Each person is asked _____.

4. The money will be used to treat _____.

5. They have lost _____.

6. Some are being _____.

Lesson 3
Of Nukes and Minefields

● ● ● **GETTING READY TO READ** ● ● ●

Key Concepts:

Match these key words or phrases from Today's Reading with the definitions/explanations below. Write the letters of the definitions on the lines.

1. ____ United States Senate
2. ____ nuclear arms [weapons]
3. ____ State Duma
4. ____ arms-control pact
5. ____ warhead
6. ____ arsenal
7. ____ disarmament
8. ____ UNICEF
9. ____ the illiterate
10. ____ Reuters

a. Russia's parliament
b. a United Nations agency that looks after children's interests
c. the bomb on top of a missile
d. one half of America's national lawmaking body
e. bombs that cause mass death and destruction
f. people who can't read or write
g. an agreement or treaty to reduce the number of weapons
h. a country's stock of guns, tanks, bombs, etc.
i. reducing the number of guns, tanks, bombs, etc.
j. an international news service

Active Reading:

As you read through Today's Reading, look for answers to these questions. Mark the sentences in the reading where the answers are found.

1. What did the agreement between Russia and the U.S. do?
2. What did the two countries' leaders have to say about it?
3. What is a landmine and what makes it so cruel?
4. Why are landmines especially dangerous for children?
5. What makes a rat such an effective anti-landmine weapon?

Words in Context:

Choose the word or phrase that is closest in meaning to the underlined word in each sentence fragment below.

1. ... the United States Senate <u>ratified</u> New START ...
   (A) signed   (B) created   (C) rejected

2. ... allows <u>mutual</u> inspection ...
   (A) secret   (B) two-sided   (C) final

3. ... other more <u>conventional</u> weapons ...
   (A) orthodox   (B) dangerous   (C) costly

4. ... any enemy soldier or <u>vehicle</u> ...
   (A) machine   (B) weapon   (C) car or truck

5. ... but to <u>maim</u> and cause terrible pain ...
   (A) cripple   (B) kill   (C) explode

6. ... a deadly <u>inheritance</u> waiting to be triggered ...
   (A) an especially dangerous weapon
   (B) a negative idea
   (C) something received from the past

7. ... waiting to be <u>triggered</u> by the innocent ...
   (A) set off   (B) set up   (C) set on

8. ... by the <u>innocent</u> and unsuspecting ...
   (A) young people
   (B) people not really involved in a situation
   (C) people not particularly intelligent

9. ... an especially <u>persistent</u> danger to children ...
   (A) cruel   (B) stubborn   (C) dangerous

10. ... an <u>acute</u> sense of smell ...
    (A) unusual   (B) useful   (C) sharp

11. ... and, more <u>crucially</u>, are too small ...
    (A) importantly   (B) interestingly   (C) confusingly

12. ... sniffing out bombs in <u>urban</u> areas ...
    (A) war-torn   (B) big-city   (C) undeveloped

Lesson 3 Of Nukes and Minefields   27

● ● ● TODAY'S READING ● ● ●

Read this essay carefully. Then do the exercises that follow.   12

On December 22, 2010, the United States Senate ratified New START, which stands for Strategic Arms Reduction Treaty, a nuclear-arms-limitation agreement between Russia and the U.S. The State Duma, Russia's parliament, is expected to soon follow suit. (Together,
5 the two countries hold 90% of the world's nuclear weapons.) The arms-control pact places a limit on the number of nuclear warheads each side can possess and, to prevent cheating, allows mutual inspection of nuclear bases and missile arsenals.

While reducing the world's stockpile of nuclear weapons is a vital
10 step towards "making us all safer," as U.S. President Obama and Russian President Dmitry Medvedev put it, other more conventional weapons call for urgent disarmament as well. Of these, landmines have to be the cruelest. Landmines are explosive devices designed to go off when stepped on or run over. Typically "planted" in minefields
15 just below the ground's surface, landmines, of which there are over 350 different types, aim to disable any enemy soldier or vehicle that comes into contact with them. What makes mines so inhuman is that their purpose is not just to take lives, but to maim and cause terrible pain and suffering. Although banned by international law,
20 landmines, cheap and easy to make, are still widely used. Once laid, a landmine can remain active for up to 50 years. More than 100 million unexploded landmines still exist in over 70 countries—"a deadly inheritance waiting to be triggered by the innocent and unsuspecting," says UNICEF. Even when a minefield is discovered,
25 it poses an especially persistent danger to children and the illiterate, who can't read signs warning them to keep away.

Removing these unexploded landmines is an expensive, time-consuming, not to mention highly dangerous process. The first and hardest step is to detect the mines, a task commonly done
30 by dogs that have been trained to sniff out the explosives in the

mines. Military robots have also been used. (Once a mine is found, experts "disarm" it by shooting a special chemical into the ground around it.) But now, says Reuters, in several African countries, a new "weapon" is being employed in the anti-landmine battle—rats. Highly intelligent, the African pouched rat is quick to learn and easy to train. Rats have an acute sense of smell and, more crucially, are too small and lightweight to trigger a mine, making them much more effective than dogs. What's more, they work faster. Fitted with a leash, a trained rat can cover an area the size of a soccer field in just 30 minutes, a job that would normally take a "canine bomb squad" at least two days. The use of rats as explosives detectors has proven so successful that they will soon be performing various other hazardous jobs like sniffing out terrorist bombs in urban areas.

● ● ● EXERCISES 1: COMPREHENSION ● ● ●

Reading for Information:

Read the sentences below. Circle T if the sentence is true, F if it is false.

1. T F START is an agreement among several countries that possess nuclear weapons.

2. T F Russia ratified START before the U.S. did.

3. T F Nine out of ten of the world's nuclear weapons belong to either America or Russia.

4. T F UNICEF says that START is making the world safer.

5. T F An area where landmines are laid is known as a minefield.

6. T F There are 100 million different types of landmine in use around the world.

7. T F Landmines often injure and kill unsuspecting children.

8. T F Until rats were used, only dogs had been used to detect landmines.

9. T F What makes rats so useful is that they weigh so little and work so fast.

10. T F Rats work freely on their own without a leash.

Listening for Ideas:

 13

Question-Response: Listen to each question and choose the best response below.

1. (A) By making it possible for them to check out each other's weapons.
   (B) By reducing the number of weapons on each side.
   (C) By having President Obama and President Medvedev both sign the agreement.

2. (A) It can destroy vehicles as well as people.
   (B) It is buried just below the surface.
   (C) It aims to cause permanent, painful injury.

3. (A) No, they are still used.
   (B) No, international law forbids their use.
   (C) No, there are still many of them that are unexploded.

4. (A) Yes, they are doing quite well.
   (B) Because they have worked out so well.
   (C) Mainly in urban areas.

● ● ● EXERCISES 2: COMPOSITION ● ● ●

Making Questions: 　　　　　　　　　　　　　　　　　14

Write the question you would need to ask to get each answer below. Use the hints. Listen to check your questions.

1. Question: _____ a cap on?
   Answer: The number of weapons each country can hold.

2. Question: When _____?
   Answer: When they are stepped on or run over.

3. Question: Why are _____?
   Answer: Probably because they are so cheap and easy to make.

4. Question: How do experts _____?
   Answer: By shooting a chemical into the ground around it.

Writing with Idioms: 　　　　　　　　　　　　　　　　15

Rewrite each sentence below by substituting one of these phrases for the underlined part. Make the necessary changes. Listen to check your answers.

> stand for　　follow suit　　go off　　call for

1. The alarm clock is set to <u>wake me up</u> at 5:30.

   _____

2. The board of directors <u>demanded</u> the CEO's resignation.

   _____

32

3. Everyone agrees. We expect you to <u>do so, too</u>.

4. To many, Kennedy <u>represented</u> youth and a better future.

Word Forms:

Choose the correct word in the parentheses.

1. Even more (crucially, crucial) is the shortage of fresh water.

2. A surprise ending is a (convention, conventionality) of an O'Henry short story.

3. The plan appears to be (mutual, mutually) beneficial.

4. I am (acute, acutely) aware of what is needed.

5. Having (inheriting, inherited) a small fortune, Lena quit her job and took up oil painting full-time.

6. Her patience and (persistence, persistently) finally paid off.

● ● ● EXERCISES 3: CHALLENGE ● ● ●

Using Key Concepts:

Complete each sentence below with one of the Key Concepts on page 26. Make the necessary changes.

1. No one knows for sure how many nuclear weapons the country has in its _____.

2. Each missile is fitted with several _____.

3. _____ is an acronym for United Nations International Children's Emergency Fund.

4. Congress is divided into two parts, the House of Representatives and the _____.

5. The library holds special classes each week to teach _____ people how to read and write.

Vocabulary Expansion:

Look at these dictionary definitions of the adjective "innocent." Then read the sentences that follow. Decide what "innocent" means in each sentence. Write the numbers of the definitions on the lines.

1. uncorrupted by evil; without sin

2. not guilty of a specific crime

3. harmless

4. not experienced or worldly; naïve

5. not familiar with or exposed to; not aware of

6. uninvolved in or not part of

a. _____ What was meant as an <u>innocent</u> joke ended up hurting many people.
b. _____ The prisoner claimed to be <u>innocent</u> right up until the time he was executed.
c. _____ Several <u>innocent</u> bystanders were killed in the attack.
d. _____ As <u>innocent</u> as a child, he wouldn't hurt a fly.
e. _____ <u>Innocent</u> of the custom, Mrs. Moore entered the temple with her shoes on.
f. _____ It is <u>innocent</u> people like you who get taken advantage of by the greedy and crooked.

Listening Activity: 16

Listen to the short talk and then choose the sentence below that best sums up the talk's main idea.

(A) Americans are less antagonistic than in the old days.

(B) More and more Americans are calling for stricter gun control.

(C) Anger and hatred combined with more and more guns will mean more and more violence in the future.

(D) The Arizona shootings have finally led to stricter gun control.

Lesson 4
Languages Lost and Found

● ● ● **GETTING READY TO READ** ● ● ●

Key Concepts:

Match these key words and phrases from Today's Reading with the definitions/explanations below. Write the letters of the definitions on the lines.

1. ___ field linguists
2. ___ dialect
3. ___ indigenous [used about people, languages, etc.]
4. ___ mythology
5. ___ ecosystems
6. ___ traditional herbalists
7. ___ Inca Empire
8. ___ Quechua
9. ___ human prehistory

a. time before the coming of human civilization
b. natural environments or surroundings
c. ancient South American civilization
d. scientists who live among local people to study their native languages
e. native language spoken in the Andes Mountains
f. minor language related to a major language
g. people who use herbs as medicines
h. native or local
i. traditional stories about gods and beginnings

Active Reading:

As you read through Today's Reading, look for answers to these questions. Mark the sentences in the reading where the answers are found.

1. Who is Dr. K. David Harrison?
2. What were researchers doing when they "discovered" the independent language known as Koro?
3. Where does most human knowledge about the natural world exist?
4. What does Dr. Harrison think the Kallawaya people have to teach us?
5. Why are Australia's aboriginal languages so important?

Words in Context:

Choose the word or phrase that is closest in meaning to the underlined word in each sentence fragment below.

1. ... in an isolated section of the foothills ...
   (A) remote   (B) unknown   (C) ancient

2. ... they were documenting a minor dialect ...
   (A) recording   (B) discovering   (C) learning

3. ... a linguistic structure and vocabulary all its own ...
   (A) sound   (B) pattern   (C) history

4. ... an entirely different perspective ...
   (A) knowledge   (B) point of view (C) detail

5. ... are facing imminent extinction ...
   (A) dangerous   (B) approaching   (C) natural

6. ... the erosion of the human knowledge base ...
   (A) destruction   (B) formation   (C) expansion

7. ... know the species' ecosystems intimately ...
   (A) secretly   (B) very well   (C) accidentally

8. ... have more sophisticated ways of classifying ...
   (A) difficult   (B) honored   (C) advanced

9. ... uses as remedies for afflictions of all kinds ...
   (A) medicines   (B) researches   (C) sources

10. ... as remedies for afflictions of all kinds ...
    (A) injuries   (B) wounds   (C) health problems

11. There, you can really glimpse human prehistory.
    (A) get a brief look at
    (B) study in depth
    (C) become excited by

Lesson 4   Languages Lost and Founds   37

● ● ● TODAY'S READING ● ● ●

Read this essay carefully. Then do the exercises that follow.   17

Field linguists, working in an isolated section of the foothills of the Himalayan Mountains in northeast India, recently chanced upon a previously unknown "hidden" language. Known as Koro, the language is spoken by fewer than 1,000 people. The researchers
5 thought they were documenting a minor dialect of another language. But they soon realized that Koro had a linguistic structure and vocabulary all its own. To Dr. K. David Harrison, the team leader and a well-known activist for the preservation of the world's indigenous languages, this discovery was especially exciting. "Koro brings an
10 entirely different perspective, history, mythology, technology, and grammar to what was known before," he said.

Sadly, though, Koro is just one of hundreds of languages around the globe that are facing imminent extinction. In fact, one language disappears every two weeks. At this rate, over half of the world's
15 approximately 7,000 languages will die out by the end of the century. Writing in *National Geographic* magazine, Dr. Harrison says that when a language dies, it takes with it "irreplaceable knowledge" about the natural world. "Most of what we know about the natural world is not written down anywhere. It's only in people's heads. We
20 are seeing right before our eyes the erosion of the human knowledge base." Some 80% of plant and animal species have been discovered not by formal science but by native peoples, Harrison points out. These people know the species' ecosystems intimately and often have "more sophisticated ways of classifying those species than science
25 does."

Harrison cites the examples of the Kallawaya, a tribe in Bolivia, and Australia's aborigines. The Kallawaya have been traditional herbalists since the time of the Inca Empire. Most of them now speak the more common Quechua language. But they also use an ancient secret
30 language, now vulnerable, to encode information about thousands of

38

medicinal plants that the tribe uses as remedies for afflictions of all kinds. When that secret language goes, that priceless information—perhaps even a cure for cancer or AIDS—will go with it.

The loss of Australia's aboriginal tongues, which are among the world's most endangered, means that another kind of human knowledge will soon disappear, Harrison believes. "Australia is amazing because humans have lived here for 50,000 years. Aborigines represent an unbroken link with the past that people in other places on Earth don't. There, you can really glimpse human prehistory. You can come into contact with the mythological beliefs and systems that people there have produced and passed on orally—with no recourse to writing of any kind."

● ● ● EXERCISES 1: COMPREHENSION ● ● ●

Reading for Information:

Write brief answers to these questions.

1. Approximately how many people speak Koro today? _____

2. At first, what did the researchers think Koro was? _____

3. Today, how often does a language die out? _____

4. Where does Dr. Harrison say most of our knowledge about the natural world exists? _____

5. What two examples of endangered languages does Harrison offer? _____

6. What language do most Kallawaya speak? _____

7. What might the information the Kallawaya have about herbs and medicinal plants contain? _____

8. Among the Aborigines, how has traditional knowledge come down to the present? _____

Listening for Ideas:

🔘 18

Listen and complete the sentences below. Then circle T if the sentence is true, F if it is false.

1. T F   The researchers thought that Koro was a separate language because _____.

2. T F   By the year 2100, there will be _____.

3. T F   According to Harrison, native peoples, not formal science, often have _____.

Lesson 4   Languages Lost and Founds   41

● ● ● EXERCISES 2: COMPOSITION ● ● ●

Making Questions: 19

Write the question you would need to ask to get each answer below. Use the hints. Listen to check your questions.

1. Question: _____ discovered?
   Answer: In the foothills of the Himalayan Mountains.

2. Question: Why did _____?
   Answer: Because Koro brings us all kinds of new knowledge.

3. Question: _____ in Australia?
   Answer: Over 50,000 years.

4. Question: What do _____?
   Answer: An unbroken link with the past, says Harrison.

Writing with Idioms: 20

Rewrite each sentence below by substituting one of these phrases for the underlined part. Make the necessary changes. Listen to check your answers.

> chance upon   point out
> come into contact with pass on

1. If you <u>meet</u> any famous people, get their autographs.

   _____

2. The lecturer <u>mentioned</u> ten simple steps to save the planet.

   _____

3. Would you kindly <u>tell</u> the staff <u>about</u> this updated information?

   _____

4. I <u>came across</u> this first edition of *Middlemarch* in Jimbocho.

   _____

Word Forms:

Fill in each blank with the correct form of one these words.

| isolated | documenting | structure |
| intimately | sophisticated | erosion |

1. I can only tell this secret to an _____ friend like you.

2. The animal was kept in an _____ ward at the airport.

3. The waves are gradually _____ the beach away.

4. Engineers found a _____ weakness in the bridge.

5. All our financial _____ were destroyed in the fire.

6. _____ comes with knowledge and experience.

● ● ● EXERCISES 3: CHALLENGE ● ● ●

Using Key Concepts:

Fill in the blank in each sentence below with one of the Key Concepts on page 36.

1. _____ are in New Zealand studying and documenting the Maori native language, which is known as "te reo."

2. The Ainu are Japan's _____ people.

3. Deforestation is destroying _____ along the Amazon.

4. Is Cantonese a _____ or a language in its own right?

5. Joyce's *Ulysses* is based on Greek and Roman _____.

Vocabulary Expansion:

Read these dictionary definitions of three words that are often confused. Then fill in the blanks in the sentences below with one of the words.

imminent: coming soon; approaching; unavoidable

immanent: existing or remaining within; inherent

eminent: of high rank; outstanding; distinguished

1. The conference was attended by some of the most _____ minds in the field of astronomy.

2. Greed is _____ in the capitalist system.

3. The patient is not at the moment in _____ danger, but we must still watch his condition carefully.

Listening Activity:

21

Listen to the short talk and then write brief answers to the questions below.

1. What two dominant languages are mentioned?

   _____

2. Who best understands that in an environment where two languages are spoken, one is less important than the other?

   _____

3. What happens when a community decides that its indigenous language prevents economic or social progress?

   _____

4. What does Harrison say is the only way to ensure that a language survives?

   _____

Lesson 5
It's About Time

● ● ● **GETTING READY TO READ** ● ● ●

Key Concepts:

Match these key words and phrases from Today's Reading with the definitions/explanations below. Write the letters of the definitions on the lines.

1. ___ gender gap
2. ___ progressive societies
3. ___ second-class citizen
4. ___ the Middle East
5. ___ slavery
6. ___ the Quran
7. ___ plaintiff
8. ___ a fair trial
9. ___ democracy
10. ___ repressive regime

a. a person who files a claim in a court of law
b. difference in status between men and women
c. a form of government where citizens vote in free elections
d. countries with advanced ideas about individual freedoms
e. a system where one person "owns" another person
f. a person who has little political power or influence
g. an area extending from southwest Asia to Northern Africa
h. a court case where the person charged with a crime is defended and judged on the evidence without prejudice
i. the holy book of the Islamic religion
j. a government that strictly controls citizens' freedoms

Active Reading:

As you read through Today's Reading, look for answers to these questions. Mark the sentences in the reading where the answers are found.

1. What does the *New York Times* call the growing power of women?
2. Why are women in the Middle East second-class citizens?
3. What is "adhl" and how does it work?
4. How are some Saudi women challenging adhl?
5. What can happen to a woman convicted of "muharabeh"?

Words in Context:

Choose the word or phrase that is closest in meaning to the underlined word in each sentence fragment below.

1. Despite welcome <u>gains</u> over the past ...
   (A) changes   (B) differences   (C) progress

2. ... women being <u>denied</u> the same rights ...
   (A) offered   (B) refused   (C) punished

3. ... is this gap more <u>visible</u> than in the countries ...
   (A) terrible   (B) frequent   (C) obvious

4. ... tradition and religion have long <u>relegated</u> women to ...
   (A) put in a lower position   (B) promoted
   (C) challenged

5. ... and <u>endeavoring</u> to create a just society ...
   (A) hoping   (B) planning   (C) working hard

6. ... to create a <u>just</u> society ...
   (A) normal   (B) fair   (C) modern

7. ... who is <u>entitled</u> by custom to beat ...
   (A) permitted   (B) forbidden   (C) requested

8. ... thanks to this <u>discrepancy</u> between law and practice ...
   (A) gap   (B) line   (C) trade

9. ... they are <u>pleading</u> their cases in the media ...
   (A) arguing for   (B) writing about   (C) hiding from

10. ... plantiffs to <u>reconcile</u> with their guardians ...
    (A) protest   (B) discuss   (C) make peace

11. ... regime is <u>notoriously</u> repressive ...
    (A) well-known for a bad reason   (B) tragically
    (C) dangerously

12. ... a woman <u>convicted</u> of this crime ...
    (A) accused   (B) found guilty   (C) found innocent

● ● ● TODAY'S READING ● ● ●

Read this essay carefully. Then do the exercises that follow.   22

Despite welcome gains over the past fifty years, the gender gap—women being denied the same rights and opportunities as men in work, school, politics, marriage and divorce, and freedom of movement—is still a reality around the globe. Even in such relatively progressive societies as those of North America and Europe, women still lag behind men in wages and salary, management positions, and representation in government.

Nowhere is this gap more visible than in the countries of the Middle East, where tradition and religion have long relegated women to the status of second-class citizen. But this is changing. "The Female Factor," as the *New York Times* calls it, is playing an increasingly important role in the Arab world. Women are challenging ancient rules and ideas. They are taking major steps toward independence and equality and endeavoring to create a more just society.

In Saudi Arabia, for example, there is an age-old practice known as "adhl." This allows male guardians, most often girls' fathers, to make all the decisions about how their single daughters conduct their lives—particularly whom they can marry and how they can spend the money they earn. Under adhl, women cannot travel, enter hospitals, or live independently without a male guardian, who is entitled by custom to beat any woman who disobeys him. "A Saudi woman can't even buy a phone without a guardian's permission," one women's rights activist told the *Times*. "It's a form of slavery."

Although adhl is illegal, forbidden by Islamic law as set down in the Quran, that doesn't keep it from being widely carried out. But thanks to this discrepancy between law and practice, many single Saudi women are now suing their guardians in courts of law and demanding the right to make their own decisions. What's more, they are pleading their cases in the media, bringing worldwide attention to the unfairness of the practice. As is to be expected, however, court

48

decisions in such cases are slow in coming. Judges, mostly male, usually just encourage plaintiffs to reconcile with their guardians. But it's only a matter of time: adhl is on the way out.

In Iran, meanwhile, where the Islamic regime is notoriously repressive, a charge known as "muharabeh" (hatred against God) is often used against female anti-government protesters. A woman convicted of this crime can be sentenced to death by stoning with nothing even resembling a fair trial. Yet despite the threat of death, more and more Irani women are standing up for their rights, and female lawyers are coming to their defense. As one attorney proudly said in the *Times*, "Mark my words. It will be women who bring democracy to Iran."

● ● ● EXERCISES 1: COMPREHENSION ● ● ●

Reading for Information:

Fill in the blanks in these sentences.

1. Female workers often don't earn the same _____ or salaries as their _____ counterparts.

2. In most companies, there aren't as many women in _____ positions as there are men.

3. In most countries, women don't have the influence in _____ and politics that men have.

4. In the Middle East, women are often kept down by _____ and _____ .

5. In the Middle East, says the *New York Times*, women are challenging ancient _____ and _____ .

6. In Saudi Arabia, most girls' guardians are their _____ .

7. According to Saudi _____ , a guardian can beat a woman if she doesn't _____ him.

8. Actually, adhl is against Islamic _____ .

9. Thanks to _____ exposure, people around the world can see how unfair adhl is.

10. If convicted of "muharabeh," a woman may be executed by having _____ thrown at her.

Listening for Ideas:

Question-Response: Listen to each question and choose the best response below.

1. (A) Yes, everyone does.
   (B) No, they don't. There are still gaps.
   (C) Yes, in North America and Europe.

2. (A) Yes, Islamic law forbids it.
   (B) No, or their guardians will beat them.
   (C) That's not true. Women have jobs, too.

3. (A) Yes, because they are usually men.
   (B) That's what they are expected to do.
   (C) No, they urge the girls to obey their guardians.

4. (A) Yes, they are.
   (B) No, they aren't.
   (C) I disagree.

5. (A) She's not sure.
   (B) That's her opinion.
   (C) Yes, it will.

● ● ● EXERCISES 2: COMPOSITION ● ● ●

Making Questions: 24

Write the question you would need to ask to get each answer below. Use the hints. Listen to check your questions.

1. Question: What has _____?
   Answer: Gains have been made in women's rights and opportunities.

2. Question: _____ endeavoring to create?
   Answer: A more just society.

3. Question: What are _____?
   Answer: They are suing them in courts of law.

4. Question: Who is _____?
   Answer: Female lawyers.

Writing with Idioms: 25

Rewrite each sentence below by substituting one of these phrases for the underlined part. Make the necessary changes. Listen to check your answers.

> lag behind   carry out   on the way out   stand up for

1. Printed books are <u>becoming a thing of the past</u>.

   _____

2. Our students <u>don't do as well as</u> those in other schools.

   _____

3. I don't need you to <u>protect</u> me. I can take care of myself.

4. Making a decision is one thing; <u>realizing</u> it is another.

Word Forms:

Choose the correct word in the parentheses.

1. The suspect entered a (plea, plead) of not guilty.

2. The actress gained (notification, notoriety) for her political activities.

3. There is no (denial, denying) that the singer is losing his voice.

4. Thanks to your (endeavors, endeavoring), we managed to hold our most successful charity drive yet.

5. The passengers were all (visibly, visible) frightened by the constant turbulence.

6. Two (convicts, convicteds) escaped from prison yesterday.

● ● ● EXERCISES 3: CHALLENGE ● ● ●

Using Key Concepts:

Fill in the blank in each sentence below with one of the Key Concepts on page 46.

1. The _____ in the trial is a patient who is suing a doctor for prescribing the wrong medicine.

2. He protested that he didn't receive _____ because the judge was prejudiced against Muslims.

3. In a _____, free and open debate of the issues is essential.

4. He spent over 30 years in prison for opposing his country's _____.

5. Even some so-called _____ like Sweden and Belgium are becoming more conservative these days.

6. Closing the _____ is one of the United Nations' highest-priority goals.

Vocabulary Expansion:

Match these types of government with the definitions below. Write the letters of the definitions on the lines.

1. _____	anarchy	2. _____	aristocracy
3. _____	autocracy	4. _____	bureaucracy
5. _____	monarchy	6. _____	meritocracy
7. _____	plutarchy	8. _____	theocracy

a. government by technicians and experts
b. government by civil servants (government workers)
c. government by one person (dictator)
d. government by no one
e. government by rich people
f. government by religious leaders
g. government by the upper class (nobility)
h. government by a king or queen (or emperor or empress)

Listening Activity: 26

As you listen to the short talk, fill in the blanks below.

The Grameen Bank is a _____ institution in _____. To fight _____, the bank loans money to poor people to allow them to start up small _____. Over _____ of its _____ are women. The bank also gives loans to women to buy a _____. Each woman then _____ others in her village to use the phone. This gives the "village phone lady" a small _____ and puts the _____ on the telephone _____.

Lesson 5 It's About Time 55

Lesson 6

Where Would We Be Without It?

● ● ● **GETTING READY TO READ** ● ● ●

Key Concepts:

Match these key words or phrases from Today's Reading with the definitions/explanations below. Write the letters of the definitions on the lines.

1. ____ human rights violations
2. ____ well-being
3. ____ living standard
4. ____ humanitarian assistance
5. ____ conflict resolution
6. ____ the rule of law
7. ____ separation of powers
8. ____ obese
9. ____ noncommunicable diseases (NCDs)

a. keeping one branch of government from becoming too powerful
b. health and happiness
c. preventing and ending wars
d. seriously overweight
e. illnesses like cancer, heart and lung disease, and diabetes that one person cannot pass on to another
f. treating citizens unfairly and cruelly; taking away people's freedoms
g. level of comfort in life
h. using legal means to keep society safe and just
i. helping people recover from natural disasters

Active Reading:

As you read through Today's Reading, look for answers to these questions. Mark the sentences in the reading where the answers are found.

1. What side of human beings does the UN represent?
2. When, by whom, and why was the United Nations established?
3. What did the UN recently tell Afghanistan?
4. How can the UN help keep peace agreements from failing?
5. What influences children's food preferences?

Words in Context:

Choose the word or phrase that is closest in meaning to the underlined word in each sentence fragment below.

1. ... ills continue to <u>plague</u> us ...
   (A) assist (B) trouble (C) encourage

2. ... at its weakest and most <u>desperate</u> ...
   (A) hopeless (B) violent (C) exciting

3. ... the side of us that <u>yearns</u> for peace ...
   (A) acts (B) wishes (C) opposes

4. ... <u>deplores</u> racial and gender inequality ...
   (A) protects (B) hates (C) prevents

5. ... <u>understands</u> the importance of creating ...
   (A) grasps (B) denies (C) suggests

6. ... to <u>inaugurate</u> the Parliament ...
   (A) elect (B) change (C) start

7. ... building up of <u>robust</u> democratic institutions ...
   (A) normal (B) perfect (C) strong

8. ... ways to <u>augment</u> its peacebuilding role ...
   (A) alter (B) improve (C) lessen

9. He <u>underscored</u> the importance of ...
   (A) stressed (B) reduced (C) explained

10. ... nations "<u>emerging</u> from conflict ..."
    (A) coming into (B) suffering (C) coming out

11. ... <u>relapse</u> into bloodshed ...
    (A) go back to a previous condition (B) cause
    (C) become a victim of

12. ... non-violent management of political <u>disputes</u> ...
    (A) solutions (B) disagreements (C) elections

13. ... a leading cause of <u>premature</u> death ...
    (A) violent (B) illness (C) early

● ● ● TODAY'S READING ● ● ●

Read this essay carefully. Then do the exercises that follow.   27

A quick glance at the headlines is enough to tell us that the world is a troubled place. War and violence, poverty and hunger, racism and human rights violations, climate change and global warming—these and other ills continue to plague us. They show mankind at
5 its weakest and most desperate. But a quick glance at the daily news also tells us that we would be much worse off if it weren't for one organization: the United Nations. The UN represents the other side of the human coin. It's the side of us that yearns for peace, seeks the health and well-being of every individual, deplores racial and gender
10 inequality, and understands the importance of creating a sustainable environment.

The UN's official website informs us that the United Nations was set up in 1945 by 51 countries "committed to maintaining international peace and security, developing friendly relations among nations,
15 and promoting social progress, better living standards, and human rights." The UN is best known for peacekeeping, conflict resolution, and humanitarian assistance. But "the UN and its specialized agencies affect our lives and make the world a better place" in many other ways, as the following recent media items show.

20 When last week President Hamid Karzai of Afghanistan refused to seat the country's newly elected Parliament, the United Nations put out a strong statement urging Karzai to inaugurate the Parliament as soon as possible. "Afghanistan's peaceful future lies in the building up of robust democratic institutions based on the rule of law and
25 clear respect for the separation of powers," the UN said.

Meanwhile, on January 11, the UN Security Council devoted the entire day to finding ways to augment its peacebuilding role. Unfortunately, half of all peace agreements fall through within five years, UN Secretary-General Ban Ki-moon said. He underscored the
30 importance of not letting nations that are "emerging from conflict

relapse into bloodshed." The UN, he said, is determined to help such nations create institutions that will strengthen their economies and allow non-violent management of political disputes.

And WHO, the UN's health agency, today called for action to keep the world's children from being taken in by television marketing messages for food with high contents of fat, sugar, or salt. TV advertising is largely responsible for influencing children's food choices. Some 43 million pre-school children worldwide are either obese or seriously overweight because of a poor diet, WHO says. And poor diet is a major factor in the risk of noncommunicable diseases and a leading cause of premature death around the globe.

Indeed, where would we be without the United Nations?

● ● ● EXERCISES 1: COMPREHENSION ● ● ●

Reading for Information:

Complete each sentence below with the correct answer choice.

1. The problem that is NOT mentioned as one that continues to plague the world is
   (A) global warming.
   (B) negative news headlines.
   (C) racism.
   (D) hunger.

2. All of the following are mentioned on the official UN website EXCEPT
   (A) providing help for victims of earthquakes, floods, etc.
   (B) helping nations get along.
   (C) making people's lives more comfortable.
   (D) promoting gender inequality.

3. All of the following are true EXCEPT
   (A) the people of Afghanistan held an election to choose a Parliament.
   (B) the United Nations refused to get involved in Afghanistan's political problems.
   (C) Ban Ki-moon wants to ensure that peace agreements are maintained.
   (D) a poor diet consists of too much fat, sugar, and salt.

4. The only piece of information that is CLEARLY STATED in the essay is
   (A) the number of member nations the United Nations has today.
   (B) in what city the United Nations Security Council met on January 11.
   (C) what influences children's food choices, giving rise to a poor diet.
   (D) the number of people who die each year from noncommunicable diseases.

Listening for Ideas:

28

Listen to the sentences. Then circle T if the sentence is true, F if it is false.

1. T F

2. T F

3. T F

4. T F

5. T F

● ● ● EXERCISES 2: COMPOSITION ● ● ●

Making Questions: 🔊 29

Write the question you would need to ask to get each answer below. Use the hints. Listen to check your questions.

1. Question: What do _____ show?
   Answer: Mankind at its weakest and most desperate.

2. Question: What is _____ ?
   Answer: For peacekeeping and conflict resolution.

3. Question: _____ Afghanistan's peaceful future _____ ?
   Answer: In the rule of law and respect for the separation of powers.

4. Question: _____ peace agreements _____ ?
   Answer: Within five years.

Writing with Idioms: 🔊 30

Rewrite each sentence below by substituting one of these phrases for the underlined part. Make the necessary changes. Listen to check your answers.

> set up   take in   put out   fall through

1. The student newspaper is <u>published</u> three times a year.

   _____

2. The elderly are often <u>deceived</u> by Internet scam artists.

   _____

3. We <u>formed</u> a committee to look into the rising drop-out rate.

_____

4. The project <u>didn't succeed</u> because of a lack of funds.

_____

Word Forms:

Fill in the blank in each sentence with the correct form of the word on the left.

1. *desperate*   We _____ need to reduce our spending.

2. *disputes*   The war broke out over a _____ island.

3. *inaugurate*   The _____ ceremony is held in January.

4. *deplores*   What a _____ situation!

5. *premature*   I think I judged him a snob _____.

6. *augment*   My accountant said I should try _____ my income by investing in stocks.

● ● ● EXERCISES 3: CHALLENGE ● ● ●

Using Key Concepts:

Rewrite each sentence below by substituting one of the Key Concepts on page 56 for the underlined part.

1. Without <u>a working legal system</u>, the country fell into chaos.

   _____

2. The man was so <u>heavy</u> that he could barely walk.

   _____

3. The government was criticized for <u>taking away its citizens' freedoms and rights</u>.

   _____

4. Raising <u>income and comfort levels</u> makes for a stronger society.

   _____

5. The university now offers a course in <u>preventing wars</u>.

   _____

Vocabulary Expansion:

Read these dictionary definitions of verbs beginning with the prefix "under." Then fill in the blank in each sentence below with the correct form of one of the verbs.

1. **underachieve:** to not be as successful as expected
2. **underestimate:** to make too low a guess or prediction
3. **undergo:** to experience or go through
4. **undermine:** to make weaker or to injure
5. **underpin:** to give support or strength

a. Our peace efforts have been _____ by greed and hatred.

b. I _____ your ability to handle such a large assignment.

c. Our students have been _____ because of a lack of motivation and teacher guidance.

d. Environmental preservation must be _____ by people's awareness of environmental problems.

e. I never want to _____ such a frightening experience again.

Listening Activity:

31

Listen to the four statements. Then circle the number of the statement that best summarizes the main idea of Today's Reading.

1.   2.   3.   4.

Lesson 7
Virtually Better

● ● ● **GETTING READY TO READ** ● ● ●

Key Concepts:

Match these key words or phrases from Today's Reading with the definitions/explanations below. Write the letters of the definitions on the lines.

1. ____ habit-forming
2. ____ virtual world
3. ____ behavioral problems
4. ____ social withdrawal
5. ____ addiction
6. ____ aggression
7. ____ field of mental health
8. ____ PTSD

a. psychological troubles
b. avoiding friends and other relationships
c. angry or hostile behavior
d. causing a person to be unable to stop doing something
e. the world inside video and computer games
f. an area of medicine working with patients with psychological problems
g. Post-Traumatic Stress Disorder, a mental affliction in people who have gone through a severe fright or shock (trauma) like war, natural disaster, or near-death experience. Patients have bad memories (flashbacks) and bad dreams (nightmares).
h. the condition of being unable to stop doing something

Active Reading:

As you read through Today's Reading, look for answers to these questions. Mark the sentences in the reading where the answers are found.

1. What are the arguments against video and computer games?
2. How are games being used in education and healing?
3. What does the *New York Times* say games are designed to do?
4. What transformation or big change is needed?
5. What does Jane McGonigal say games can do?

Words in Context:

Choose the word or phrase that is closest in meaning to the underlined word in each sentence fragment below.

1. ... inability to <u>distinguish</u> fantasy from ...
   (A) tell one thing from another (B) accept as true
   (C) escape from
2. ... some studies <u>contend</u> that playing ...
   (A) oppose (B) argue (C) wish
3. Games have great <u>potential</u> as learning ...
   (A) possibility (B) reason (C) trouble
4. ... an experimental <u>curriculum</u> being tried ...
   (A) method (B) treatment (C) school course
5. ... effective in decreasing the <u>symptoms</u> of PTSD ...
   (A) patients (B) suffering (C) signs
6. ... feel far less <u>anxiety</u> overall ...
   (A) pain (B) comfort (C) worry
7. ... the skills, <u>determination</u>, optimism, and confidence ...
   (A) decision (B) belief (C) will
8. ... they remain <u>motivated</u> to keep going ...
   (A) inspired (B) defeated (C) undecided
9. Effort is <u>rewarded</u>, not just success.
   (A) praised (B) stressed (C) scolded
10. ... we need to <u>emulate</u> these basic gaming assets ...
    (A) increase (B) copy (C) practice
11. ... we need to emulate these basic gaming <u>assets</u> ...
    (A) benefits (B) ideas (C) situations
12. One of the most <u>profound</u> transformations we can learn ...
    (A) difficult (B) unlucky (C) deep
13. ... games can <u>instill</u> a "sense of productivity" ...
    (A) introduce (B) increase (C) involve

● ● ● **TODAY'S READING** ● ● ●

Read this essay carefully. Then do the exercises that follow. 32

We've all heard all the arguments against video and computer games. Like gambling, drugs, and alcohol, games can be habit-forming. Playing them constantly (by age 21, the average person in a developed country will have put in more than 10,000 hours in virtual worlds) can cause a variety of behavioral problems. These include loss of personal control, social withdrawal, dishonesty (lying to family and friends), and the inability to distinguish fantasy from reality. Addicted gamers can even resort to criminal activity to support their addiction. There's also the problem of aggression: some studies contend that playing violent video games is directly linked to violent behavior in the real world.

But there's another side to the story, too. Games have great potential as learning and healing tools. For instance, First Things First, an experimental curriculum being tried out in several schools in the United States, presents high-school math as a series of levels that encourage students to master basic concepts, as they would in a game, before advancing to the next level. The program has been highly successful: participating students have scored impressive increases in statewide tests, with some improving by as much as 40%. And in the field of mental health, game-playing (using puzzle-solving games like Tetris in particular) is effective in decreasing the symptoms of PTSD. Patients experience fewer flashbacks and nightmares and feel far less anxiety overall.

A recent article in the *New York Times* asks if games might not have other important functions as well. Is there some way the skills, determination, optimism, and confidence games develop can be used to make us better people and to solve real-world problems? Games are designed to provide instantaneous feedback and continual encouragement. Though players may fail over and over (failing takes up 80% of game-playing time), they remain motivated to keep going. Effort is rewarded, not just success. Short-term goals lead to long-term achievement. To make work, school, and other social institutions as attractive as games, the Times suggests, we need to emulate these basic gaming assets: "One of the most profound transformations we can learn from games is how to turn the sense that someone has 'failed' into the sense that he or she 'hasn't succeeded yet.'"

Speaking at the London Nokia World Forum, respected game-designer and futurist Jane McGonigal backed this idea up. Used effectively, she said, games can instill a "sense of productivity and purpose" in our lives. Games can work to build a strong "social fabric" and create a sense of "epic meaning" in society, making each member feel like part of a much bigger picture.

● ● ● EXERCISES 1: COMPREHENSION ● ● ●

Reading for Information:

Follow the instructions below. Write brief answers on the lines.

1. Name three things besides gaming that can be habit-forming.

   _____

2. Define "dishonesty" as used in the reading.

   _____

3. Name an experimental curriculum being used in the U.S.

   _____

4. Explain why the curriculum can be seen as successful.

   _____

5. Tell us what kind of game Tetris is.

   _____

6. Name four things that games develop in players, as pointed out in the *New York Times*.

   _____

7. Tell us what games are designed to provide.

   _____

8. Explain what short-term goals can lead to.

   _____

9. Explain what big change or transformation the *New York Times* says we can learn from games.

_____

Listening for Ideas: 🔘 33

As you listen, write what you hear to complete each statement below.

1. By a "sense of productivity and purpose," Jane McGonigal means _____.

2. The term "social fabric," as used by Jane McGonigal, means _____.

3. "Creating a sense of 'epic meaning' in society" means _____.

● ● ● EXERCISES 2: COMPOSITION ● ● ●

Making Questions: 🔊 34

Write the question you would need to ask to get each answer below. Use the hints. Listen to check your questions.

1. Question: By age 21, how many _____?
   Answer: More than 10,000 hours.

2. Question: What _____ contend?
   Answer: That playing violent games causes people to be violent in the real world.

3. Question: _____ high-school math _____?
   Answer: As a series of levels like in a game.

4. Question: What percentage _____?
   Answer: 80%.

Writing with Idioms: 🔊 35

Rewrite each sentence below by substituting one of these phrases for the underlined part. Make the necessary changes. Listen to check your answers.

> put in   resort to   take up   back up

1. We may have to <u>end up</u> suing the polluters in court.

_____

2. How many hours did <u>it take</u> you <u>to write</u> this report?

_____

72

3. If you complain to the teacher, I'll go along with you.

_____

4. Making calls to clients consumes half my day.

_____

Word Forms:

Write each sentence with the correct form of the word in brackets.

1. If not taken correctly, the drug is [potential → _____] deadly.

2. It is my [contend → _____] that capital punishment should be banned.

3. I want a job that is [reward → _____] and makes me feel useful.

4. The suspect has a [distinguish → _____] scar on his left cheek.

5. She is [determination → _____] to succeed at no matter what cost.

6. I was so [anxiety → _____] before the interview that I had trouble breathing.

7. As a [motivated → _____] speaker, he attracts huge audiences.

● ● ● EXERCISES 3: CHALLENGE ● ● ●

Using Key Concepts:

Decide which of this lesson's Key Concepts each of the following lists or phrases refers to. Write the concepts on the lines.

1. psychologists, psychiatrists, counselors   _____

2. alcoholism, workaholics, compulsive gamblers   _____

3. loneliness and isolation   _____

4. fears, depression, eating disorders   _____

5. uncontrollable anger   _____

Vocabulary Expansion:

Look at this list of verbs related to "copy" and their definitions. Then fill in the blank in each sentence below with the correct form of one the verbs.

imitate:	to use or follow as a model
emulate:	to try hard to equal or excel by imitation
mimic:	to imitate, usually in order to make fun of
impersonate:	to pretend to be another person
simulate:	to serve as a model of something
duplicate:	to make an exact copy

1. They cruelly _____ the new foreign student's poor English.
2. You can't go wrong _____ Jack's courage and determination.
3. This machine _____ space flight to train astronauts.
4. The thieves _____ cleaning workers to get into the art museum.

5. No one will ever _____ Oh's career home-run record.

6. This diamond looks real, but it's actually an _____.

Listening Activity: 36

Listen to the four ways in which futurist Jane McGonigal thinks games can improve people's lives. Then circle A if you AGREE with what she says about each way, or D if you DISAGREE.

1. A D

2. A D

3. A D

4. A D

Lesson 8
It's Never Too Late

● ● ● **GETTING READY TO READ** ● ● ●

Key Concepts:

Match these key words or phrases from Today's Reading with the definitions/explanations below. Write the letters of the definitions on the lines.

1. ____ Inuit, Indian, and Metis
2. ____ mental and physical abuse
3. ____ Bataan Peninsula
4. ____ POWs
5. ____ Manchuria
6. ____ forced laborers
7. ____ the apartheid era
8. ____ racist ideology

a. an area in the Philippines that was the site of one of the most painful incidents of World War II
b. indigenous or native peoples of Canada
c. the belief that one race is superior to another
d. prisoners of war; enemy soldiers captured and imprisoned
e. a period in South African history (from 1948 to the early 1980s) when ruling whites denied black South Africans all rights and freedoms
f. slave workers
g. an area in China that was a colony of Japan during much of the first half of the 20th century
h. treating people cruelly and unfairly

Active Reading:

As you read through Today's Reading, look for answers to these questions. Mark the sentences in the reading where the answers are found.

1. What in general did Canadian Prime Minster Stephen Harper apologize for and to whom?
2. What happened to Canada's native children who were forced to go to residential schools?
3. What was the Bataan Death March?
4. What were South African and Maori rugby players the victims of?

Words in Context:

Choose the word or phrase that is closest in meaning to the underlined word in each sentence fragment below.

1. ... standing humbly before Inuit, Indian, and Metis representatives
   (A) proudly   (B) modestly   (C) sadly

2. ... many were inadequately fed, clothed, and housed ...
   (A) poorly   (B) suddenly   (C) angrily

3. All were deprived of the care ...
   (A) provided with
   (B) made to get along without
   (C) forced to give to others

4. ... the care and nurturing of parents ...
   (A) feeding   (B) teaching   (C) cherishing

5. Thousands perished ...
   (A) vanished   (B) survived   (C) died

6. ... apology was later reiterated by ...
   (A) denied   (B) repeated   (C) argued

7. ... their deep remorse for excluding ...
   (A) regret   (B) responsibility   (C) confusion

8. This acknowledgement of the mistakes ...
   (A) knowledge   (B) reality   (C) admission

9. ... the mistakes of our predecessors ...
   (A) superiors   (B) forerunners   (C) enemies

10. ... apology for our sport's culpability ...
    (A) history   (B) blame   (C) error

11. ... such apologies are superficial and insincere ...
    (A) temporary   (B) untrue   (C) shallow

12. ... the terrible wrongs that were perpetrated ...
    (A) committed   (B) discovered   (C) reported

13. ... the resentful feelings of the past ...
    (A) bitter   (B) permanent   (C) sad

● ● ● **TODAY'S READING** ● ● ●

Read this essay carefully. Then do the exercises that follow.   37

Public apologies have been making headlines recently. In June 2008, Canadian Prime Minister Stephen Harper, standing humbly before Inuit, Indian, and Metis representatives, apologized for Canada's past treatment of its indigenous children. Starting in the
5 late 1800s, Canada had an official government policy that aimed to "kill the Indian in the child." Thousands of native children were taken away from their families and shipped off to far-away boarding schools, where many suffered severe mental and physical abuse. "Many were inadequately fed, clothed, and housed," Harper said. "All
10 were deprived of the care and nurturing of parents, grandparents, and communities. Native languages and cultural practices were prohibited. Tragically, some of these children died." Harper then went on: "The government of Canada asks the forgiveness of the aboriginal peoples of this country for failing them so profoundly."
15 In May 2009, Japan's U.S. ambassador, Ichiro Fujisaki, apologized in person to the 73 remaining American survivors of the Bataan Death March. Fujisaki said that his country was truly sorry for the "tremendous damage and suffering" it had caused. The incident occurred in April 1942, after Japanese military forces took over the
20 Bataan Peninsula in the Philippines. Some 80,000 American and Filipino soldiers were captured and made to walk 80 kilometers in intense heat without food or water. Thousands perished. Those POWs who survived were sent to Japan and Manchuria to work as forced laborers. Fujisaki's apology was later reiterated by then
25 Foreign Minister Katsuya Okada: "On behalf of the government of Japan, I offer my heartfelt apology over the inhumane treatment and suffering you experienced."

In May 2010, New Zealand's and South Africa's rugby unions expressed in a published statement their deep remorse for excluding
30 Maori and black players from their teams during the apartheid era.

South African Rugby president Oregan Hoskins apologized to the "innocent victims of the racist ideology of our former government." He stressed the importance of apologizing to "black South Africans who were denied the opportunity to represent their country during those long, dark years. This acknowledgement of the mistakes of our predecessors and apology for our sport's culpability is another step in attempting to lift that shadow."

Critics may complain that such apologies are superficial and insincere. How can a simple "I'm sorry" ever make up for the terrible wrongs that were perpetrated? Maybe it can't. But apologies do at least show that we have the ability to learn from our mistakes: that we recognize that easing the resentful feelings of the past is the best way to keep history from repeating itself.

● ● ● EXERCISES 1: COMPREHENSION ● ● ●

Reading for Information:

Write a brief answer to each question below.

1. Where was Stephen Harper standing when he made his apology?

   _____

2. What did Canada's official government policy of the time aim to do?

   _____

3. What were children in the boarding schools not allowed to do?

   _____

4. What did Ichiro Fujisaki say his country had caused?

   _____

5. When Fujisaki apologized, how many years had passed since the Bataan Death March?

   _____

6. What did survivors of the march do in Japan and Manchuria?

   _____

7. What did Oregan Hoskins say black South African players were the innocent victims of?

   _____

8. What do some critics of public apologies often say about them?

   _____

Listening for Ideas:

🔘 38

Listen and write what you hear. Then circle T if the sentence is true, F if it is false.

1. T F

2. T F

3. T F

4. T F

5. T F

● ● ● EXERCISES 2: COMPOSITION ● ● ●

Making Questions: 　　　　　　　　　　　　　　　　39

Write the question you would need to ask to get each answer below. Use the hints. Listen to check your questions.

1. Question: When did _____?
   Answer: In the late 1800s.

2. Question: _____ were deprived of?
   Answer: The care and nurturing of parents.

3. Question: _____ forced to do?
   Answer: To walk 80 kilometers in intense heat.

4. Question: _____ the era of apartheid?
   Answer: Those long, dark years.

Writing with Idioms: 　　　　　　　　　　　　　　　40

Rewrite each sentence below by substituting one of these phrases for the underlined part. Make the necessary changes. Listen to check your answers.

   in person　　take over　　on behalf of　　make up for

1. Are you speaking <u>for</u> all the class members?

   _____

2. In June 1940, Nazi troops <u>captured and occupied</u> Paris.

   _____

3. How can I ever <u>atone for</u> what I did?

   _____

4. He's much shorter <u>when you meet him</u> than he looks on the screen.

   _____

Word Forms:

Write the correct form of the word in brackets.

1. A person who doesn't brag or boast is a [humbly → _____] person.

2. A person who commits a crime is called a [perpetrated → _____].

3. Fruits and vegetables are known as [perished → _____] foods because they soon go bad.

4. A [remorse → _____] person feels bad because he did something wrong.

5. Going without sleep is known as sleep [deprived → _____].

6. A person who doesn't like you [resentful → _____] you.

● ● ● EXERCISES 3: CHALLENGE ● ● ●

Using Key Concepts:

Fill in the blank in each sentence A below so that it is similar in meaning to sentence B. Use Key Concepts from page 76.

1. A: They say that the canal was dug by slaves.
   B: I've heard that _____ dug the canal.

2. A: The paper says that prisoners there are being treated inhumanely.
   B: According to the paper, the people being held prisoner there are victims of _____.

3. A: That political party stands for prejudice and discrimination.
   B: That political party has a _____.

Vocabulary Expansion:

Look at this list of words related to "ability" and their definitions. Then fill in the blank in each sentence below with one of the words.

capacity: ability to develop mentally or physically
faculty: general natural ability
talent: natural ability, especially in the arts
skill: ability developed through practice
competence: satisfactory but not excellent ability

1. I don't want mere _____; I want the best!
2. Yes, you have _____, but I cannot promise that you have what it takes to become a professional musician.
3. Humans have the _____ to apologize as well as to err.
4. Her _____ at handling difficult customers makes her indispensable to our company.

84

5. He was born without the _____ of self-criticism.

Listening Activity: 41

Listen to and write the quotations by the Indian freedom fighter Mahatma Gandhi and the British poet Alexander Pope. Then circle A below if the two writers appear to AGREE with each other, or D if they seem to DISAGREE.

"_____.

_____." Mahatma Gandhi

"_____." Alexander Pope

Answer: A   D

Lesson 9
Global Concepts 1: People

● ● ● GETTING READY TO READ ● ● ●

Key Concepts:

Match these key words or phrases from Today's Reading with the definitions/explanations below. Write the letters of the definitions on the lines.

1. ____ gynecologist
2. ____ tank shell
3. ____ Gaza Strip
4. ____ conjoined twins
5. ____ charitable foundation
6. ____ botanical garden
7. ____ biodiversity
8. ____ doomsday

a. the wide variety of plant and animal species in a specific ecosystem or on Earth as a whole
b. an explosive device launched from a large military vehicle
c. the end of the world as we know it
d. a narrow strip of land along the eastern coast of the Mediterranean Sea between Egypt and Israel; when Israel was created in 1948, thousands of Palestinians, the area's residents, were forced to move into the tiny Gaza area, which has been the center of the ongoing Israeli-Palestinian conflict; Gaza has high unemployment and political instability; under the control of Israel, the area seeks independence, with militants frequently carrying out anti-Israel violence, to which Israel responds with violence of its own
e. a doctor specializing in female health problems
f. an organization that carries out good deeds
g. two babies born with parts of their bodies stuck together
h. a public park displaying a large variety of plants and flowers

Active Reading:

As you read through Today's Reading, look for answers to these questions. Mark the sentences in the reading where the answers are found.

1. Who is Dr. Izzedin Abuelaish and what is his tragedy?
2. How has Dr. Abuelaish responded to the tragedy?
3. Who is Stephen Hopper and what is his goal?

Words in Context:

Choose the word or phrase that is closest in meaning to the underlined word in each sentence fragment below.

1. ... allowing his grief to torment him ...
   (A) pain   (B) soothe   (C) excite

2. ... immunized me against suffering ...
   (A) convinced   (B) protected   (C) protested

3. ... their shared, precarious humanity ...
   (A) valuable   (B) permanent   (C) not secure

4. ... *Road to Peace and Human Dignity*.
   (A) self-awareness (B) self-doubt   (C) self-respect

5. ... on death and history and revenge is a waste of time ...
   (A) repaying someone money
   (B) repaying someone for a favor
   (C) repaying someone for a cruel or harmful act

6. ... must not be spoiled by revenge ...
   (A) damaged   (B) remembered   (C) forgotten

7. ... they will adorn the doors of institutions ...
   (A) close   (B) open   (C) decorate

8. Conserving this precious biodiversity ...
   (A) Studying   (B) Enjoying   (C) Maintaining

9. ... this precious biodiversity ...
   (A) ancient   (B) valuable   (C) threatened

10. ... involves interacting with plants ...
    (A) exchanging   (B) working together (C) growing

11. ... letting these plants die would be catastrophic ...
    (A) dangerous   (B) disastrous   (C) foolish

12. ... stave off such an eventuality ...
    (A) result   (B) tragedy   (C) concept

● ● ● TODAY'S READING ● ● ●

Read this essay carefully. Then do the exercises that follow.   42

(1) Izzeldin Abuelaish is a Palestinian gynecologist. On January 16, 2009, a series of Israeli tank shells exploded in his Gaza Strip home. Sifting through the rubble, Dr. Abuelaish discovered to his horror that three of his daughters had been killed outright. Another had lost the sight in one eye. But instead of allowing his grief to torment him, Dr. Abuelaish has transformed the tragedy into a quest for peace. His daughters' deaths, he told Joseph Berger of the *New York Times*, "immunized me against suffering." He believes that the Israeli-Palestinian conflict, which has dragged on for decades, can only be put right when the two sides recognize "their shared, precarious humanity. We are like conjoined twins with one heart and one brain," he says. "Any harm to one will affect the other." Dr. Abuelaish has now written an autobiography, *I Shall Not Hate: A Gaza Doctor's Journey on the Road to Peace and Human Dignity*. In the book, he reaffirms the message that he has been spreading around the globe and that has made him a candidate for the Nobel Peace Prize: Hatred is an illness. Dwelling on death and history and revenge is a waste of time. "Revenge will not return my daughters," he writes. "The innocence of those girls must not be spoiled by revenge. I can keep their memories alive with good deeds." And that is just what Dr. Abuelaish has been doing. Since 2009, he and his surviving children have lived in Canada, where he teaches global health at the University of Toronto. He has also established a charitable foundation called Daughters for Life that supports girls' education. He is determined that his daughters' "names will not only be written on their gravestones," but that they will adorn the doors of institutions and other "good places."

(2) According to the BBC and Professor Stephen Hopper, director of the U.K.'s Royal Botanic Gardens at Kew, one-fifth of the world's plants could soon die out. The earth is home to some 380,000 plant

species, of which those in the tropical rainforests are in the most danger. Conserving this precious biodiversity for future generations is vital, says Hopper. "We cannot sit back and watch plant species disappear. Plants are the basis of all life on Earth, providing clean air, water, food, and fuel. Every breath we take involves interacting with plants." He added that in the world's poorest countries, plant remedies are the only source of healthcare; letting these plants die would be catastrophic. To help stave off such an eventuality, Hopper oversees Kew's Millennium Seed Bank. This is a "doomsday" vault where 1.8 billion samples of plant and crop seeds from around the world are stored in deep, underground, refrigerated rooms to keep them safe from natural and manmade disasters.

● ● ● EXERCISES 1: COMPREHENSION ● ● ●

Reading for Information:

Read these statements. Circle T if the statement is true, F if it is false.

1. T F All of Dr. Abuelaish's children were killed or injured in the explosions.

2. T F The Israeli-Palestinian conflict started in 2009 when Israeli tanks attacked the Gaza Strip.

3. T F The new book about Dr. Abuelaish's story was written by Joseph Berger of the New York Times.

4. T F Dr. Abuelaish now lives in Canada, where he teaches a class in the history of the Gaza conflict.

5. T F Daughters for Life works to improve educational opportunities for young women.

6. T F Nearly 80,000 plant species are on the verge of extinction.

7. T F Stephen Hopper says plants provide us with everything except drugs and medicines.

8. T F The Millennium Seed Bank is open to visitors to Kew Botanical Gardens.

Listening for Ideas:

Question-Response: Listen to each question and choose the best response below.

1. (A) By doing good deeds.
   (B) By moving to Canada.
   (C) By being a candidate for the Nobel Peace Prize.

2. (A) Death.
   (B) Revenge.
   (C) Illness.

3. (A) Preserving biodiversity for the future.
   (B) Increasing the world's stock of crops and plants by developing new kinds of seeds.
   (C) Keeping seeds safe if an earthquake, say, or nuclear war should occur.

● ● ● EXERCISES 2: COMPOSITION ● ● ●

Making Questions: 44

Write the question you would need to ask to get each answer below. Use the hints. Listen to check your answers.

1. Question: What happened _____?
   Answer: She lost the sight in one eye.

2. Question: _____ been going on?
   Answer: For decades.

3. Question: What would _____?
   Answer: The doors of institutions and other good places.

4. Question: _____ stored?
   Answer: In deep, undergound, refrigerated rooms.

Writing with Idioms: 45

Rewrite each sentence below by substituting one of these phrases for the underlined part. Make the necessary changes. Listen to check your answers.

> drag on   put right   dwell on   stave off

1. Perhaps apologizing will help <u>make</u> the situation <u>less uncomfortable</u>.

   _____

2. Japanese baseball games would often <u>keep going</u> for four hours.

   _____

3. Some say it may be too late to <u>keep</u> further global warming <u>from happening</u>.

---

4. Don't <u>think about</u> what happened <u>so much</u>.

Word Forms:

Choose the correct word in the parentheses.

1. New evidence led to the suspect's (eventually, eventual) capture.

2. We need to respond more quickly to floods, earthquakes, and other natural (catastrophe, catastrophes).

3. In the film, the little boy's (torment, tormentor) is a tiny gremlin named Pester.

4. The buildings lining the streets were (adorning, adorned) with national flags, banners, and bunting.

● ● ● EXERCISES 3: CHALLENGE ● ● ●

Using Key Concepts:

Fill in the blank in each sentence below with one of the Key Concepts on page 86.

1. The surgery to separate the ____ lasted more than fourteen hours.

2. I would prefer working for a ____ where I know that I'm helping to make the world a better place.

3. In the novel, ____ comes about because a huge meteor crashes into Earth, killing every living thing on the planet.

4. Destruction of plant and animal habitats and ecosystems is the main cause of loss of ____.

5. There is widespread poverty in the ____, which many residents compare to a prison with Israeli guards.

Vocabulary Expansion:

Look at these explanations of how to use adjectives similar in meaning to "artificial." Fill in the blank in each sentence below with one of the words.

synthetic: refers to a substance produced chemically to look, feel, or taste like the original

counterfeit: refers to money made by professional criminals that they try to pass off as real

forged: refers to paintings, documents, or signatures that copy the real thing

sham: refers to something that people do or say that only seems honest or real

ersatz: refers to an imitation product that is obviously inferior to the real thing

1. It was a _____ marriage, done so the wife could get her U.S. green card.
2. The _____ letters were made by a literary critic as a hoax to fool one of his rivals.
3. She came in wearing a(n) _____ mink coat that everyone knew wasn't real.
4. _____ rubber has virtually taken the place of real rubber.
5. Store clerks have to watch out for _____ $20 bills.

Listening Activity: 46

Listen to the short talk and questions. Write answers to the questions on the lines below.

1. _____

2. _____

3. _____

4. _____

Lesson 10
Global Concepts 2: Trends

● ● ● **GETTING READY TO READ** ● ● ●

Key Concepts:

Match these key words or phrases from Today's Reading with the definitions/explanations below. Write the letters of the definitions on the lines.

1. ___ philanthropy
2. ___ conglomerate
3. ___ multiple sclerosis
4. ___ financier
5. ___ liberal causes
6. ___ Associated Press
7. ___ low profile
8. ___ nouveau riche
9. ___ economic downturn
10. ___ loss of public confidence

a. recession; slow or poorly functioning economy
b. donating large sums of money to charity
c. a large corporation made up of many companies
d. things like human rights, gender equality, social welfare, etc.
e. people feeling pessimistic about the future and dissatisfied with the way their government runs the nation
f. a disease where nerves and muscles grow weaker and weaker
g. a person involved in large-scale money-making affairs
h. a person or persons who have recently become rich
i. a well-known international news service
j. staying out of the public eye; keeping away from attention

Active Reading:

As you read through Today's Reading, look for answers to these questions. Mark the sentences in the reading where the answers are found.

1. Who are three philanthropists who recently made large donations to various causes?
2. What were billionaires Bill Gates and Warren Buffet doing in China?
3. What are some "austerity measures" governments are taking?
4. Why does one economist think austerity measures don't work?

Words in Context:

Choose the word or phrase that is closest in meaning to the underlined word in each sentence fragment below.

1. ... large chunks of their "<u>decadent</u>," as some see it, wealth ...
   (A) immoral (B) enviable (C) admirable

2. The <u>reclusive</u> billionaire Esther Koplowitz ...
   (A) well-known
   (B) not often seen in public
   (C) having a difficult character

3. ... to help it <u>revamp</u> its struggling school system ...
   (A) recover (B) reverse (C) remake

4. ... growth is <u>spawning</u> a large number of billionaires ...
   (A) delivering (B) producing (C) accepting

5. ... believed to have <u>reaped</u> their fortunes through illegal ...
   (A) gathered (B) stolen (C) cheated

6. ... nouveau riche are <u>wary</u> of attracting too much attention ...
   (A) cautious (B) eager (C) hurt

7. ... to <u>pledge</u> his entire fortune to charity ...
   (A) inherit (B) lend (C) promise

8. ... I don't want to be a <u>miser</u> ...
   (A) poor person
   (B) famous person
   (C) cheap or stingy person

9. ... and the U.K. are all <u>drastically</u> cutting ...
   (A) immediately (B) eventually (C) dramatically

10. ... in an effort to reduce public <u>debt</u> ...
    (A) state of owing money; money that is owed
    (B) earned income
    (C) safety and security

11. ... and mounting public anger and <u>unrest</u> ...
    (A) lack of sleep (B) trouble; protest
    (C) opinion

● ● ● TODAY'S READING ● ● ●

Read this essay carefully. Then do the exercises that follow.

(1) Philanthropy is "in" these days. The world's richest people are making headlines for giving away large chunks of their "decadent," as some see it, wealth. The reclusive billionaire Esther Koplowitz, head of a Spanish construction conglomerate, recently donated $21 million to a Barcelona biomedical research center that seeks treatments for cancer and multiple sclerosis. Last year, billionaire financier and philanthropist George Soros, known for his contributions to liberal causes, donated $100 million to Human Rights Watch. Mark Zuckerberg, the twenty-something founder of Facebook, gave $100 million to Newark, New Jersey, to help it revamp its struggling school system. China, with its explosive economic growth, is spawning a large number of billionaires of its own. Not too long ago, Bill Gates and Warren Buffet, two of America's richest men and most generous donors, called on Beijing to try to convince their Chinese counterparts to give most of their fortunes to charity. The Associated Press (AP) reports that many rich Chinese like to keep a low profile. With a widening gap between rich and poor, there is "growing resentment against those believed to have reaped their fortunes through illegal means," the report said. These nouveau riche are wary of attracting too much attention. Nevertheless, Gates and Buffet's "pitch" inspired one multimillionaire, Chen Guangbiao, CEO of a large recycling company, to pledge his entire fortune to charity upon his death. "I'm a rich man," Chen told AP, "but I don't want to be a miser."

(2) Speaking of money, another trend is making headlines these days: austerity. In fact, Merriam-Webster Dictionary named "austerity," defined as "enforced or extreme economy," as its 2010 Word of the Year. It's easy to see why. Governments everywhere, especially in Europe, have been announcing strict austerity measures to cope with the present global economic downturn. Greece, Ireland,

Portugal, and the U.K. are all drastically cutting government spending in an effort to reduce public debt. What this means is that less money is available for education, welfare benefits, healthcare, and other social-improvement programs. And more often than not, it is the poorest and neediest members of society who suffer the most. But austerity doesn't work, or so says economist David Blanchflower. In short, austerity means a loss of public confidence. Businesses and consumers see what is coming and cut back on spending and investing accordingly, Blanchflower says. Shops and factories go out of business. Schools close. Unemployment goes up, real estate prices come down. The result? Deeper and deeper recession and mounting citizens' anger and unrest. As the recent London riots showed.

● ● ● EXERCISES 1: COMPREHENSION ● ● ●

Reading for Information:

Complete each sentence with the correct answer choice.

1. All of the following are mentioned as having donated money to SPECIFIC charities EXCEPT
   (A) Bill Gates.
   (B) Esther Koplowitz.
   (C) George Soros.
   (D) Mark Zuckerberg.

2. The statement that is OPINION and not FACT is
   (A) Newark's schools really needed the donated money.
   (B) Chinese billionaires earned their money illegally.
   (C) Mr. Chen was impressed by what Gates and Buffet had to say.
   (D) George Soros is interested in the cause of human rights.

3. The information that is NOT CLEARLY STATED in the reading is
   (A) what "austerity" means according to Merriam-Webster.
   (B) what countries are taking austerity measures.
   (C) who suffers most from spending cuts.
   (D) where David Blanchflower expressed his opinion.

4. The problem caused by government austerity that David Blanchflower does NOT MENTION is
   (A) loss of jobs.
   (B) reduced company investments.
   (C) poor public health.
   (D) loss of educational opportunity.

Listening for Ideas:

48

Listen to the possible answers to each question below. Circle the letter of the correct answer.

1. What do some people think of the wealth of the world's richest people?
   (A)   (B)   (C)

2. Why is there growing resentment against rich people in China these days?
   (A)   (B)   (C)

3. Which of these is NOT MENTIONED as a reason governments are adopting austerity measures?
   (A)   (B)   (C)

● ● ● EXERCISES 2: COMPOSITION ● ● ●

Making Questions: 49

Write the question you would need to ask to get each answer below. Listen to check your questions.

1. Question: What two diseases _____?
   Answer: Cancer and multiple sclerosis.

2. Question: Why did _____?
   Answer: To try to convince their Chinese counterparts to give most of their fortunes to charity.

3. Question: What doesn't _____?
   Answer: A miser.

4. Question: What does _____?
   Answer: It doesn't work.

Writing with Idioms: 50

Rewrite each sentence below by substituting one of these phrases for the underlined part. Make the necessary changes. Listen to check your answers.

> call on
> more often than not
> cope with
> go out of business

1. Donna seems to be <u>handling</u> her new duties very well.

   _____

2. Many small companies have <u>closed their doors</u> recently.

   _____

3. <u>Usually</u>, Ian is practicing the piano at this time of day.

_____

4. Thanks for <u>visiting</u> my mother in the hospital yesterday.

_____

Word Forms:

Write the correct form of the word in brackets.

1. A person who owes a lot of money is called a [debt → _____].

2. A [miser → _____] person likes to keep his money to himself.

3. If you enter a dark room very carefully because you aren't sure who or what is in it, you enter the room [wary → _____].

4. To take [drastically → _____] action to solve a problem is to believe that this is your last chance to solve it.

5. A time in history when people are self-indulgent and spend money foolishly is often called an age of [decadent → _____].

● ● ● EXERCISES 3: CHALLENGE ● ● ●

Using Key Concepts:

Complete each sentence with one of the Key Concepts on page 96.

1. You can read the latest headlines by checking out _____.

2. A big corporation like Mitsubishi is called a _____.

3. When citizens lose faith in their leaders, they suffer from _____.

4. A financial crisis often leads to an _____.

5. People who protect their privacy keep a _____.

6. A progressive politician tries to promote _____.

Vocabulary Expansion:

Look at this list of adjectives that are similar in meaning to "generous" but that are used to express different things. Then fill in the blank in each sentence below with the correct NOUN FORM of one of the adjectives.

lavish:	generous, but often for show only
magnanimous:	generous in forgiving others; kind
munificent:	generous with gifts of money
altruistic:	generous without concern for oneself
tolerant:	generous in understanding others' beliefs and ideas

1. The university thanked the wealthy donor for his _____.
2. The movie star is known for the _____ of his parties.
3. In the camp, the kids learn _____ for other religions and

cultural practices.

4. The _____ that the doctor showed by not hating those who had caused him such grief should be a model for us all.

5. Bats also display _____, helping wounded or sick members of their group despite danger to themselves.

Listening Activity: 51

Listen to the short talk. Then decide which statement below best sums up the talk's main idea.

1. The University of Pittsburgh recently received a large donation from a major financial conglomerate.

2. Corporate social responsibility (CSR) programs at the University of Pittsburgh will give students a better moral education and deeper understanding of the needs of our interconnected world.

3. Students at the University of Pittsburgh will learn how to use technology to provide clean water, produce abundant electricity, and create job opportunities.

Lesson 11
Psychology

● ● ● **READY TO READ** ● ● ●

The exercises below will help you get the most out of this lesson's reading.

KEY VOCABULARY:

Match the words on the left with the definitions/synonyms on the right. Write the letters on the appropriate lines.

1. _____ abuse
2. _____ definitive
3. _____ inept
4. _____ inevitable
5. _____ inherited
6. _____ mediate
7. _____ pessimistic
8. _____ predilection
9. _____ resist
10. _____ vulnerability

a. handed down from parent to child
b. lacking skill; lacking judgment; clumsy
c. using something or someone in a bad way
d. weakness; openness to attack
e. bound or destined to happen; unavoidable
f. potential; possibility
g. to not be tempted to do or try; refuse
h. solid; proven beyond a doubt
i. having a dark or hopeless worldview
j. to act as a go-between; negotiate

Active Reading:

As you read the essay for this lesson, do the following.

(A) Choose the correct word in each numbered parentheses to make a common phrase.

(B) Look for these details. Draw a circle around each detail as you find it.

1. what "wired" people are compared to
2. an idea proposed by an ancient Greek philosopher
3. two brain-imaging technologies
4. What Sir Francis Bacon called knowledge
5. who conducted a study on introspection
6. how introspection is defined
7. another name for the brain's "gray matter"
8. a serious mental disease
9. what drug addicts cannot control
10. what the brain's frontal lobe "mediates"

(C) Look for and underline the answers to these questions.

1. Why can the term "wired" be seen as pessimistic? Why can it be seen as optimistic?
2. What do the University College London researchers hope their discoveries will lead to?
3. What makes it possible for some siblings with "inherited brain abnormalities" NOT to become addicted to drugs?

● ● ● READING ● ● ●

WIRED

[1] Although it appears to **go (1. through, against)** the humanistic—and, by extension, the democratic—concepts of free will, individual choice, and the possibility of personal change, the term "wired" is used more and more often these days. To say that a person is "wired for" a particular character trait or flaw or attitude toward life is to say that that person was born with that particular predilection and that there's nothing he or she can do about it. It is to say that something in that person's mental or genetic makeup makes it inevitable that he or she will grow up to be a drunk or drug addict, say, or will be unlucky in love, or will always be shy and socially inept. To put it more bluntly, it is to say that people are like machines or gadgets, designed and built (wired) to do one thing and one thing only. At first, this may sound like a pretty pessimistic way of looking at things, an echo of the "A man's character is his fate" idea first proposed by the Greek philosopher Heraclitus over 2,500 years ago. But let's take a closer look.

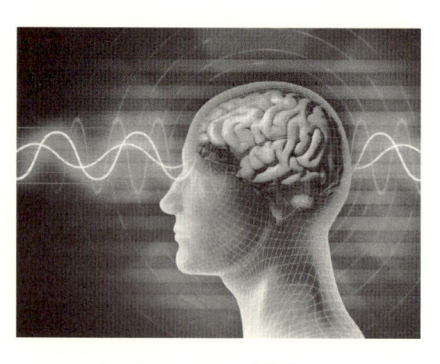

[2] The term "wired" has come into common usage these days thanks to recent advances in neuroscience and brain-imaging technology like PET scans and fMRI. Originally developed to help surgeons pinpoint brain abnormalities caused by disease or stroke, these new techniques have now made it possible to watch the brain in action, to better see how it works, and to monitor which brain regions control which actions and behaviors. This new knowledge gives us a sort of early-warning system—not only for medical purposes but also

for detecting problematic aspects of character. Knowing **(2. ahead, before) of time**, for instance, that the area of a person's brain that controls violent behavior is out of control, so to speak, can help him or her resist such behavior. Knowledge is power, as another philosopher, the Englishman Sir Francis Bacon, once put it. So the term "wired" isn't all bad **(3. after, in) all**: it appears it can have an optimistic aspect as well.

[3] Here's an example: The Associated Press (AP) reports that scientists at University College London have just published the results (in the journal *Science*) of brain-scan findings that offer hope to people who lack an essential function of consciousness— introspection, the ability to examine and judge your own thoughts and actions. "There may be different levels of consciousness," said the lead author of the study, "ranging from simply having an experience to reflecting on that experience. Introspection is on the higher end of the spectrum—by measuring this process and relating it to the brain, we hope to gain insight into the biology of conscious thought." In the study, the team measured self-awareness by asking volunteers certain questions, and then asking the subjects to rate how much confidence they had in the correctness of their answers. The researchers used brain scans to watch the subjects' brains as they made and defended their responses. The idea behind the experiment, says AP, was that strongly introspective people would be more confident when they got the answers right, "and more likely to second-guess themselves when they really were wrong." And this proved to be the case. People who were just "brash and overconfident," on the other hand, "might lead an outsider to think they were right, but in reality would not show that correlation." According to the report, the study revealed that strong introspective ability is linked to the size of the brain's prefrontal cortex, the "gray matter" region usually associated

with "higher thinking skills" like introspection: in other words, the larger our prefrontal cortex, the better we are at self-analysis. Brain scans also showed that introspective ability is also bolstered by "stronger functioning white matter," that is, the nerve fibers that allow brain cells to **keep in (4. relation, touch) with** one another. It is hoped that the study's findings will one day help "tackle brain injuries or diseases that rob people of self-reflection—such as schizophrenia patients who are not aware that they are ill and thus do not take their medication." Related studies have shown that schizophrenia, at least in part, **stems (5. out, from)** impaired "gray matter" functioning.

[4] The team leader, though encouraged by the experiment's outcome, concluded that the study raised some important questions and that more research would be needed to **come (6. up, down) with** definitive answers: Are these differences in brain size and function innate, or do they mean that the prefrontal cortex gets stronger as a result of people spending more time and effort "exercising" it? Is improved introspection an ability that we can **pick (7. up, out)** through training? If the answer to the latter question is yes, that's very good news indeed.

[5] In another brain-scan study, also published in *Science*, British scientists at Cambridge University have revealed that drug addicts have "inherited abnormalities" in regions of the brain that control rash behavior. Until now, there has been some doubt about whether these brain abnormalities were the result of brain damage caused by the drugs or were already present in the brain, thereby "wiring" a person for drug abuse. To conduct the study, the Cambridge researchers compared pairs of siblings, one of whom was addicted to drugs, the other addiction-free. They found that the siblings shared many weaknesses in the structure of the brain's frontal lobe, the region that "mediates motor control, cognition, and behavior," thus indicating that addictive behavior had a family origin. Presumably, said the study's leader, the non-addictive siblings have some "other resilience factors"—either environmental or **brought (8. around,**

about) by other differences in brain structure—that "counteract the familial vulnerability to drug dependence." The results of this study offer hope that those "wired" for drug dependence can be detected early on and helped before they fall victim to the "ravages of drug addiction."

READING COMPREHENSION

READING COMPREHENSION 1:

Complete each sentence with the correct choice.

1. The author probably sees free will, individual choice, and personal change as
   (A) character traits that make for certain personal attitudes.
   (B) aspects of our mental and genetic makeup.
   (C) essential to a democratic society.

2. It is implied that PET scans and fMRI technologies were originally used
   (A) to make brain surgery surer and safer.
   (B) as tools to study mental function and processes.
   (C) for detecting violent and other negative behavior.

3. The underlined expression "were more likely to second-guess themselves when they were really wrong" as used in paragraph 3 means that the subjects
   (A) hated to admit their mistakes.
   (B) reflected on why they made their mistakes.
   (C) asked permission to change their answers.

4. If a stronger predilection for introspection is not indeed innate, it means that the ability to "think about one's thoughts"
   (A) runs in families.
   (B) can be learned and developed.
   (C) cannot be developed in some people.

5. Until the Cambridge study proved otherwise, some scientists thought that drug addicts' brain abnormalities
   (A) were found in other regions of the brain.
   (B) could be overcome by early detection.
   (C) were caused by the drugs themselves.

READING COMPREHENSION 2:

🔘 53

Listen to the sentences. Circle T if the sentence is true, F if it is false.

1. T F   2. T F   3. T F   4. T F   5. T F

READING COMPREHENSION 3:

Go back to the ACTIVE READING questions on page 107. Write full-sentence answers in your own words as much as possible.

1. _____

2. _____

3. _____

Lesson 12
The Environment

● ● ● READY TO READ ● ● ●

The exercises below will help you get the most out of this lesson's reading.

KEY VOCABULARY:

Match the words on the left with the definitions/synonyms on the right. Write the letters on the appropriate lines.

1. _____ acutely
2. _____ cogent
3. _____ deplorable
4. _____ dire
5. _____ dread
6. _____ forfeit
7. _____ invalidate
8. _____ precarious
9. _____ sustainable
10. _____ tirade

a. to not look forward to; fear what is coming
b. capable of being continued; secure
c. to make or render untrue; to nullify
d. an outburst of anger; long, angry speech
e. keenly; felt deeply and strongly
f. sad and miserable; highly regrettable
g. not safe or secure; lacking stability; easily affected
h. clever; convincing; appealing to the intellect
i. having terrible or disastrous consequences
j. to give up or put off; sacrifice

ACTIVE READING:

As you read the essay for this lesson, do the following.

(A) Choose the correct word in each numbered parentheses to make a common phrase.

(B) Look for these details. Draw a circle around each detail as you find it.

1. the year the first Earth Day was held
2. a foreign phrase that means "reason for being"
3. what "Green" is
4. what Elisabeth Rosenthal compares Earth Day to
5. how many people shot One Day on Earth, how many languages it is in, and how many hours of footage were shot
6. what "climate injustice" means
7. whom Dinah Shelton represents
8. where Dipi Moni comes from
9. how often and to whom the Goldman Prize is awarded
10. what Ma Jun means by "transparency"

(C) Look for and underline the answers to these questions.

1. What does the author of the essay say is the goal for our planet?
2. What kind of place does Kyle Ruddick say that One Day on Earth shows the world to be?
3. What does Dipi Moni say that the advanced countries that are responsible for the greenhouse effect and global warming are obligated to do?

● ● ● READING ● ● ●

EVERY DAY SHOULD BE EARTH DAY

[1] Today is Earth Day. In 175 countries, millions of people are celebrating our planet and the progress that has been made since 1970 (when the first Earth Day was held) to preserve and protect it. But as a deluge of daily headlines makes us acutely, and **(1. at, in) times** depressingly, aware, we still have a long way to go to bring about our goal of a healthy and humane, secure and sustainable global environment and economy. Thus, another of Earth Day's raisons d'etre is to **(2. call, move) attention to** pressing environmental issues like carbon emissions and climate change, habitat destruction and endangered species, and water and air pollution, and to get us to think about how we can **go (3. after, about)** tackling them.

[2] Sure, we could be cynical about Earth Day and, like Elisabeth Rosenthal in "Green," her *New York Times* energy and environment blog, see it as just another day like Valentine's Day, "a colossal marketing opportunity—a paradoxical way to promote consumption and sell stuff." As an environmental reporter, Rosenthal says she has come to "dread the Earth Day avalanche of deals and promotions that arrive via e-mail (or worse, environmentally speaking) in my office or home mailbox." Shouldn't, she asks, Earth Day be a chance to seriously **think (4. of, about)** forfeiting purchases and giving up habits that are "environmentally questionable or that we could happily **(5. have, do) without**" rather than just another occasion for hitting the local mall or superstore looking for "green" bargains?

Rosenthal ends her Earth Day tirade by making this cogent and thought-provoking comment: "Earth Day is transient. If you only showed love on Valentine's Day, would that really mean anything at all?"

[3] But let's put our cynicism on the back burner for a while and try to see Earth Day in a more positive light. And what better way to do that than to catch a screening of a new film entitled *One Day on Earth*, a remarkable video album of our planet that was filmed in every country of the world on just a single day—October 10, 2010? With financial and technological support from 60 non-profit organizations and the United Nations (the film is being shown today at U.N. headquarters in New York City), and with 19,000 professional and amateur filmmakers **(6. pitching, throwing) in** on the project, accumulating over 3,000 hours of footage in more than 70 languages, the movie, as its director Kyle Ruddick told the London *Telegraph*, is "a simple big idea." Ruddick hopes that the film, which can be seen at movie theaters, on university campuses, and at "makeshift outdoor venues" around the world, will help people see that "the world is this enormous, powerful, sometimes dangerous, sometimes wonderful place, and that they will realize that their life is connected to everyone else's and that, for lack of better words, we are all in this together, more or less."

[4] And while we're being upbeat about Earth Day and optimistic about our planet's ability to reverse courses and invalidate all the dire, coming-disaster predictions that have been made about our ecological future, let's take a look at a couple of new ideas that offer hope on the environmental front.

[5] At a recent Human Rights Council meeting in Geneva, Switzerland, experts proposed a novel approach to environmental protection—getting those advanced industrial countries most

responsible for climate change to **(7. look, see) upon** it as a human rights issue. The approach is based on a deplorable "climate injustice"—the fact that many of the nations who have contributed the least to the greenhouse effect are the worst affected by global warming. As the online news service OneWorld.net explained: "The impact of climate change would be most acutely felt by those whose rights protections were already precarious, including the poor, migrants, the disabled, indigenous people, and women." One participant in the Geneva meeting, Dinah Shelton, chairperson of the Inter-American Commission on Human Rights, summed up the idea like this: "Why take a human rights approach to climate change? First, in a rather cynical way, because nothing else is working." Efforts to curb global warming through the "environmental law regime" and the promotion of "sustainable development," she says, have largely **(8. fallen, gone) through** because the emphasis has been "more on development than sustainable." Human rights can address environmental problems in a more effective manner, Shelton believes, because of the "very high place human rights law holds in the global community." Another meeting participant, Dipi Moni, Foreign Minister of Bangladesh, concurs: "Customary international law says it is the obligation of every state not to allow itself knowingly to be used for acts contrary to the rights of other states. Historically responsible countries must not turn a blind eye to the denial of the human rights of millions affected in vulnerable countries. There are sufficient reasons to affirm that emission reduction and compensatory financing constitute human rights obligations."

[6] Meanwhile, one of the recipients of the 2012 Goldman Environmental Prize, an annual award given to six "grassroots environmental heroes," was Ma Jun, who has come up with a novel approach of his own for cleaning up China's polluted lakes, streams, and rivers. Ma, arguably China's best-known ecological warrior, set up a nonprofit group, the Institute of Public and Environmental Affairs, which he now uses to "shame" the country's polluters

into environmental accountability. Although China has laws and regulations against polluting, "enforcement," Ma told the *Christian Science Monitor*, "is very weak." So Ma decided that "transparency"— informing the Chinese public about who is responsible for fouling China's waters—was key. If the people have the right information, they will use it to put pressure on polluters, Ma reasoned, and he was right. Already, nearly 600 companies have been punished for pollution-law violations, and many of the largest international corporations doing business in China now "check their suppliers against Ma's list of violators" to make sure they are operating aboveboard.

READING COMPREHENSION

READING COMPREHENSION 1:

Complete each sentence with the correct choice.

1. The author says that daily headlines about the environment can sometimes be depressing most likely because
   (A) there are so many of them that they are difficult to keep up with.
   (B) we have read and heard them so many times before.
   (C) they can make us feel as if the situation is without hope.

2. The environmental problem that is NOT mentioned in paragraph 1 is
   (A) an increase in the earth's atmospheric temperature.
   (B) animals being forced out of their homes and dying out as a result.
   (C) people being forced to migrate to other countries.

3. When Elisabeth Rosenthal calls Earth Day "transient," she means that
   (A) it only comes once a year.
   (B) people forget what it means soon after it's over.
   (C) it is too commercial these days.

4. In paragraph 5 it is implied that
   (A) most countries are more likely to observe and enforce human rights laws than laws designed to protect the environment.
   (B) countries that are responsible for denying human rights in other countries aren't usually aware that they are doing it.
   (C) the greenhouse effect should affect only those nations responsible for creating it.

5. It can be inferred that
   (A) Ma Jun personally inspects each company suspected of polluting water.
   (B) the more Chinese people know about what is going on, the more involved they will become in environmental matters.
   (C) only foreign companies have been punished so far.

READING COMPREHENSION 2: 55

Listen to the sentences. Circle T if the sentence is true, F if it is false.

1. T F   2. T F   3. T F   4. T F   5. T F

READING COMPREHENSION 3:

Go back to the ACTIVE READING questions on page 115. Write full-sentence answers in your own words as much as possible.

1. _____

2. _____

3. _____

Lesson 13
History

● ● ● **READY TO READ** ● ● ●

The exercises below will help you get the most out of this lesson's reading.

KEY VOCABULARY:

Match the words on the left with the definitions/synonyms on the right. Write the letters on the appropriate lines.

1. _____ adversity
2. _____ advocate
3. _____ arcane
4. _____ certifiable
5. _____ chronological
6. _____ devastating
7. _____ extermination
8. _____ heinous
9. _____ succinctly
10. _____ terrain

a. wicked; evil; nefarious
b. in sequence or order of time
c. an area of land; region; landscape
d. said in a few words; tersely
e. mass killing; annihilation
f. hardship; ill fortune; suffering
g. person who fights for a cause; activist
h. genuine; provable
i. very damaging; destructive; ruinous
j. known by only a few people; mysterious; esoteric

ACTIVE READING:

As you read the essay for this lesson, do the following.

(A) Choose the correct word in each numbered parentheses to make a common phrase.

(B) Look for these details. Draw a circle around each detail as you find it.

1. a word in paragraph 1 that means professor
2. what kind of topics Robert Tombs says U.K. history pupils must study
3. what era in U.K. history he says pupils often miss out on
4. who Henry Ford was
5. a word in paragraph 2 that means "not commonly accepted"
6. three advantages of history according to David Hume
7. what history shows us, according to Edward Gibbon
8. what Norman Cousins campaigned for
9. what Michael Berenbaum specializes in
10. where Adolf Eichmann was when he was captured

(C) Look for and underline the answers to these questions.

1. What does Robert Tombs say about U.K. history teachers?
2. In what way in particular does the American Historical Association agree with David Hume's comments about the uses of history?
3. How does the author of the essay say history is taught in most schools?

● ● ● READING ● ● ●

THE "STORY" IN HISTORY 56

[1] In what has been called a devastating report, Professor Robert Tombs, a history fellow at Cambridge University, charged that history teaching in the U.K. is among the worst in the western world, adding that it was difficult to name a European country that teaches history so poorly, "so that the majority of school-leavers are **left in the (1. dark, black)** about the unfolding story of their past." History education in U.K. schools has "little in common with real historical study," Tombs complained, because pupils are required to study "obscure topics in absurdly arcane detail." Taught a "miscellany of disconnected fragments," pupils **(2. left, miss) out on** vast sections of history, particularly the history of the British Empire, to which "scant attention" is paid, Tombs said, despite its "far-reaching implications in global history." Much of the problem lies with history instructors, who focus not on the teaching of the story of history but on developing "artificial historical skills such as evaluating sources." And if that's not bad enough, Tombs says, most teachers have little real knowledge of the topics they teach. In his report, Tombs demanded that the history teaching system be "overhauled" and attached an alternative curriculum made up of 36 events in British history that he said all secondary-school pupils should **be (3. known, familiar) with**. He also recommended that Britain emulate France, Germany, and Australia, countries that offer students a "broad chronological sweep of world and national history."

[2] Though not expressly stated, between the lines of Tombs's report is the assumption that history matters, that its study is vital to us in

some profound way, that time spent learning about the past is never wasted. But what is it about history that makes it so crucial? Why, indeed, do we need to study it?   Henry Ford, the American automobile and manufacturing pioneer, didn't think we needed to **(4. do, bother) with** history at all. "History is more or less bunk," he said, then went on: "It's tradition. We don't want tradition. We want to live in the present, and the only history that is worth a tinker's damn is the history we make today." But Ford's view is a heretical one, and most serious historians (and most people in general, thank goodness) dismiss it is as more or less, well, bunk (the only history Ford wanted to make was a historically huge profit). In the 18th century, David Hume, the great British philosopher and historian, stated quite succinctly what has become the standard view of the value of historical study—that it makes us better people: "The advantages found in history seem to be of three kinds, as it amuses the fancy, as it improves the understanding, and as it strengthens virtue."

[3] On its website, the American Historical Association backs Hume up: "History provides a terrain for moral contemplation. Studying the stories of individuals and situations in the past allows us to test our own moral sense, to hone it against some of the real complexities individuals have faced in difficult settings. People who have weathered adversity can provide inspiration. History teaching by example is one phrase that describes the study of the past— a study not only of certifiable heroes, great men and women who successfully **(5. tried, worked) through** moral dilemmas, but also of more ordinary people who provide lessons in courage, diligence, or constructive protest." Another 18th-century British historian, however, Edward Gibbon, author of the immortal *The Rise and Fall of the Roman Empire*, thought history could be instructive in a

different way: "History is indeed little more than the register of the crimes, follies, and misfortunes of mankind." In other words, history provides us with all kinds of negative models as well, examples of historical mistakes and reprehensible acts that we must never forget if we are to **(6. keep, stay) from** repeating them. Looked at in this way, "History is a vast early warning system," as Norman Cousins, the 20th-century American journalist, professor, and advocate for world peace put it.

[4] Now that we know *why* we study history the next question is: *How* do we study it? Most of us "slog through" history in school, where it is often the driest of subjects, a rote chore of memorizing historical people, places, and dates—facts and figures that we forget almost as soon as we are tested on them. Rarely are we told the "story" in history. So: how can we make history come alive and make it more relevant to our own lives? One way, says Michael Berenbaum, a noted scholar who specializes in the study of the Holocaust, is to visit a good historical museum, which he calls "a storytelling institution" that shows the "power of the story in all its elements." Take the Museum of the Jewish People at the University of Tel Aviv in Israel, for example, which is currently **(7. having, putting) on** an exhibition that chronicles the top-secret Mossad (Israeli's "CIA") operation that led to the capture of the infamous Nazi war criminal, Adolf Eichmann. Eichmann was one of the chief architects of Adolph Hitler's Final Solution, which called for the extermination of all Europe's Jews. After the Second World War, Eichmann escaped to Argentina, where he lived and worked under a false identity until he was **(8. followed, tracked) down** by Mossad agents in 1960 and flown under cover to Israel. There, in a trial broadcast around the globe and what was to become one of the greatest news stories of the twentieth century, Eichmann was convicted of war crimes and heinous crimes against humanity and sentenced to death by hanging.

The museum exhibition, says *Time* magazine, is "satisfying in every possible way: Not only seeing justice done, but laying eyes on all the homespun artifacts of early spycraft"—all the "James Bond" stuff, as

AP calls it, that made the operation possible. The exhibition is the most thrilling of spy thrillers, a story that visitors can walk through and feel as if they were both learning history and living it, something which only a good historical museum can do for us, says Michael Berenbaum.

READING COMPREHENSION

READING COMPREHENSION 1:
Complete each sentence with the correct choice.

1. Robert Tombs says that
   (A) U.K. pupils should focus more on the history of France, Germany, and Australia in order to understand western society better.
   (B) history instruction in the U.K. needs to be changed from top to bottom.
   (C) if U.K. pupils learn about the 36 British historical events he recommends, they won't need to study global history.

2. What Tombs's report hints at but does not expressly state is that
   (A) history is too vital a subject to be taught in elementary school.
   (B) the study of history as it is now taught is a waste of time.
   (C) we need to know about history to know about ourselves.

3. The difference between the American History Association's view of the examples history gives us and that of Edward Gibbon is that
   (A) the former is negative while the latter is positive.
   (B) the latter is negative while the former is positive.
   (C) Gibbon's is profound while the former is shallow.

4. Norman Cousins sees history
   (A) as something to be studied for its own sake.
   (B) as a practical guide to avoiding present-day dangers.
   (C) as the record of mankind's most glorious achievements.

5. It can be inferred from the essay that
   (A) the author visited the Eichmann exhibition in person.
   (B) Eichmann's trial, like his capture, took place in secret.
   (C) Eichmann escaped to Argentina after the war because he knew he was wanted as a war criminal.

READING COMPREHENSION 2:

57

Listen to the sentences. Circle T if the sentence is true, F if it is false.

1. T F   2. T F   3. T F   4. T F   5. T F

READING COMPREHENSION 3:

Go back to the ACTIVE READING questions on page 123. Write full-sentence answers in your own words as much as possible.

1. _____

2. _____

3. _____

Lesson 14
Space

● ● ● READY TO READ ● ● ●

The exercises below will help you get the most out of this lesson's reading.

KEY VOCABULARY:

Match the words on the left with the definitions/synonyms on the right. Write the letters on the appropriate lines.

1. _____ acclaimed
2. _____ affliction
3. _____ compile
4. _____ comprise
5. _____ depletion
6. _____ fatal
7. _____ hypothetically
8. _____ precious
9. _____ probe
10. _____ sovereignty

a. in theory; possibly; theoretically
b. reducing to a very low amount; loss
c. national independence; self-government
d. highly praised; respected; lauded
e. to gather or collect; amass
f. to be made up of; contain; constitute
g. to explore; investigate
h. deadly; terminal
i. a mental or physical health problem
j. very valuable; priceless

ACTIVE READING:

As you read the essay for this lesson, do the following.

(A) Choose the correct word in each numbered parentheses to make a common phrase.

(B) Look for these details. Draw a circle around each detail as you find it.

1. by how many times our chances of finding alien life have increased
2. what the "A" in HARPS means
3. estimated percentage of red dwarfs in our galaxy
4. what Diane Ackerman compares stars to
5. how she says the planets should be used
6. Stephen Hawking's area of expertise
7. the name of a crippling affliction
8. what terraforming would make Mars, according to Hawking
9. the name of a new company formed by billionaires
10. when the Outer Space Treaty became effective

(C) Look for and underline the answers to these questions.

1. What are two drawbacks to finding habitable planets near Red Dwarfs?
2. What "perils" does Stephen Hawking see for mankind?
3. What, in essence, does the Outer Space Treaty say about to whom "outer space" belongs?

Lesson 14   Space   131

GALAXY QUEST

[1] The chances of finding alien life somewhere in our galaxy other than on Earth just **(1. came, went) up** astronomically, "by a factor of 8 or 10," or so says a new study conducted by the Search for Extraterrestrial Intelligence Institute in Mountain View, California. The study **(2. makes, takes) use of** data compiled by the European Space Agency's HARPS (which stands for High Accuracy Radial-velocity Planet Searcher: no wonder they shortened it to HARPS!) spectrograph at the La Silla Observatory in Chile. HARPS has been scanning the southern skies for the last decade looking for potentially inhabitable planets outside the solar system (so far, astronomers have spotted more than thirty candidates). According to the new study, tens of billions of planets in orbit around red dwarfs, stars that are smaller, fainter, and cooler than our sun, could contain liquid water and thus are hypothetically capable of supporting life. These stars, which have longer lives than our sun, are thought to comprise up to 80 percent of the stars in the Milky Way. But one participant in the project warned that it might be a bit premature to **get our (3. dreams, hopes) up** too far. "The habitable zone (known as 'Goldilocks') around these stars would be very, very small. Consequently, the chances that you would actually find any planet at the right distance from the red dwarf to be attractive to life was likely to be small, too," Seth Shostak told Yahoo News. He also speculated that the harsh, perhaps fatal, environment surrounding these suns, particularly the high levels of radiation,

raised some concern about whether these stars' planets could be livable. **Be that as it (4. must, may)**, Shostak believes that even with these drawbacks, the "sheer influx of tens of billions of potentially habitable planets improves the chances of finding alien life." The search, he says, must go on.

[2] In an essay in the *New York Times*, Diane Ackerman, a best-selling and critically acclaimed American fiction and non-fiction author, agrees. "We're explorers by design," she writes, "right down to our cells, and we thrive on quests. Stars flare like distant campfires overhead, and we wonder if they're home to other worlds like our own. Or made of diamond. I'm hoping NASA will continue to find the boosters it needs, will continue sending scouts around our solar system, and use the planets as stepping stones to the stars," because, Ackerman concludes, "that's where our compass points."

[3] Stephen Hawking, **without a (5. worry, doubt)** the most recognized name and face in the world of theoretical physics, also believes we must **(6. pull, carry) on** our exploration of outer space, but not just because we're "explorers by design." Probing space is essential for our very survival, he says. Mankind is in peril, Hawking warns. Resource depletion, overpopulation, climate change, a global pandemic (possibly caused by a bio-engineered disease), nuclear holocaust, or even collision with an asteroid or comet—these are some of the "great dangers" he sees for the human race. "Our only chance of long-term survival is not to remain inward-looking on Planet Earth but to expand into space." This, he said in a recent radio interview through the computer he uses to communicate, means colonizing first the moon and then Mars, which Hawking maintains could be made inhabitable through "terraforming," techniques by which the Red Planet could be **(7. fixed, turned) into** "an analogue of Earth." Despite being a victim of Lou Gehrig's disease, an affliction

that has left him all but paralyzed and is usually associated with early death, Hawking recently celebrated his 70th birthday, which might help explain why he remains an optimist. "Though we face great dangers," he says, "if we can avoid disaster for the next two centuries, our species should be safe, as we spread into space."

[4] A small group of world-famous billionaires has just announced that they have other, more immediate designs on space, though with an eye on the future survival of mankind as well. They have formed a company called Planetary Resources that plans to send robotic spacecraft to asteroids to mine minerals and precious metals like platinum and palladium and then ship them back to Earth. This, they believe, will add trillions of dollars to the global economy. And they mean business. As one of the co-founders of the company, Eric Anderson, told ABC News: "If you believe it's important to have continued prosperity for future generations, we need resources from somewhere. Near-Earth asteroids are way, way more appealing than just about any other place we might look." According to ABC, Anderson envisions "whole fleets of robotic 'droids' approaching asteroids," of which there are more than 1,500 that pass close to Earth, and "scouring their surfaces" for valuable resources.

[5] But is what the company is planning legal? To whom do those precious resources and potential trillions of dollars belong? Isn't space and everything in it the communal property of everyone here on Earth, of all nations equally? These are the questions many law and international relations professors are asking. The answer might seem to lie in the Outer Space Treaty, which was ratified by all space-probing nations in 1967 and established that outer space, "including the moon and other celestial bodies, is not subject to national appropriation by claim of sovereignty, by means of use or occupation, or by any other means." In other words, outer space *does* belong to everyone. But what about resource exploitation? To whom do the universe's vast resources belong? Unfortunately, the treaty does not **(8. come, go) into** this question. But as *Wired* magazine puts it: "This question is too far in the future to answer. But the day that question

arrives, we can all pop the champagne corks to celebrate: Mankind will have become a truly space-faring species. We will have taken the first steps toward bringing the nearly limitless resources of space into the economic sphere of humanity."

● ● ● READING COMPREHENSION ● ● ●

READING COMPREHENSION 1:
Complete each sentence with the correct choice.

1. It can be inferred that a red dwarf is all of the following EXCEPT
   (A) longer lived than our sun.
   (B) brighter than our sun.
   (C) not as hot as our sun.

2. By saying "that's where our compass points," Diane Ackerman implies that
   (A) NASA needs our support.
   (B) outer space is our destiny.
   (C) Earth will not be our home for much longer.

3. The author of the essay implies that
   (A) Stephen Hawking's own survival makes him optimistic about the survival of mankind.
   (B) Hawking doesn't believe we are "explorers by design."
   (C) Hawking is not a true optimist.

4. The main goal of the billionaires who formed the new company Planetary Resources is largely
   (A) exploratory in nature.
   (B) ecological in scope.
   (C) economic oriented.

5. Wired concludes that the question of to whom outer space's resources belong
   (A) doesn't really matter.
   (B) will never be definitively answered.
   (C) must await an answer until the billionaires' plan becomes reality.

READING COMPREHENSION 2: 🔊 59

Listen to the sentences. Circle T if the sentence is true, F if it is false.

1. T   F   2. T   F   3. T   F   4. T   F   5. T   F

READING COMPREHENSION 3:

Go back to the ACTIVE READING questions on page 131. Write full-sentence answers in your own words as much as possible.

1. _____

2. _____

3. _____

Lesson 15
Education

● ● ● **READY TO READ** ● ● ●

The exercises below will help you get the most out of this lesson's reading.

KEY VOCABULARY:

Match the words on the left with the definitions/synonyms on the right. Write the letters on the appropriate lines.

1. _____ academic
2. _____ acquisition
3. _____ assessment
4. _____ credentials
5. _____ engaging
6. _____ erode
7. _____ median
8. _____ strain
9. _____ supersede
10. _____ torture

a. pain or the inflicting or causing of pain
b. to reduce or wear away gradually
c. to replace or take over
d. average; normal
e. stress; pressure; tension
f. judgment; evaluation; test
g. causing to pay close attention; fascinating
h. qualifications; required documents
i. obtaining; gaining
j. having to do with school and study

ACTIVE READING:

As you read the essay for this lesson, do the following.

(A) Choose the correct word in each numbered parentheses to make a common phrase.

(B) Look for these details. Draw a circle around each detail as you find it.

1. a word in paragraph 1 that means "selling for profit"
2. in the future, what information will do, according to Eli Noam
3. the name of an ancient city that is now in modern-day Iraq
4. what David Brooks says online courses were not too long ago
5. what Harvard and MIT's project costs and what it is called
6. the name of a course created by Stanford teachers
7. how many students have enrolled in the Stanford course so far
8. in what country a huge university building program is under way
9. who conducted a study on the effectiveness of online teaching
10. what John Updike compared schools to

(C) Look for and underline the answers to these questions.

1. What three things did Eli M. Noam say might happen to universities because of free online courses?
2. What other traditional fields besides higher education did David Brooks say have been altered by the onset of the Internet?
3. What was the conclusion of a study that compared online instruction and traditional classroom education?

● ● ● READING ● ● ●

ADVENTURES IN LEARNING

[1] Back in 1995, Eli M. Noam, a professor of Finance and Economics at Columbia University, delivered a lecture (later published in *Science* as an essay, which is available online, by the way) about what he saw as a far from "cheerful scenario for higher education." Noam agreed that the non-profit sharing of information online rather than "commercializing" it was a positive step forward for people everywhere, and that research would no doubt be strengthened by it. But he also felt that there was a growing possibility that the Internet and other communications-technology tools would "supersede" the traditional functions of the university as an institution of higher learning, "erode" its financial base, and reduce its role in intellectual inquiry. "In the past," said Noam, "people came to the information, and the information was at the university. In the future, the information will come to the people, wherever they are. What then is the role of the university? Will it be in the future more than a collection of remaining physical functions, such as science labs and the football team? Will electronics do to the university what printing did to the medieval cathedral, ending its central role in information transfer? Have we reached the end of the line of a model that **(1. turns, goes) back to** Nineveh, more than 2,500 years ago? Can we self-reform the university, or must things get much worse first?"

[2] Universities around the globe, but particularly in Britain and the United States, reacted to Noam's worries and warnings at first with

alarm and then with the realization that to avert his "bleak scenario," they would have to open their arms to and accommodate the new technologies—or, rather, learn to cohabit with them. And that is exactly what they are doing. As David Brooks put it in a recent *New York Times* column, "The elite, pace-setting universities have embraced the Internet. Not long ago, online courses were interesting experiments. Now online activity is at the core of how these schools envision their future. What happened to the newspaper and magazine business is about to happen to higher education: a rescrambling around the Web."

[3] Take Harvard and MIT (the Massachusetts Institute of Technology), for example. The two schools—both ranked in the top ten of the world's best universities—have now teamed up in a project, budgeted at $60 million and dubbed "edX," to offer free online courses that they expect to **(2. draw, come) in** millions of Internet users worldwide. Scholars at both institutions will develop the special courses, and other leading universities have been invited to join the project and adopt and adapt the courses for their own purposes. (For the last decade, MIT has, in fact, already been making material from more than 2,000 of its classes available free online.) Another good example of the rush to Internet education is the **(3. setting, making) up** of a free online course entitled "Introduction to AI" created by several Stanford scholars. According to John Naughton, writing in the London *Observer*, 160,000 students from more than 190 countries have already **(4. registered, signed) up** for the course, "with a median age of around 30." Naughton says that another big change is about to take place: "Up to now, universities have **held (5. up, back) from** offering qualifications for their online offerings. But starting this spring, MIT will give academic credentials to students

Lesson 15   Education   141

taking its free online courses, if they pass the assessment," which, of course, is also given online.

[4] Could anything be more wonderful? Now millions of people across the globe will have access to the world's best teachers and greatest scholars. India, for example, has just announced that it is planning to expand higher education to every corner of the country, where many of its most poverty-stricken citizens live, and is already building hundreds of model universities that could incorporate Harvard's or Stanford's or Oxford's online courses into their curricula, reaching millions of people who until now had no hope of going to college. Amazing! But the trend has its doubters, too, and rightly so, since it raises all kinds of important questions. What will happen to face-to-face learning? Isn't there a big difference between watching a lecture on a computer screen and listening to it in person, sharing the experience with other learners and then taking part in passionate discussions about its contents? Will academic standards be maintained, or will they sink to the lowest common denominator, as many people fear? But the main question is: Is online education as effective as classroom learning? That, of course, **(6. remains, leaves) to be seen**, but one study, conducted in 2009 by the U.S. Department of Education, concluded that "students in online learning conditions performed better than those receiving face-to-face instruction." The real promise of online education, the study said, is that it provides learning experiences that, unlike traditional classroom instruction, are more "engaging and useful because they stress learning by doing and can be tailored to individual students."

[5] John Updike, the late, great American novelist, once said: "The founding fathers in their wisdom decided that children were an unnatural strain on parents. So they provided jails called schools, equipped with torture called education." An exaggeration, of course, but Updike was right in implying that traditional classroom teaching at all levels has often been less than engaging. Could online instruction be what we're looking for? In his column, David Brooks hints that e-education can never **(7. get, take) the place**

of live learning. The challenge now is to find ways to "blend online information acquisition with face-to-face discussion, tutoring, debate, coaching, writing, and projects," turning it into real learning, which Brooks calls a complex social and emotional process. "My guess," he concludes," is that it will be easier to be a terrible university on the wide-open Web, but it will be possible for committed schools and students to be better than ever." In other words, online education is **here to (8. keep, stay)**. So let's make the best of it.

● ● ● READING COMPREHENSION ● ● ●

READING COMPREHENSION 1:
Complete each sentence with the correct choice.

1. Eli Noam concedes that having information available for free online will
   (A) be good for research.
   (B) spell the end of the line for the university as a physical place.
   (C) force universities to get rid of their science labs and football teams.

2. John Naughton implies that
   (A) until recently, most online university courses did not lead to formal degrees.
   (B) online courses have reached the limit of their popularity.
   (C) assessment will never be a part of online learning.

3. What is NOT mentioned about India's ambitious college building program is
   (A) whom the project is aimed at.
   (B) what courses the curricula might offer.
   (C) how the project is being funded or paid for.

4. It is suggested that some people are afraid that
   (A) only poor, disadvantaged people will study online.
   (B) online education standards will not be what they should be.
   (C) online lectures will be less than engaging because they won't be given by top-notch instructors.

5. It can be inferred that both David Brooks and the author of the essay believe that
   (A) live learning will be limited to the elite universities.
   (B) online education may only be a passing fad.
   (C) the best universities will be enhanced by the online boom.

READING COMPREHENSION 2:

Listen to the sentences. Circle T if the sentence is true, F if it is false.

1. T F   2. T F   3. T F   4. T F   5. T F

READING COMPREHENSION 3:

Go back to the ACTIVE READING questions on page 139. Write full-sentence answers in your own words as much as possible.

1. _____

2. _____

3. _____

VOCABULARY

A

- aboveboard 公明正大に
- abuse 乱用
- acclaimed 絶賛された
- accordingly それに応じて
- accountability 責任
- achievement 達成
- acknowledgement 承認
- activist 活動家
- acute 鋭い
- addicted 中毒になった
- adorn ～を飾る
- advertising 広告
- affliction 苦痛
- aggression 攻撃性
- ailment 病気
- amazing 驚くべき
- ameliorate ～を改善する
- analogue 類似体
- anti-landmine 対地雷の
- apartheid アパルトヘイト；人種差別政策
- apology 謝罪
- appealing 魅力的な
- appropriation 私用
- approximately およそ
- architect 考案者
- armed 武装した
- arms-control 軍備制限の
- arsenal 兵器工場；兵器の貯蔵量
- assistance 援助；支援
- asteroid 小惑星
- astronomer 天文学者
- attorney 弁護士
- augment ～を拡大させる
- austerity 緊縮；緊縮政策
- autobiography 自伝

B

- bankruptcy 破たん；倒産
- beast 動物；獣
- behavioral 行動の
- benefits 手当
- big-game 大物狙いの
- billionaire 億万長者
- biodiversity 生物の多様性
- bio-engineered 生物工学による
- biomedical 生物医学の
- bleak 暗い
- bluntly 遠慮なく
- booster 熱狂的な支持者
- brink 瀬戸際
- bunk くだらない話

C

- candidate 候補者
- canine 犬の
- capture ～を捕らえる；逮捕
- catastrophic 大惨事の
- chainsaw チェーンソー；電動鎖のこ
- charitable 慈善の
- charity 慈善団体
- chemical 化学物質
- chronicle ～を記録にとめる

☐ chronological	年代順の		☐ decorative	装飾用の
☐ cite	～を引用する		☐ defense	弁護
☐ classify	～を分類する		☐ deluge	氾濫
☐ cogent	説得力のある		☐ den	私室
☐ cohabit	共存する		☐ denominator	基準
☐ colonize	～を植民地化する		☐ depletion	枯渇
☐ commonly	通例は		☐ deplore	～を遺憾に思う
☐ communal	共有の		☐ detect	～を見つけ出す
☐ comprise	～を構成する		☐ detector	探知機
☐ concept	概念		☐ determination	決断力
☐ conflict	紛争		☐ determined	固く決心した
☐ conglomerate	複合企業		☐ device	装置
☐ conjoin	～を結合させる		☐ diet	食べ物
☐ consequently	したがって		☐ dire	深刻な
☐ conserve	～を保護する		☐ director	責任者
☐ constantly	絶えず		☐ disable	～を身体障碍者にする；～を運転不能にする
☐ construction	建設		☐ disarm	～を安全にする
☐ consumer	消費者		☐ disarmament	軍備縮小
☐ content	含有量		☐ disaster	災害
☐ continent	大陸		☐ discrepancy	不一致
☐ continual	継続的な		☐ disfigure	～を醜くする
☐ contribution	貢献		☐ disobey	～に服従しない
☐ conventional	通常の		☐ dispute	紛争；論争
☐ convict	～に有罪の判決を下す		☐ distribution	配給
☐ convince	～を納得させる		☐ divorce	離婚
☐ counterpart	相手方		☐ donate	～を寄付する
☐ critically	批判的に		☐ donor	寄贈者
☐ crucially	決定的に		☐ doomsday	地球滅亡の日
☐ culpability	とがめられるべきこと		☐ downturn	下降
☐ cynical	ひねくれた		☐ drag	だらだら長引く
☐ cynicism	冷笑		☐ dramatically	劇的に
			☐ drastically	思い切って
D			☐ drawback	障害
☐ dagger	短剣		☐ droid	アンドロイド；人造人間
☐ decade	10年間			
☐ decadent	モラルの低下した		☐ dub	～と呼ぶ
☐ decisively	決定的に		☐ dwarf	矮星

Vocabulary 147

E

- early-warning 早期警戒の
- ecosystem 生態系
- embark 乗り出す
- emerge 抜け出す
- emulate ～を規範として見習う
- encode ～を符号化する
- encouragement 励まし
- endangered 絶滅の危機にさらされた
- endeavor ～しようと努力する
- enforcement 執行
- entire 全部の
- envision ～を心に描く
- epic 壮大な
- equality 平等
- erosion 衰退
- eventuality 不測の事態
- explode 爆発する
- explorer 探検家
- explosive 爆発物；爆発性の；激増する
- extinction 絶滅
- extraterrestrial 地球圏外の

F

- fabric 構造
- feedback フィードバック（行動の結果からその後の行動に修正を加えること）
- fighter 闘う人
- financier 投資家
- flashback フラッシュバック（突然鮮明に思い出すこと）
- follow-up 追跡調査の
- foothills 山麓の丘
- forbid ～を禁じる
- forgiveness 許し
- foundation 基金
- founder 創設者
- futurist 未来派の人

G

- gadget 道具
- gender 性差
- glance ちらっと見ること
- glimpse ～をちらりと見る
- grandparents 祖父母
- gravestone 墓石
- gray matter タンパク質
- guardian 保護者
- gynecologist 産婦人科

H

- habitable 生息可能な
- habit-forming 常習性の
- hazardous 危険な
- headline （記事の）見出し
- headquarters 本部；本社
- healthcare 健康管理；保健医療
- heartfelt 心からの
- heinous 極悪非道な
- herbalist 薬草医
- heretical 異端の
- highly 非常に
- holocaust 大破壊
- horror 恐ろしさ
- humanitarian 人道的な
- humanity 人間性；人類
- humbly 謙虚に
- hypothetically 仮説上は

I

- illegal 違法の；不法な
- illiterate 読み書きができない
- imminent 差し迫った

- immortal 不朽の
- immunize ～に免疫を与える
- impair ～を弱める
- implication 影響
- impressive すばらしい
- inadequately 不十分に
- inaugurate ～を開始する
- increasingly ますます
- independently 独立して
- indigenous 固有の；土着の
- inequality 不平等
- inevitable 避けられない
- influx 殺到
- inheritance 遺産
- inhuman 残忍な
- initially 最初は
- innate 生まれつきの
- insincere 不誠実な
- inspection 査察
- instantaneous 瞬間的な
- instill ～を徐々に浸透させる
- institution 制度；施設
- intense 猛烈な
- interact 影響を及ぼし合う
- intimately 親密に
- introspection 自己分析
- irreplaceable かけがえのない
- isolated 独立した

L

- landmine 地雷
- lead author 主筆者
- leash ヒモ
- lightweight 軽量の
- linguist 言語学者
- link きずな
- lucrative もうかる；利益の大きい

M

- maim 肢体不自由にする
- makeshift 間に合わせの
- mammal 哺乳類
- mankind 人類
- manmade 人口の
- massive どっしりした；巨大な
- meanwhile その一方では
- measles はしか
- measures 政策；対策
- medication 薬物治療
- medicinal 薬用の
- migrant 移住者
- mine 地雷
- minefield 地雷原
- miscellany 寄せ集め
- miser けちん坊
- missile ミサイル
- mortality 死亡者数
- mounting 高まる
- multimillion-aire 大富豪
- multiple 多様な
- mutual 相互の
- mythological 神話の
- mythology 神話

N

- nevertheless それにもかかわらず
- nightmare 悪夢
- noncommuni-cable 非伝染性の
- non-violent 非暴力的な
- notoriously 悪名高く
- novel 斬新な

O

- official 当局者；公式の
- optimism 楽観性
- optimistic 楽観的な
- orally 口述で
- outcome 結果
- overhaul 〜を徹底的に調べる
- overly あまりに

P

- pace-setting 先導的な
- pact 条約
- palladium パラジウム
- pandemic 病気の広範囲の流行
- paradoxical 矛盾した
- paralyze 〜を麻痺させる
- participant 参加者
- patrol 巡回する
- peacebuilding 平和構築の
- peacekeeping 平和維持
- peril 危険；危険物
- perpetrate 〜を犯す
- persistent 持続する
- perspective 観点
- pessimistic 悲観的な
- philanthropist 慈善活動家
- philanthropy 慈善活動
- pinpoint 〜を正確に示す
- plague 〜を絶えず悩ます
- plaintiff 原告
- platinum プラチナ
- plead 〜を弁護する
- pledge 〜を誓約する
- poacher 密猟者
- poaching 密猟
- potential 可能性のある
- poverty 貧困
- poverty-stricken 非常に貧乏な
- precarious 不安定な
- precious 貴重な
- predecessor 前任者
- predictably 予想通りに
- predilection 好み
- prefrontal cortex 前頭前皮質
- prehistory 先史時代
- premature ふつうより早い
- pre-school 就学前の
- preservation 保護
- presumably たぶん
- previously 以前に
- priceless 非常に貴重な
- productivity 生産性
- profound 深遠な
- progressive 進歩した
- prohibit 〜を禁止する
- project 研究課題
- prosperity 繁栄
- protester 抗議者
- puzzle-solving パズル式の

Q

- quest 探求

R

- racism 人種差別
- rainforest 多雨林；熱帯雨林
- ratify 〜を批准する
- realistic 現実的な
- real-world 現実社会の
- recession 景気後退
- reclusive 他人との交際を拒む
- reconcile 〜と和解させる

☐ recourse	頼りになるもの	☐ sift	じっくり調べる
☐ refrigerate	〜を冷凍する	☐ slaughter	〜を殺す
☐ regime	（非民主的手段による）政権	☐ slavery	奴隷制度
		☐ so-called	いわゆる
☐ reiterate	〜を繰り返して言う	☐ social-improvement	社会改善の
☐ relapse	逆戻りする		
☐ relevant	関連がある	☐ sophisticated	洗練された
☐ remedy	治療薬	☐ sovereignty	主権
☐ remorse	自責の念	☐ spawn	〜を生み出す
☐ reprehensible	非難されるべき	☐ species	種
☐ repressive	弾圧的な	☐ specifically	具体的には
☐ rescrambling	再び大慌てで集まること	☐ spectrograph	分光写真機
		☐ speculate	〜を推測する
☐ resentful	憤慨した	☐ spending	支出
☐ resentment	憤慨；怒り	☐ squad	チーム；分隊
☐ resolution	解決	☐ standard	水準
☐ resources	資源	☐ statewide	州全体の
☐ revamp	〜を改造する	☐ stepped-up	増大した
☐ revenge	復讐	☐ stockpile	備蓄
☐ rhinoceros [rhino]	サイ	☐ strengthen	〜を強くする
		☐ sue	〜を訴える
☐ riot	暴動	☐ surpass	〜を超える
☐ roam	歩き回る	☐ sustainable	生態系を破壊しない
☐ robust	確固たる	☐ symptom	症状
☐ role	役割		
☐ rubble	がれき		

S

T

☐ scan	〜を走査する	☐ tempting	魅力的な
☐ scheme	計画	☐ terraforming	天体環境の地球化
☐ schizophrenia	統合失調症	☐ terrorist	テロリスト
☐ school-leaver	卒業予定者	☐ thought-provoking	示唆に富む
☐ sclerosis	硬化症		
☐ scour	〜を探し回る	☐ thrive	栄える
☐ secondary-school	中等学校の	☐ time-consuming	時間のかかる
		☐ tragedy	悲劇
☐ sentence	〜に判決を下す	☐ tragically	痛ましいことに
☐ sibling	兄弟；姉妹	☐ tranquilizer	鎮静剤；精神安定剤
		☐ transformation	転換

☐ transmitter	送信機			
☐ transparency	透明性		**W**	
☐ treaty	条約	☐ wage	賃金	
☐ tremendous	非常に大きい	☐ warhead	弾頭	
☐ trial	裁判	☐ wary	警戒している	
☐ trigger	〜を引き起こす	☐ weather	〜を切り抜ける	
☐ trillion	兆	☐ website	ホームページ；サイト	
☐ trophy	狩猟記念品	☐ welfare	生活保護	
☐ tropical	熱帯の	☐ well-being	福祉；幸福	
☐ tuberculosis	結核	☐ widespread	広範囲にわたる	
☐ tutoring	個人指導	☐ wildlife	野生動物	
☐ twenty-something	20代の	☐ wired	運命づけられた	
☐ typically	典型的に	☐ withdrawal	引きこもり	
		☐ worldwide	世界的な	

U

☐ unbroken	途切れない；連続した
☐ underground	地下の
☐ underscore	〜を強調する
☐ unexploded	不発の
☐ unfairness	不公平
☐ unrealistic	現実的でない
☐ unrest	不安
☐ unsuspecting	疑いもしない
☐ urban	都会の
☐ urge	〜に強く迫る
☐ urgently	緊急に

Y

☐ yearn	切望する

V

☐ vault	地下貯蔵庫
☐ venue	開催地
☐ violation	侵害
☐ virtual	仮想の
☐ visible	目に見える
☐ vital	不可欠な
☐ vocabulary	語彙
☐ vulnerable	無防備な

VERBAL CONSTRUCTIONS AND PHRASES

A ＝ 名詞・代名詞
B ＝ 名詞・代名詞
C ＝ 形容詞・副詞など
… ＝ 節（＜主語＋動詞＞がある形）

A

- [ ] add that ...
  He added that he would go there too.
  …と付け加えて言う
  （彼は自分もそこへ行く，と付け加えた）

- [ ] advance to A
  We advanced to the finals.
  A に進む
  （私たちは決勝戦へ進んだ）

- [ ] affirm that ...
  He affirmed that she was innocent.
  …であると断言する
  （彼は彼女が潔白だと断言した）

- [ ] agree that ...
  I agree that I was in the wrong.
  …ということで意見が合う
  （私は自分が間違っていたことを認めます）

- [ ] aim to *do*
  The company aims to branch out into China.
  〜することを目指す
  （その会社は中国への進出を目指している）

- [ ] allow A to *do*
  Her parents allowed her to go to the movies.
  A が〜するのを許す
  （両親は彼女が映画に行くのを許した）

- [ ] announce that ...
  The management announced that there would be 1,000 layoffs.
  …だと発表する
  （経営側は 1,000 人の一時解雇を発表した）

- [ ] apologize for A
  I apologized for my carelessness.
  A について謝罪する
  （私は自分の不注意をわびた）

- [ ] apologize to A
  You should apologize to your wife.
  A に謝る
  （奥さんに謝ったほうがいいよ）

- [ ] appear to be C
  She appeared to be tired that night.
  C のように見える
  （その晩，彼女は疲れているように見えた）

- [ ] ask if ...
  He asked if we were students.
  …かどうか尋ねる
  （彼は私たちが学生かと尋ねた）

Verbal Constructions and Phrases 153

- [ ] ask A of B
  May I ask a favor of you?

  A を B に頼む
  (ちょっとお願いしたいことがあるのですが)

- [ ] assess how ...
  It is difficult to assess how the plan could be improved.

  どのように…かを見極める
  (どのようにその計画を改善できるか見極めるのは難しい)

B

- [ ] back up A
  They backed her up in everything.

  A を支持する；A を支援する
  (彼らはすべての面で彼女を支援した)

- [ ] base A on B
  My opinion is based on facts.

  A の基礎を B に置く
  (私の意見は事実に基づいたものです)

- [ ] become C
  Detroit became known as the automobile capital of the world.

  C になる
  (デトロイトは世界の自動車産業の中心地として知られるようになった)

- [ ] believe in A
  He believes in getting plenty of exercise.

  A をよいと思う
  (彼はたくさん運動するのがよいと思っている)

- [ ] believe that ...
  I believe that you have the wrong number.

  …と考える；…だと信じる
  (番号のかけ間違えだと思います)

- [ ] believe A to *do*
  He is widely believed to have been killed in the accident.

  A が〜すると思う
  (彼はその事故で死んだとみんなに思われている)

- [ ] belong to A
  This ship belongs to Mr. Smith.

  A のものである
  (この船はスミス氏のものです)

- [ ] blend A with B
  He blended the sugar with the flour.

  A を B と混ぜる
  (彼は砂糖と小麦粉を混ぜ合わせた)

- [ ] bother with A
  Don't bother with that.

  A を気にかける
  (そんなことでくよくよするなよ)

- [ ] break out
  The Korean War broke out in 1950.

  急に始まる
  (朝鮮戦争は 1950 年に起こった)

- [ ] bring A B
  Her new business has brought her a lot of money.

  A に B をもたらす
  (新しい事業で彼女は大儲けした)

- [ ] bring about A
  Computers have brought about many changes in our life.

  A をもたらす
  (コンピューターは私たちの生活に多くの変化をもたらした)

- [ ] **bring out A** — Aを引き出す
  Her parents tried to bring out the best in her.（彼女の両親は彼女のよいところを引き出そうとした）

- [ ] **bring B to A** — AにBをもたらす
  His home run brought victory to the team.（彼のホームランがチームに勝利をもたらした）

C

- [ ] **call A B** — AをBと呼ぶ
  What do you call this tree?（この木は何というのですか）

- [ ] **call for A** — Aを必要とする；Aを要求する
  This situation calls for prompt action.（この事態は迅速な行動を必要とする）

- [ ] **call on A** — Aを訪問する
  I'll call on you around three, if that's convenient.（もしご都合がよろしければ，3時ごろお伺いします）

- [ ] **campaign for A** — Aに賛成の運動を起こす
  They campaigned for women's right.（彼女らは女性の権利獲得のために運動を起こした）

- [ ] **care for A** — Aを世話する
  I will care for the children.（私が子どもたちの面倒をみましょう）

- [ ] **carry on A** — Aを続ける
  The discussion was carried on.（討論は続けられた）

- [ ] **carry out A** — Aを実行する
  She always carries out her duties properly.（彼女は常に義務をきちんと果たす）

- [ ] **cause A B** — AにBをもたらす
  His careless words caused me a lot of trouble.（彼の不注意な言葉が私にとって非常に迷惑となった）

- [ ] **chance upon A** — Aをたまたま見つける
  As I was cleaning the yard, I chanced upon my wife's missing ring.（庭を掃除していたら，妻のなくした指輪をたまたま見つけた）

- [ ] **charge that ...** — …であると非難する
  The manager charged that I had lied about the contract.（部長は私が契約のことでうそをついたと非難した）

- [ ] **check out A** — Aを調べる
  I'll check out the mailbox later.（後で郵便受けを見ておくよ）

- [ ] **clean up A** — Aをきれいにする
  Clean up the kitchen.（キッチンをきれいにしなさい）

Verbal Constructions and Phrases

- [ ] **come about** 起こる
  How did the accident come about?
  (その事故はどのようにして起こったのですか)

- [ ] **come across as A** Aという印象を与える
  She came across as a dependable person.
  (彼女は頼りになる人のように見えた)

- [ ] **come down** 低下する
  Unemployment came down last quarter.
  (失業率は先の四半期に低下した)

- [ ] **come from A** Aに由来する
  Many English words come from Latin.
  (多くの英単語はラテン語に由来する)

- [ ] **come in** 入る
  May I come in?
  (入ってもいいですか)

- [ ] **come to A** Aに達する
  The bill came to fifty dollars.
  (勘定は50ドルになった)

- [ ] **come up with A** Aを思いつく
  I hope someone will come up with a good solution.
  (誰かうまい解決法を考え出してくれることを望みます)

- [ ] **compare A to B** AをBにたとえる
  Life is often compared to a voyage.
  (人生はよく航海にたとえられる)

- [ ] **complain that ...** …だと不平を言う
  He complained that the taxi driver was driving too slowly.
  (彼はタクシーの運転手の運転が遅すぎると文句を言った)

- [ ] **conclude that ...** …と結論を下す
  From his explanation, I conclude that he is right.
  (説明を聞いて彼が正しいと考える)

- [ ] **continue to** *do* ～し続ける
  We continue to learn new things throughout life.
  (私たちは生きている限り新しいことを学び続ける)

- [ ] **contribute A to B** AをBに提供する
  Every member was asked to contribute some money to the fund-raising.
  (会員はみなその募金への寄付を求められた)

- [ ] **convict A of B** AにBの有罪判決を下す
  He was convicted of theft.
  (彼は窃盗罪で有罪とされた)

- [ ] **convince A to** *do* Aに～するように勧める
  Who convince you to choose this college?
  (誰がこの大学を選ぶように勧めたのですか)

- ☐ cope with A
  How can we cope with our present difficulties?

  A に対処する
  (どのように私たちは今日の難局を切り抜けることができますか)

- ☐ crash into A
  A car crashed into the building last night.

  A に衝突する
  (昨夜その建物に車が激突した)

- ☐ cut back on A
  My doctor told me to cut back on sweets.

  A を減らす
  (医者に甘いものを控えるように言われた)

D

- ☐ decide that ...
  I decided that it would be fun to do some shopping.

  …と考える
  (少し買い物をすれば楽しいだろうと私は考えた)

- ☐ decide whether ...
  I couldn't decide whether he was telling the truth or not.

  …かどうかを決める
  (私は彼が本当のことを言っているのかどうか判断がつかなかった)

- ☐ define A as B
  Ice can be defined as solid water.

  A を B と定義する
  (氷は個体の水と定義できる)

- ☐ demand that ...
  The loser in the election demanded that the votes be counted again.

  …せよと要求する
  (選挙の落選者は投票数を数え直すよう要求した)

- ☐ deprive A of B
  They were deprived of their rights.

  A から B を奪う
  (彼らは権利を奪われた)

- ☐ describe A as B
  He described my plan as a failure.

  A を B であると言う
  (彼は私の計画を失敗だと言った)

- ☐ determine A to *do*
  The failure determined her to be more careful.

  A に〜するよう決心させる
  (その失敗のため彼女はもっと注意しようと決心した)

- ☐ devote A to B
  He has devoted all his life to biological studies.

  A を B にささげる
  (彼は生涯を生物研究にささげてきた)

- ☐ die from A
  The flowers in the garden died from frost.

  A で死ぬ
  (庭の花が霜で枯れてしまった)

- ☐ die out
  This species of bird died out some time ago.

  絶滅する
  (この鳥の種はだいぶ前に絶滅した)

Verbal Constructions and Phrases

- [ ] discover that ...
  He discovered that all his money had been stolen.
  …であることに気づく
  (彼はお金を全部盗まれたことに気づいた)

- [ ] distinguish A from B
  Can you distinguish a poisonous mushroom from an edible one?
  A を B と区別する
  (毒キノコを食用キノコと見分けられますか)

- [ ] divide A into B
  Divide this cake into 8 equal parts.
  A を B に分ける
  (このケーキを 8 等分しなさい)

- [ ] do without A
  We cannot do without computers in our business.
  A なしで済ませる
  (私たちのビジネスはコンピューターなしではできない)

- [ ] donate A to B
  I donated money to the refugee fund.
  A を B に寄付する
  (私はその難民基金にお金を寄付した)

- [ ] drag on
  The war dragged on for many long years.
  だらだら続く
  (戦争は長々と何年も続いた)

- [ ] dwell on A
  Don't dwell on your past mistakes.
  A をくよくよ考える
  (過去の失敗をくよくよ考えるな)

E

- [ ] embark on A
  Our company embarked on several new projects.
  A を始める
  (わが社はいくつかの新企画を打ち出した)

- [ ] emerge from A
  At last the country has emerged from the recession.
  A から抜け出す
  (ついにその国は不況から抜け出した)

- [ ] encourage A to *do*
  The teacher encouraged his students to ask questions.
  A に～するよう励ます
  (先生は生徒たちに質問するように促した)

- [ ] endeavor to *do*
  He endeavored to arrange an agreement between the two countries.
  ～しようと努力する
  (彼は両国間の協定をまとめようと努力した)

- [ ] ensure that ...
  I can't ensure that the report will be ready in time.
  …ということを確実にする
  (私は報告書が時間に間に合うとは約束しかねます)

- [ ] establish that ...
  The police established that she was at the scene of the crime.
  …ということを立証する
  (警察は彼女が事件現場にいたことを立証した)

- [ ] exclude A from B
  They excluded the boy from their group.

  AをBから除外する
  (彼らはその少年を仲間からのけ者にした)

- [ ] expect to *do*
  I expect to see you again soon.

  〜すると思う
  (また近いうちにお会いしたいものです)

- [ ] expect A to *do*
  You are expected to return the books within two weeks.

  Aが〜することを期待する
  (2週間以内に本を返却してください)

F

- [ ] fall into A
  These methods fell into disuse.

  Aになる
  (これらの方法は用いられなくなった)

- [ ] fall through
  My plans to go to Europe fell through at the last minute.

  だめになる
  (私のヨーロッパ行の計画はどたん場でだめになってしまった)

- [ ] feel as if ...
  I felt as if I had been there before.

  まるで…かのような感じがする
  (私は以前そこに行ったことがあるような気がした)

- [ ] feel like A
  I felt like a prisoner in that uniform.

  Aのような感じがする
  (その制服を着たら囚人になったような気がした)

- [ ] feel that ...
  I feel that she's the best person for the job.

  …と思う
  (私は彼女がその仕事に適任だと思う)

- [ ] find A C
  I found him asleep in the classroom.

  AがCであることを見つける
  (私が授業中に彼が眠っているのを見つけた)

- [ ] fit A with B
  The room was fitted with an air conditioner.

  AにBを取り付ける
  (その部屋にエアコンが設置された)

- [ ] force A to *do*
  You shouldn't force him to study.

  Aに無理に〜させる
  (彼に無理やり勉強させるべきではない)

G

- [ ] get A C
  Have you got everything ready for the trip?

  AをCにする
  (旅行の準備はすべて整いましたか)

- [ ] get by on A
  It's hard to get by on my husband's salary.

  Aでどうにか暮らしていく
  (夫の給料で暮らしていくのは大変だ)

Verbal Constructions and Phrases

- [ ] **get rid of A** — Aを取り除く；Aを処分する
  I have finally got rid of my bad cold.
  (悪い風邪がやっと治った)

- [ ] **get A to** *do* — Aに〜させる；Aに〜してもらう
  The United Nations got the two countries to stop the war.
  (国際連合はその二つの国に戦争をやめさせた)

- [ ] **give A B** — AにBを与える
  Give me liberty, or give me death.
  (我に自由を与えよ，さもなくば死を)
  ＊アメリカ独立戦争当時の愛国者 Patrick Henry の言葉。

- [ ] **give away A** — Aをただであげる
  We don't need these things. Let's give them away.
  (こういった物はうちには必要ない。人にあげてしまおう)

- [ ] **give rise to A** — Aを引き起こす
  Her conduct gave rise to another problem.
  (彼女の行為はまたやっかいなことを引き起こした)

- [ ] **give B to A** — AにBを与える
  She gave her collection to the museum.
  (彼女は収集品を博物館に寄贈した)

- [ ] **give up A** — Aをやめる
  She didn't give up her job when she got married.
  (彼女は結婚しても仕事を辞めなかった)

- [ ] **go about A** — Aに取りかかる
  I don't know how to go about this problem.
  (私はどうやってこの問題に取り組んだらいいのかわからない)

- [ ] **go against A** — Aに反対する
  She went against her father's wishes.
  (彼女は父親の意向に逆らった)

- [ ] **go into A** — Aを調査する；Aを詳細に論じる
  We went into the problem in detail.
  (私たちはこの問題を詳しく調査した)

- [ ] **go off** — 爆発する
  A bomb went off, injuring several people.
  (爆弾が爆発して，何人かが負傷した)

- [ ] **go on** — 続けて言う；続ける
  Please go on with your story.
  (どうぞお話を続けてください)

- [ ] **go up** — 上がる
  The nation's standard of living has been going up every year.
  (その国の生活水準は年々上がってきている)

H

- [ ] **hand down A** — A を伝える
  This story has been handed down for generations.
  (この物語は何世代にもわたって語り継がれてきた)

- [ ] **happen to A** — A に起こる
  What happened to your arm?
  (腕をどうしたの)

- [ ] **have A *done*** — A が〜される；A を〜してもらう
  I had my bag stolen at the airport.
  (空港でカバンを盗まれた)

- [ ] **have A in mind** — A を考えている
  Tell me if you have anything in mind.
  (決めていることがあれば言ってください)

- [ ] **hear of A** — A のことを聞き知る
  I've never heard of such a ridiculous offer.
  (そんなばかばかしい申し出は聞いたことがない)

- [ ] **help (to) *do*** — 〜するのに役立つ
  Help promote peace.
  (平和運動促進に協力してください)

- [ ] **help A (to) *do*** — A が〜するのに役立つ；A が〜するのを手伝う
  The bridge helped the city develop.
  (その橋は町の発展に貢献した)

- [ ] **hint at A** — A をほのめかす
  He hinted at the engagement of his daughter to a young architect.
  (彼は娘が若い建築家と婚約していることをほのめかした)

- [ ] **hint that ...** — …ということをほのめかす
  She hinted that she was not satisfied with her work.
  (彼女は仕事に不満があることをほのめかした)

- [ ] **hope that ...** — …であることを願う
  We hope that you'll come a little earlier.
  (少しばかり早めにおいでいただければと思います)

I

- [ ] **imply that ...** — …であることを暗示する
  Are you implying that I told a lie?
  (私がうそをついたとでもおっしゃるんですか)

- [ ] **incorporate A into B** — A を B に組み入れる
  We incorporated his idea into our new product.
  (私たちは彼のアイディアを新製品に取り入れた)

- [ ] **indicate that ...** — …であることをはっきりさせる
  He indicated that he might resign.
  (彼は辞職するかもしれないことを明らかにした)

- [ ] **inform A about B** — A に B を知らせる
  I have to inform her about the change of plan.
  (私は彼女に計画の変更を知らせなければならない)

Verbal Constructions and Phrases

- inform A that ...
  His email informed me that he had passed the exam.

  Aに〜だと通知する
  (彼のメールで彼が試験に合格したことがわかった)

- inspire A to *do*
  His promotion inspired me to make a greater effort.

  Aを奮起させて〜させる
  (私は彼の昇格に奮起してよりいっそう努力した)

- instill A in B
  The new manager tried to instill confidence in every player.

  AをBに吹き込む
  (新監督は選手全員に自信を持たせようとした)

- invite A to *do*
  He was invited to join the club.

  Aを〜するように誘う
  (彼はそのクラブの入会を誘われた)

- involve A in B
  Do not try to involve me in your problems.

  AをBに関わらせる
  (君の問題に私を巻き込もうとしないで)

J

- judge A C
  Nobody judged the problem serious.

  AをCと判断する
  (誰もその問題を深刻なものと考えなかった)

K

- keep A C
  These socks will keep you warm.

  AをCに保つ
  (この靴下をはくと暖かいよ)

- keep away
  It's dangerous here! Tell those kids to keep away.

  近寄らないでいる
  (ここは危険なんだ！その子供たちに近寄るなと言って)

- keep *doing*
  He keeps changing his plans.

  〜し続ける
  (彼は計画を変えてばかりいる)

- keep down A
  The government will not be able to keep the people down for much longer.

  Aを抑圧する
  (政府はこれ以上国民を抑え込むことはできないだろう)

- keep A from *doing*
  The heavy snow kept us from going out.

  Aに〜させないようにする
  (大雪で私たちは外出できなかった)

- keep A to *oneself*
  I'll keep the secret to myself until death.

  Aを内緒にしておく
  (死ぬまでその秘密は口外しない)

- keep track of A
  I kept track of expenses.

  Aの跡をたどる
  (私は出費を丹念に記録した)

- keep up with A
  I try to keep up with the other students in the class.
  Aに遅れずについていく
  （私はクラスの他の学生に勉強で遅れないように努力している）

- know about A
  How did you know about it?
  Aについて知っている
  （どうしてそのことを知っているの）

- know A as B
  I know him as a musician.
  AがBであると知っている
  （私は彼が音楽家であることを知っている）

L

- lag behind A
  Salary increases are lagging behind the rate of inflation.
  Aに後れをとる
  （賃上げはインフレ率に比べて立ち遅れている）

- lead to A
  Hard work led to his success.
  Aとなる；Aに至る
  （努力が彼に成功をもたらした）

- learn about A
  I'd like to learn about the history of my hometown.
  Aについて知る
  （私は故郷の町の歴史について学びたい）

- learn from A
  He never learns from his mistakes.
  Aから学ぶ
  （彼は失敗から少しも学ばない）

- learn to *do*
  He learned to swim at last.
  〜することを学ぶ
  （彼はようやく泳げるようになった）

- leave A C
  Leave the door open.
  AをCにしておく
  （ドアをあけておいてください）

- let A *do*
  Don't let my dream be destroyed.
  Aに〜させる
  （私の夢を壊さないで）

- let me *do*
  Let me ask you a question.
  私に〜させてください
  （質問をさせてください）

- lie in A
  The secret of success lies in persistence.
  Aにある
  （成功の秘訣は粘り強さにある）

- lie to A
  She lied to me about her age.
  Aにうそをつく
  （彼女は私に年齢をごまかした）

- lie with A
  The decision lies with you.
  Aの責任である
  （決めるのはあなたです）

- link A to B
  The Seikan Tunnel links Hokkaido to Honshu.
  AをBにつなぐ
  （青函トンネルは北海道と本州をつないでいる）

- [ ] live on A Aで暮らしていく
  It is hard to live on such a small salary. (そんな少ない給料で生活していくのは難しい)

- [ ] look for A Aをさがす
  I'm looking for a new job. (私は新しい仕事をさがしている)

- [ ] look into A Aを調査する
  A committee was formed to look into the accident. (その事故の調査のため委員会がつくられた)

- [ ] look on [upon] A as B AをBであると考える
  She looked on her husband as a good friend. (彼女は夫をよい友だちと考えていた)

M

- [ ] make A B AをBにする
  Her coach made her a really great marathon runner. (コーチは彼女を超一流のマラソンランナーに育て上げた)

- [ ] make A C AをCの状態にする
  What makes you so sad? (何がそんなに悲しいの)

- [ ] make A *do* Aに〜させる
  This photo makes her look much younger than she really is. (この写真だと彼女は実際よりずっと若く見える)

- [ ] make for A Aに寄与する
  Calcium makes for strong bones. (カルシウムは強い骨をつくる)

- [ ] make A of B AをBでつくる
  These gloves are made of real leather. (この手袋は本革でできている)

- [ ] make sure (that) ... 必ず…するようにする；…ということを確認する
  Make sure that you come back by eight o'clock. (8時までに必ず戻ってきなさい)

- [ ] make up for A Aの埋め合わせをする
  She made up for lost time by driving fast. (彼女は車のスピードを上げて遅れを取り戻した)

- [ ] make up A of B AをBから構成する
  A car is made up of a lot of different parts. (自動車はたくさんのパーツからできている)

- [ ] mean (that) ... …ということを意味する
  That sign means that you must drive slowly. (あの標識は徐行運転を意味している)

- [ ] miss out on A
  I missed out on all the fun because I stayed at home.
  Aを逃す
  (家にいたので楽しいことに参加できなかった)

- [ ] mix A into B
  Mix some salt into the flour.
  AをBに加える
  (小麦粉に塩を少し加えなさい)

- [ ] move A to B
  All the children were moved to the safety zone.
  AをBに移動する
  (子どもたちはみんな安全地帯に移された)

N

- [ ] need to *do*
  All you need to do is write down your name here.
  〜する必要がある
  (ここに名前を書くだけでいいのです)

O

- [ ] obligate A to *do*
  I was obligated to pay the expenses.
  Aに〜する義務を負わせる
  (私には経費を支払う義務があった)

- [ ] offer A B
  She offered me a good position.
  AにBを提供する
  (彼女は私によい地位を用意した)

P

- [ ] pass A off as B
  He passed himself off as a surgeon.
  AをBだとして通す
  (彼は自分を外科医であると偽った)

- [ ] pass on A
  Farming skills are generally passed on to the children by the parents.
  Aを伝える
  (農業技術は一般に親によって子供たちに伝えられる)

- [ ] pay for A
  The book has been paid for.
  Aのお金を払う
  (その本の代金はいただきました)

- [ ] pay off
  The effort paid off handsomely.
  よい結果を生む
  (苦労が見事に実った)

- [ ] pick up A
  Children pick up a new language easily.
  Aを身につける
  (子どもは新しい言葉を簡単に聞き覚える)

- [ ] plan to *do*
  They planned to climb Mt. Everest.
  〜する計画を立てる
  (彼らはエベレスト登山を計画した)

Verbal Constructions and Phrases

- [ ] point out that ... …ということを指摘する
  Experts point out that oil resources are not limitless.
  (石油資源は無尽蔵ではないと専門家たちは指摘している)

- [ ] pose A to B AをBに引き起こす
  Global warming poses a serious threat to the world.
  (地球温暖化は世界に重大な脅威を与えている)

- [ ] prefer *doing* 〜するほうを好む
  I prefer living in the city.
  (私は都会生活のほうが好きだ)

- [ ] prevent A from *doing* Aが〜するのを妨げる
  We tried to prevent the fact from leaking out.
  (私たちはその事実が漏れるのを防ごうとした)

- [ ] prove (to be) C Cであるとわかる
  Her remarks proved correct.
  (彼女に意見は正しいことがわかった)

- [ ] provide A with B AにBを供給する
  Cows provide us with milk.
  (雌牛はミルクを供給する)

- [ ] punish A for B AをBで罰する
  The teacher punished him severely for cheating.
  (先生は彼のカンニングを厳しく罰した)

- [ ] put on A Aを催す
  They put on a special performance for senior citizens.
  (彼らは高齢者のために特別公演を行った)

- [ ] put out A Aを発表する
  A flood warning has been put out for this area.
  (この地域に洪水警報が出されている)

- [ ] put A right Aを正常な状態にする
  It is difficult to put misunderstanding right.
  (誤解を正すのは難しい)

R

- [ ] range from A to B AからBまでに及ぶ
  Her lecture ranged from child rearing to women's rights.
  (彼女の講演は子育てから女性の権利にまで及んだ)

- [ ] react to A Aに反応する
  The ears react to sounds.
  (耳は音に反応を示す)

- [ ] realize that ... …だとわかる
  I didn't realize that he was joking.
  (私は彼が冗談を言っているのがわからなかった)

- [ ] **recognize that ...**
  You should recognize that you made a mistake.
  …だと認める
  (君は自分がミスしたことを認めるべきだ)

- [ ] **recommend that ...**
  The doctor strongly recommends that she get exercise every day.
  …ということを勧める
  (医者は彼女に毎日運動をするよう強く勧めている)

- [ ] **reconcile with A**
  I reconciled with her briefly, then divorced.
  A と和解する
  (私は彼女と一時的に和解した後，離婚した)

- [ ] **refer to A**
  She never referred to her illness.
  A のことを言う
  (彼女は決して病気のことを口にしなかった)

- [ ] **refuse to *do***
  He refused to accept my advice.
  〜することを拒む
  (彼は私のアドバイスを受け入れるのを拒んだ)

- [ ] **relapse into A**
  She relapsed into silence.
  A に逆戻りする
  (彼女はまた黙ってしまった)

- [ ] **relate A to B**
  The teacher related my improving grades to better study habits.
  A を B と関連づける
  (先生は私の成績向上は学習習慣の改善にあると言った)

- [ ] **relegate A to B**
  He has been relegated to a post on the fringes of the diplomatic service.
  A を B に追いやる
  (彼は外交官勤務の末端の地位に左遷された)

- [ ] **remain C**
  The weather will remain cold for several days.
  C のままである
  (気温はここ数日間は依然として寒いでしょう)

- [ ] **repay A for B**
  No thanks can repay you for your help.
  A に B で報いる；A に B で報復する
  (あなたの援助にはいくら感謝しても足りません)

- [ ] **report that ...**
  The newspaper reports that the missing child was found safe and sound.
  …だと報告する
  (新聞は行方不明の子供が無事発見されたと伝えている)

- [ ] **respond to A**
  It is said that plants respond to music.
  A に反応する
  (植物は音楽に反応すると言われている)

- [ ] **result from A**
  This kind of disease results from an unsanitary environment.
  A によって生じる
  (この種の病気は不衛生な環境のために起こる)

- [ ] **reveal that ...**
  The paper revealed that the minister was hospitalized.
  …だと明らかにする
  (新聞は大臣が入院したことを明らかにした)

Verbal Constructions and Phrases

- ☐ run out of A
  His car has run out of gas.
  Aがなくなる
  (彼の車はガス欠になってしまった)

- ☐ run over A
  I think I just ran over something.
  Aを車でひく
  (今,何かひいた気がするんだ)

S

- ☐ save A from B
  We managed to save some of the documents from the fire.
  AをBから救う
  (なんとか書類の一部を火事から救うことができた)

- ☐ say that ...
  Nobody can say that natural resources are inexhaustible.
  …と言う
  (天然資源が無尽蔵だとはだれも断言できない)

- ☐ see A as C
  He sees health as the most important thing.
  AをCと考える
  (彼は健康を一番大切なものと考えている)

- ☐ see A *done*
  I saw a police car parked in front of her house.
  Aが〜されるのが見える
  (パトカーが彼女の家の前に止まっているのが見えた)

- ☐ seem (to be) C
  The mission seems too dangerous.
  Cのように思われる
  (その任務は危険すぎるようと思われる)

- ☐ seem to *do*
  He doesn't seem to care about his future.
  〜するように見える
  (彼は自分の将来のことを気にしていないようだ)

- ☐ send A to B
  Are you going to send your daughter to college?
  AをBに送り込む;AをBに送る
  (あなたは娘さんを大学にやるおつもりですか)

- ☐ sentence A to B
  He was sentenced to life imprisonment for murder.
  AにBの判決を宣告する
  (彼は殺人罪で終身刑の判決を下された)

- ☐ set back A
  Set your watch back one hour.
  Aを遅らせる
  (時計の針を1時間戻しなさい)

- ☐ set down A
  In order to avoid later dispute, we set the rules down in writing.
  Aを規定する
  (後のなって争いが起こらないように,私たちは規則を定めて文書にした)

- ☐ set up A
  The police set up a road block to catch the thieves.
  Aを設置する;Aを始める;Aを設立する
  (警察は泥棒を捕まえるために道路にバリケードを設けた)

- [ ] **shame A into B**
  She was shamed into apologizing.
  AをBじさせてBさせる
  (彼女は恥じ入って謝罪した)

- [ ] **ship off A**
  In the old days, British criminals were often shipped off to America or Australia.
  Aを送り込む
  (昔はイギリスの犯罪者たちはよくアメリカやオーストラリアへ流刑されたものだ)

- [ ] **shorten A to B**
  Daniel is shortened to Dan.
  Aを短くしてBにする
  (ダニエルはダンと略される)

- [ ] **show that ...**
  Research shows that excessive exercise is harmful to the health.
  …だと示す
  (研究によると過度の運動は健康に害を及ぼすということだ)

- [ ] **show A to be C**
  He has shown the hypothesis to be correct.
  AがCであることを明らかにする
  (彼はその仮説が正しいことを証明した)

- [ ] **show up**
  John did not show up at the party.
  姿を見せる
  (ジョンはパーティーに顔を出さなかった)

- [ ] **sift through A**
  He sifted through the documents.
  Aをじっくり調べる
  (彼は念入りに書類に目を通した)

- [ ] **sign up for A**
  I've signed up for an English conversation class.
  Aに登録する
  (英会話のクラスに登録した)

- [ ] **sit back**
  This is an emergency! We can't just sit back and do nothing.
  何もしないでいる；傍観する
  (これは緊急事態だ！何もせずにただ傍観してはいられないぞ)

- [ ] **sniff out A**
  This dog has been trained to sniff out illegal drugs.
  Aをかいで見つけ出す
  (この犬は違法薬物をかぎ出す訓練を受けている)

- [ ] **sound C**
  That sounds interesting to me.
  Cに聞こえる
  (それは面白そうだ)

- [ ] **sound like A**
  It sounds like a good idea to me.
  Aのように聞こえる
  (それは私にはいい考えのように思われる)

- [ ] **specialize in A**
  I specialize in modern European history.
  Aを専門にする
  (私は近代ヨーロッパ史を専門にしています)

- [ ] **speculate that ...**
  He speculated that they were in trouble.
  …であると推測する
  (彼らは困っているのだと彼は推測した)

Verbal Constructions and Phrases

- [ ] **stand for A** — Aを表す
  "UN" stands for "United Nations." (UNは「国際連合」を表す)

- [ ] **stand up for A** — Aを支持する；Aを弁護する
  All the members stood up for her. (すべてのメンバーが彼女を支持した)

- [ ] **start up A** — Aを始める
  My grandfather started up this bakery. (祖父がこのパン屋を始めた)

- [ ] **stave off A** — Aを食い止める
  The company struggled desperately to stave off bankruptcy. (会社は倒産を食い止めようと必死に努力した)

- [ ] **stem from A** — Aから生じる
  Most of his worries stemmed from his imagination. (彼の心配のほとんどは妄想から生じた)

- [ ] **suffer from A** — Aに苦しむ
  He is suffering from a bad cold. (彼はひどい風邪で苦しんでいる)

- [ ] **suggest that ...** — …してはどうかと提案する
  May I suggest that you extend your stay for a few days? (滞在をあと2, 3日延ばすというのはどうですか)

- [ ] **sum up A** — Aを要約する
  Sum up what we've discussed so far. (これまで論じてきたことをまとめなさい)

- [ ] **suspect A of B** — AにBの容疑をかける
  The police will suspect him of the murder. (警察は彼をその殺人の容疑者と思うだろう)

T

- [ ] **take A B** — AにBを必要とさせる
  My homework took me the whole night. (宿題をするのにまる一晩かかった)

- [ ] **take away A** — Aを連れ去る；Aを持ち去る
  The tow truck took away the wrecked car. (レッカー車が事故車を引っぱって行った)

- [ ] **take care of A** — Aの面倒を見る
  You must take good care of yourself. (体を大切にしなければならない)

- [ ] **take A off B** — AをBから離す
  Take your hand off the gun. (銃から手を離せ)

- [ ] **take over A** — Aを支配する；Aを占領する
  The army took over the government. (軍が政府を乗っ取った)

- [ ] **take part**
  The most important thing in the Olympic Games is not to win but to take part.
  参加する
  (オリンピック競技において最も大切なことは勝つことではなく参加することだ)

- [ ] **take place**
  Where will the wedding ceremony take place?
  行われる
  (結婚式はどこで行われるのですか)

- [ ] **take A to *do***
  She took two years to write this novel.
  〜するのに A が必要である
  (彼女はこの小説を書くのに 2 年間かかった)

- [ ] **take up A**
  Most of my day was taken up with meetings.
  A を占める；A を趣味として始める
  (今日はほとんど一日中, 会議ばかりだった)

- [ ] **team up**
  Local people teamed up against the gang.
  協力する
  (地域住民は暴力団に対抗して団結した)

- [ ] **tell A (that) ...**
  She told me that she likes you.
  A に…だと話す
  (彼女が君のこと好きだって言ってたよ)

- [ ] **thank A for B**
  I thanked them for their assistance.
  A に B に対して感謝する
  (私は彼らに援助してもらったお礼を言った)

- [ ] **think about A**
  He thought carefully about the offer.
  A について考える
  (彼はその申し出についてじっくり考えた)

- [ ] **think of A as C**
  Dogs think of themselves as members of the family.
  A を C だと思う
  (飼い犬は自分を家族の一員だと思っている)

- [ ] **think (that) ...**
  I don't think it's a good idea.
  …と思う
  (それはよい考えとは思わない)

- [ ] **track down A**
  The police finally tracked down the source of the calls.
  A を苦労して見つける
  (警察はついに電話の発信源を突き止めた)

- [ ] **train A to *do***
  The dog is trained to carry a newspaper.
  A を〜するように訓練する
  (その犬は新聞を持ってくるように訓練されている)

- [ ] **transform A into B**
  The snow transformed the town into a white plain.
  A を B に変える
  (雪で町は銀世界に一変した)

- [ ] **try out A**
  You can try this product out for free for two weeks.
  A を試しに使ってみる
  (この製品は無料で 2 週間試用できます)

Verbal Constructions and Phrases

- try to *do* — 〜しようと努力する
  Try not to make any noise. (物音を立てないようにしてくれ)
- turn A into B — A を B に変える
  Heat turns ice into water. (熱は氷を水に変える)

U

- urge A to *do* — A に〜するよう強く勧める
  His parents urged him to go on to college. (両親は彼に大学に進学するように強く勧めた)

W

- wait to *do* — 〜するのを待つ
  I was waiting to use a pay phone. (私は公衆電話の順番待ちをしていた)
- want A *doing* — A に〜してもらいたい
  I don't want you coming so late. (そんなに遅く来られては困る)
- want to *do* — 〜したい
  What do you want to buy? (あなたは何を買いたいのですか)
- want A to *do* — A に〜してもらいたい
  My parents wanted me to be a doctor. (両親は私を医者にしたいと思っていた)
- warn A about B — A に B を警告する
  The radio warned us about a tsunami. (ラジオは私たちに津波への注意を呼びかけた)
- warn that ... — …ということを警告する
  They warn that the typhoon is approaching. (予報では台風が接近していると警告している)
- warn A to *do* — A に〜するよう警告する
  She warned me not to go there. (彼女は私にそこに行かないように警告した)
- watch A *do* — A が〜するのを見る
  He watched his children climb the tree. (彼は子供たちが木に登るのを見つめていた)
- watch out for A — A に注意する
  Watch out for cars when you cross the street. (通りを渡るときには車に注意しなさい)
- wipe out A — A を全滅させる
  The whole village was wiped out by the floods. (洪水で全村が壊滅した)
- wonder if ... — …かしらと思う
  I wonder if it will be fine tomorrow. (明日は晴れるかしら)

- [ ] work for A
  My father works for a trading company.
  Aに勤めている
  (父は貿易会社に勤めている)

- [ ] would rather (that) ...
  I'd rather he stopped smoking.
  むしろ…だといいのに
  (私は彼にタバコをやめてもらいたい)

- [ ] write down A
  I wrote down his telephone number in my pocket diary.
  Aを書きとめる
  (彼の電話番号を手帳に書きとめた)

Y

- [ ] yearn for A
  We yearns for world peace.
  Aを切望する
  (私たちは世界平和を切望している)

● 著者プロフィール

Jim Knudsen　　（ジム・カヌーセン）

40 年以上日本で生活し，活動している。
ワシントン州立大学で政治学（1971）と英文学（1975）の学位を取得。英国サセックス大学で，20 世紀英文学の修士号（1978）を取得。他に高校・大学向けの 100 冊以上の英文テキストの著者でもある。

小中 秀彦　　（こなか ひでひこ）

日本大学准教授。ハンボルト州立大学（カリフォルニア州）に留学後，日本大学で英文学の修士号（1984）を取得。専門は日英語比較。『日本語に惑わされない英語表現』（南雲堂），『スヌーピーと学ぶライティングとリスニング』（南雲堂）の他，大学テキストを多数執筆。

著作権法上、無断複写・複製は禁じられています。

英語リーディングの王道

	2014 年 2 月 28 日	1 刷
著　者	ジム・カヌーセン	Jim Knudsen
	小中 秀彦	Hidehiko Konaka
発行者	南雲 一範	
発行所	株式会社　南雲堂	

〒162-0801　東京都新宿区山吹町 361
TEL　03-3268-2311（営業部）
TEL　03-3268-2387（編集部）
FAX　03-3269-2486（営業部）
振替　00160-0-4686

印刷所／日本ハイコム株式会社　　　　製本所／松村製本所
カバー写真撮影／松蔭浩之

Printed in Japan　　乱丁・落丁本はお取り替えいたします。
ISBN978-4-523-26522-1　　C0082　　　　　　[1-552]

　　　　　E-mail　　nanundo@post.email.ne.jp
　　　　　URL　　　http://www.nanun-do.co.jp

音声で学ぶリーディングで得点力アップ！

TOEFL® Test iBT リーディング 実践編
TOEFL® Test iBT Reading: Practice for Success

Jim Knudsen／生井　健一

A5判　320ページ　定価（本体2200円＋税）　CD2枚付

TOEFL iBTのリーディング・セクションの効果的練習教材！
合わせてリスニングにも使えるCD音声を用意した。

特徴

- 比較・対照、因果関係など、北米大学での勉強の際に必ず読むことになる文章のパターンを研究し、様々な読解難易度のオリジナル・パッセージを多様な分野から用意した。
- 練習問題はマルティプル・チョイスはもちろん、iBTより始まった新しい形式の設問（情報を類別する、サマリーを完成する等）も備えている。
- iBTでは難しい単語はクリックして、その定義を参照できるようになっているが、本書でもGlossaryを用意して、必要に応じて活用できるようにした。

南雲堂
NAN'UN-DO

英語リーディングの王道

The Royal Road to
Current English Reading

Jim Knudsen 著
日本大学准教授 小中秀彦 解説

解答・解説

南雲堂

The Royal Road
to Current English Reading

英語リーディングの王道

【解答・解説】

NAN'UN-DO

解答・解説目次

Lesson 1	What the World Needs Now	4
Lesson 2	The Horns of a Dilemma	13
Lesson 3	Of Nukes and Minefields	24
Lesson 4	Languages Lost and Found	34
Lesson 5	It's About Time	43
Lesson 6	Where Would We Be Without It?	52
Lesson 7	Virtually Better	61
Lesson 8	It's Never Too Late	72
Lesson 9	Global Concepts 1: People	81
Lesson 10	Global Concepts 2: Trends	91
Lesson 11	Psychology	101
Lesson 12	The Environment	109
Lesson 13	History	117
Lesson 14	Space	125
Lesson 15	Education	132

Lesson 1   What the World Needs Now
国際社会の支援を必要とする課題

> **NOTES**
> name A as B「B を A と指定する」　get by「どうにか暮らしていく」　the Earth Institute of Columbia University「コロンビア大学地球研究所」　antiretroviral treatment「坑レトロウイルス治療」

● ● ● GETTING READY TO READ ● ● ●

Key Concepts:

リーディングの重要語句と下の定義や説明を結びつけなさい。定義や説明の文字を空所に書きなさい。

1. h　貧困＝非常に貧しい状態
2. a　男女平等＝男性と女性が同じ権利や機会をもっていること
3. g　子どもの死亡率＝早死にする子供の割合
4. e　生態系を破壊しない環境をつくりだすこと＝自然界を守り, 保護する
5. b　破たん＝経済的・財政的な難局
6. c　民族間戦争や内戦＝国内での少数派民族間の暴力行為
7. d　援助＝富める国々から貧困国への金銭や融資の贈り物
8. f　坑レトロウイルス治療＝エイズ患者のための薬品の組み合わせ

Active Reading:

リーディングを読み, 質問の答えをさがしなさい。答えが見つかった箇所の文をマークしなさい。

1. 国際連合は 2000 年に世界のための目標を決めた。その目標の大まかなねらいや目的は何か?

    解答 Generally, the MDGs aimed to ameliorate social and economic conditions in the world's poorest countries.

2. ある人たちはこれらの目標をどう思ったか?

    解答 Many critics looked upon them as unrealistic and overly optimistic—impossible, in fact.

3. その人たちは，特にアフリカに関してなぜそう考えたのか？

   解答 After all, the situation at the time, particularly in Africa, seemed hopeless.

4. ジェフリー・ザックスは誰か，また今日の状況に関して何と言っているか？

   解答 Sachs is the director of the Earth Institute of Columbia University and a long-time fighter in the war against world poverty. Sachs believes that now, cynicism has been replaced by hope.

5. 2010年に開催された国連の会議ではどんな結論が下されたか？

   解答 Although there is still a long way to go, the summit concluded, the Millennium Development Goals are now "within reach."

Words in Context:

文の一部の下線部に最も意味が近い語句を選びなさい。

1. (B)　これらの目標を達成する目標期日
   (A) 〜を保持する　　　(B) 〜に達する　　　(C) 〜を決定する

2. (B)　社会的・経済的状況を改善すること
   (A) 〜を悪くする　　　(B) 〜を良くする　　　(C) 〜を起こられる

3. (B)　具体的には，それらの目標には…がある
   (A) 実際は　　　　　　(B) 詳しく見ると　　　(C) 実のところ

4. (C)　そして男女平等を促進する
   (A) 〜を要求する　　　(B) 〜を頼む　　　　　(C) 〜を育てる

5. (C)　最初はこれらの目標は
   (A) とうとう　　　　　(B) せいぜい　　　　　(C) 初めのうちは

6. (A)　そして，あまりに楽観的である
   (A) 希望を持った　　　(B) バカな　　　　　　(C) 危険な

7. (B)　その状況は劇的に変わってきている
　　　(A) ほとんど〜ない　　　(B) 非常に　　　　　　(C) たびたび

8. (C)　冷笑は希望に代わってきている
　　　(A) 怒り　　　　　　　　(B) 誇り　　　　　　　(C) 疑い

9. (B)　貧困と飢えは減少してきている
　　　(A) 改善されて　　　　　(B) 下がって　　　　　(C) 増えて

10. (B)　より広範囲への蚊帳の供給
　　　(A) 工場生産　　　　　　(B) 使用可能，または提供　(C) 理解

11. (B)　どの程度の前進かを見極めること
　　　(A) を批判する　　　　　(B) を評価する　　　　(C) を報告する

12. (A)　今すぐ最も差し迫って必要なもの
　　　(A) ぜひとも　　　　　　(B) 肯定的に　　　　　(C) 静かに

● ● ● TODAY'S READING ● ● ●

エッセイを注意深く読み，それに続く練習問題を解きなさい。

試訳

① さかのぼって 2000 年に，国際連合（国連）がニューヨーク市の本部で特別サミットを開催した。およそ 192 の国々と 23 の国際組織が参加した。その会議の目的は，国連が「ミレニアム開発目標」，略して MDGs と呼んでいる目標を設定することであった。サミットの参加者たちは，これらの目標を達成する到達期限をはっきり 2015 年と決めた。

② 一般的に言って，MDGs は世界の最貧の国々の社会的・経済的状況の改善を目指すものだった。具体的には，開発目標には次のようなものがある。
　　貧困とひどい飢えをなくすこと。
　　あらゆる国々の子どもたちに，せめて小学校教育を提供すること。
　　女性に権利を与え，男女平等を促進すること。
　　子どもの死亡率を減らすこと。
　　エイズ，マラリアなどの病気と闘うこと。
　　生態系を破壊しない環境をつくり出すこと。

③ 最初は，これらの開発目標は冷笑を浴びた。多くの批評家はそれらを非現実的であまりにも楽観的である―事実上，達成不可能である―と思っていた。何といっても，当時の状況は，特にアフリカでは絶望的に思えたからだ。ほとんどのアフリカ諸国が破たんの危機に瀕していた。たいていのアフリカ人は 1 日 1 ドルに満たないお金でどうにか暮ら

していた。エイズ，マラリア，結核，はしかが手に負えなくなっていた。民族間戦争や内戦も 12 か所で行われていたのである。
④ しかし，今日ではその状況が劇的に変化している，とジェフリー・ザックスは言う。ザックスはコロンビア大学地球研究所の所長で，世界の貧困との闘いを長年にわたって続けている。ザックスは今や，冷笑は希望に代わってきている，と信じている。アフリカ諸国の政府による努力が増大し，富める国々からの援助が増えたおかげで，本当の進歩がなされた，と彼は言う。経済状態がアフリカ大陸中でよくなってきている。極貧と飢えが減少している。何百万ものアフリカ人が坑レトロウイルス治療を受けることで，エイズも衰えつつある。さらに，より広範囲に蚊帳を配給することで，マラリアによる死亡者数を「決定的に」減らすことができたのだ。
⑤ 2010 年 9 月に，追跡調査のサミットが国連で開催された。今回，会議の目的はこうした開発目標を実現するためにどの程度，前進したかを見極めることである。まだまだかなり長い道のりが先にあるが，ミレニアム開発目標は今や「手の届くところに」あると，今回のサミットで結論が出された。さらに，それらの開発目標は，今すぐ最も差し迫って必要なものを世界に与えることにつながる，私たちの最も「現実的な進路」を今でも示している，とジェフリー・ザックスは語る。

● ● ● EXERCISES 1：COMPREHENSION ● ● ●

Reading for Information:

文の空所を埋めなさい。

1. 15
   ミレニアム開発目標を達成する到達期限は今後 15 年間と決められた。

2. food
   開発目標の 1 つは人々のために十分な食料を確保することだ。

3. six
   国連によると，すべての子供が少なくとも 6 年間の教育を受けるべきである。

4. 2000 / women / men
   2000 年のサミットは女性に男性と同じ権利や機会を与えることを目指した。

5. world / worse
   もう 1 つの開発目標は自然界をこれ以上破壊しないようにすることだ。

6. Africans / 365

   2000年には，ほとんどのアフリカ人は1年間365ドルで暮らしていかなければならなかった。

7. Columbia / poor

   コロンビア大学で教鞭をとるかたわら，ジェフリー・ザックスは世界の貧しい人々を援助しようとしている。
   * in addition to doing「～するほかに」

8. governments

   アフリカ諸国の政府は自国の問題を解決するために何らかの行動をとってきた。

9. antiretroviral

   坑レトロウイルスのおかげでエイズは減少している。
   * in decline「衰えて」

10. 10

    第2回の国連サミットは第1回の10年後に開催された。

Listening for Ideas:

音声を聞き，文の空所を埋めなさい。文がリーディングの内容に合っていればTに，合っていなければFに○をつけなさい。

1. T [target / conference / deaths]

   2000年の会議の到達目標の1つは子供の死亡率を減らすことだった。

2. T [social / economic / hopeless]

   2000年にはアフリカの社会的・経済的状況は絶望的のように思われた。

3. F [Professor / wars / fought]

   ザックス教授によると，アフリカでは今はもう内戦は行われていない。
   * no longer ~「もはや～でない」

4. F [nations / nothing / improve / situation]

   富める国々からのアフリカへの金銭援助は，状況を改善するのに全然役立っていない。

5. F [2010 / decided / reached]

   2010年のサミットでは，ほとんどのミレニアム開発目標はすでに達成されたと判断された。

6. T [way / serious / efforts]
   ザックスは世界で最も深刻な諸問題を解決する最善の方法は，ミレニアム開発目標を達成するため私たちがもっと努力することだと信じているようだ。

● ● ● EXERCISES 2: COMPOSITION ● ● ●

Making Questions:

下の ANSWER が答えとなる疑問文を完成させなさい。音声で疑問文をチェックしなさい。

1. Q. 2000 年と 2010 年にどこでサミットが開催されたか？
   A. ニューヨーク市で。

   解答 the 2000 and 2010 summits held

2. Q. ある批評家たちはミレニアム開発目標をどう考えていたか？
   A. あまりにも楽観的で非現実的。

   解答 some critics look upon the MDGs

3. Q. ジェフリー・ザックスによると冷笑は何に代わってきたか？
   A. 希望に。

   解答 What does Jeffrey Sachs say cynicism has been

4. Q. どのようにマラリアによる死亡を削減したか？
   A. より広範囲に蚊帳と薬を配給することによって。

   解答 deaths from malaria been cut

Writing with Idioms:

下線部の代用として下の語句を用いて，文を書き換えなさい。語句や直後の語の語形を変える必要があることもある。音声で答えをチェックしなさい。

1. I wish I could <u>get rid of</u> this stubborn cold.
   このしつこい風邪が早く治ればいいのに。

2. <u>Thanks to</u> your advice, I was able to choose the best career for me.
   あなたのアドバイスのおかげで，私にとって最高の職業を選ぶことができた。

Lesson 1　What the World Needs Now　9

3. She is <u>looked upon</u> by many as a possible candidate for president.
   彼女は多くの人から大統領になりそうな候補者とみなされている。

4. Many species are <u>on the brink of</u> dying out.
   多くの種が絶滅の危機に瀕している。

Word Forms:

左の語を適当な形に直して，文の空所を埋めなさい。

1. cynical

   その批評家は<u>冷笑的な</u>世界観で有名だ。

2. achievements

   その賞は彼の多くの<u>業績</u>を評価したものだ。

3. promotion

   上司は，来年私は<u>昇進</u>すると言っていた。

4. distribute

   これらのテスト用紙をクラスのみんなに<u>配って</u>ください。

5. specific

   どこか<u>心当たりの</u>レストランはありますか？

6. assessment

   その映画に対するあなたの<u>評価</u>に同意できない。

7. Optimistically

   <u>楽観的に</u>言えば，経済復興に最低1年はかかるだろう。

8. urgency

   その<u>緊急</u>状況を過度に強調することはできない。

● ● ● EXERCISES 3: CHALLENGE ● ● ●

Using Key Concepts:

Aの文と意味が同じになるように，Bの文の空所を埋めなさい。KEY CONCEPTSの語句を使いなさい。

1. bankruptcy
   今日，多くの会社が破たんを申請している。

2. create a sustainable environment
   私たちは生態系を破壊しない環境をつくり出す必要がある。

3. gender equality
   その新しい法律は男女平等を保障している。

4. child mortality rate
   栄養状態がよくなれば子供の死亡率は下がる。

Vocabulary Expansion:

単語 "poor" の辞書定義を見て，下の文を読みなさい。それぞれの poor がどの意味かを判断し，辞書定義の番号を空所に書きなさい。

a. 5　出席状況が悪いため，その講座は中止された。　＊ because of A 「A のために」
b. 4　給料が安いため，彼女はその仕事を辞めた。
c. 6　かわいそうなその男性は事故で家族全員を亡くした。
d. 1　貧しい家庭の子どもたちは学校の成績もよくない。
e. 7　その新しい計画は町の貧困者を援助することを目指している。
f. 2　石油が乏しいため，日本はその供給を海外からの輸入に頼らなければならない。
g. 3　その女優は感動を与えない下手な演技をした。

辞書定義
1. （形容詞）　お金や財産がほとんど，またはまったくない
2. （形容詞）　ある特定の素質，または品質が劣っている
3. （形容詞）　すぐれていない；劣っている
4. （形容詞）　金銭的価値がない；よくない
5. （形容詞）　量と数で劣っている
6. （形容詞）　哀れみに値する；かわいそうな
7. （名詞）　　お金や財産がほとんど，またはまったくない人々

Listening Activity:

「マラリア」に関するショートトークを聞いて，下の文を読みなさい。話の内容に合っていればTに，合っていなければFに○をつけなさい。

1. F　マラリアはサルに噛まれることで発症する。
2. F　マラリアはラテン語で「不運」という意味である。
3. T　マラリアはたいてい高温多湿の場所で発症する。
4. T　マラリアは特に子どもには危険なものだ。
5. F　マラリアの症状の1つに激しい空腹感がある。
6. F　すべてのタイプのマラリアは同様に危険なものだ。
7. T　治療は可能だが，それでもマラリアは多くの人の命を奪っている。

Listening Script

　Malaria is an infectious disease caused by mosquito bites. The word "malaria" comes from Italian and means "bad air." Malaria is found in about 100 countries worldwide. It most often occurs in tropical and subtropical environments. The disease's symptoms include high fever, chills, severe pain, and sweating. Pregnant mothers and small children are especially susceptible to the disease. There are many types of malaria. The most serious is Plasmodium falciparum, which, if not treated, usually leads to death. Today, about two million people die from malaria each year, despite the fact that there are various drugs for treating the disease. The sooner treatment is begun after infection, the better the chance the patient has to fully recover.

　マラリアは，蚊にさされることが原因でかかる伝染病だ。「マラリア」という単語はイタリア語から由来し，「悪い空気」を意味する。マラリアは世界中の約100か国で発症している。マラリアは熱帯，または亜熱帯の環境で最も多く発症する。マラリアの症状には，高熱，悪寒，激痛，発汗がある。特に，妊婦や小児がマラリアに感染しやすい。マラリアにはいろいろなタイプがある。最も危険なタイプは熱帯熱マラリア原虫だ。このタイプは治療を受けないとたいてい死に至る。今日，マラリア治療のためのいろいろな薬剤があるという現実にもかかわらず，約200万人が毎年，マラリアで死亡する。感染後に早く治療を始めれば始めるほど，患者が全治する確率が高くなるのである。

　＊ Plasmodium falciparum「熱帯熱マラリア原虫」
　＊ despite the fact that ...「…という事実にもかかわらず」
　＊＜the ＋比較級, the ＋比較級＞「〜すればするほど，ますます…」

Lesson 2   The Horns of a Dilemma
角か命かの二者択一を迫られて

NOTES

in the wild「野生の状態で」 the World Wildlife Fund「世界野生動物基金」
dodo「ドードー」17 世紀に絶滅した飛べない鳥

● ● ● GETTING READY TO READ ● ● ●

Key Concepts:

リーディングの重要語句と下の定義や説明を結びつけなさい。定義や説明の文字を空所に書きなさい。

1. f   哺乳類＝恒温の脊椎動物［脊椎のある動物］
2. d   絶滅の恐れのある種＝まもなく地球から消滅するかもしれない植物や動物
3. e   国際禁止令＝世界中であるものを不法にする［法に反する］こと
4. a   密猟＝法に反して動物を狩ったり作物を収穫すること
5. h   法執行官＝法律が守られているかどうかを確認するために雇われた人；警察官
6. i   絶滅＝死滅すること；地球からの消滅
7. b   GPS 送信機＝後を追ったり，居場所がわかるように物体に取り付ける広範囲位置特定のための送信装置
8. c   鎮静剤の付いた矢＝動物を診察したり治療したりできるように精神を落ち着かせる薬を撃つために使用される小さな矢
9. g   ドードー＝ 17 世紀に狩猟され，絶滅したオーストラリアの鳥

Active Reading:

リーディングを読み，質問の答えをさがしなさい。答えが見つかった文をマークしなさい。

1. アジアではサイの角は何のために使われているか？

   解答 For centuries, Asian tradition has coveted the horns of the "rhino," believing they can heal a variety of medical and sexual ailments.

2. 世界中でサイの狩猟が違法になると何が起きたか？

   解答 But predictably, this gave rise to widespread illegal hunting, or poaching.

Lesson 2   The Horns of a Dilemma   13

3. 今日では誰がサイを「密猟している」か？

    解答 Gangs of professional poachers, armed with powerful rifles, have become increasingly aggressive.

4. WWFとは何か？また，どのようにサイを守ろうとしているか？

    解答 The World Wildlife Fund. Game officials are fitting rhinos with GPS transmitters to make it easier to keep track of them. Foot soldiers, themselves heavily armed, are on duty 24 hours a day, seven days a week, patrolling for poachers.

5. 独特なサイ救出新計画はどのように機能しているか？

    解答 And in a unique new program, wildlife "police" are finding rhinos, shooting them with tranquilizer darts from helicopters and then, when the animal is down, removing its horns with chainsaws.

Words in Context:

文の一部の下線部に最も意味が近い語句を選びなさい。

1. (B)　これらの<u>どっしりと大きい</u>アフリカの動物
    (A) 醜い　　　　　　　(B) 巨大な　　　　　　(C) 危険な

2. (B)　伝統が角を<u>欲しがっている</u>
    (A) 〜を使用している　(B) 〜を望んでいる　　(C) 〜を捕らえている

3. (C)　<u>疾病</u>や性病
    (A) 治療　　　　　　　(B) なぞ　　　　　　　(C) 病気

4. (C)　いろいろな装飾品をつくるために<u>彫られる</u>
    (A) 針で縫われる　　　(B) 刷毛で塗られた　　(C) ナイフで形作られる

5. (B)　しかし，<u>予想通りに</u>これは〜を引き起こした
    (A) ふつうは　　　　　(B) 予期したように　　(C) やがて

14

6. (A)　そこではかつて何千ものサイが歩き回っていたが，たった～
   (A) さまよっていた　　　(B) 死滅した　　　(C) エサを食べていた

7. (C)　サイを殺すだろう
   (A) ～を狩る　　　　　　(B) ～を捕らえる　　(C) ～を殺す

8. (A)　それは何と利益の大きい取引だろう
   (A) 利益になる　　　　　(B) 違法な　　　　　(C) 邪悪な

9. (B)　ますます攻撃的になってきて
   (A) 意地の悪い　　　　　(B) 厚かましい　　　(C) 巧みな

10. (C)　積極的な運動に乗り出している
    (A) ～を発明する　　　　(B) 努力している　　(C) 取りかかっている

11. (A)　密猟団に対して無防備な状態を少なく
    (A) 弱い　　　　　　　　(B) 有益な　　　　　(C) 能力がある

12. (B)　その計画は費用がかかり
    (A) 製品　　　　　　　　(B) 計画　　　　　　(C) 道具

● ● ● TODAY'S READING ● ● ●

エッセイを注意深く読み，それに続く練習問題を解きなさい。

試訳
① しわが寄った厚い皮と角がついた突き出た鼻をもったサイは，最も醜い哺乳類であろう。だからと言って，このどっしりしたアフリカの動物たちがそれほど珍重されていないということではない。数世紀の間，アジアでは伝統的にいろいろな疾病や性病を治療できると信じて，「サイ」の角をむやみに欲しがった。他の様々な文化においても，中東の短剣の柄のような様々な装飾品を作るのに角が彫られてきた。そして，ほぼ200年の間，いわゆる大物狙いのハンターである，狩猟旅行中の裕福なヨーロッパ人やアメリカ人が，その野外活動としてサイを殺し，後で私室の壁に剥製の狩猟記念品をつるしてきた。その結果，現在残存する5種すべてのサイが絶滅の危機にさらされている。
② 1976年までに，サイの境遇が大変深刻になり，サイ狩猟やサイの諸器官の商取引に対して国際禁止令が出された。だが予想通り，この禁止令が広範囲に及ぶ不法狩猟や密猟を引き起こすことになった。それ以降20年，30年にわたって，アフリカのサイ総数の90パーセントが殺された。2010年には，サイの密猟がこれまでのピークに達した。まさに適切な例として，ジンバブエでは数千頭のサイが，かつて野生の状態で歩き回って

いたが，現在生き残っているのはわずか700頭にすぎない。
③ サイの角は，金の値段以上の，1キロ2万ドルに達することもある。密猟者たちはほんの1,2インチの角を手に入れるためにサイを殺すのだが，それだけでもすごい儲けとなる。昔は，密猟者は，主に生計を立てようとする貧しい地元の人だった。しかし，世界野生動物基金によると，今日のサイ密猟は非常に組織化されているという。強力なライフル銃で武装したプロの密猟団は，ますます攻撃的になり，邪魔しようとしたり，自分たちが欲しがっているものを手に入れるのを妨害しようとする者は誰でも，「目に入るとすぐに撃ってくる」。密猟者と法執行官との銃撃戦もよく起こり，双方に死者が出ることもある。まるで映画の一場面のようである。
④ 現在，サイを絶滅から救うために，世界野生動物基金が独自の積極的な運動に乗り出している，とヤフーニュースが報じている。猟場管理官たちはサイの跡をつけやすくするために，サイにGPS送信機を取り付ける。重武装した歩兵たちは密猟者を巡察して，1日24時間，週に7日，その任務についている。そして，この独特な新計画では，野生動物「警備隊」はサイを発見すると，鎮静剤付きの矢をヘリコプターから撃ち，サイが倒れると，チェーンソーで角を切除する。これはやり過ぎに思えるが，専門家たちは，とても必要なことだ，と言う。痛みを感じさせないその方法は，密猟に対してサイを「魅力的に」，そして無防備にすることを避ける結果になる―「見た目は悪いが，生きている」と世界野生動物基金の当局者は言う。この計画は費用も時間もかかるが，サイをドードーと同じ道をたどらせないようにするのに役立っている。

● ● ● EXERCISES 1：COMPREHENSION ● ● ●

Reading for Information:

下の質問に対して簡潔に答えなさい。下線上に答えを書きなさい。

1. snout
   サイの鼻を表す語は何か？

2. dagger handles
   中東の人々はサイの角で何をつくるか？

3. on the walls of their dens
   大物狙いのハンターたちが自分が殺したサイの頭をどこにかけるのが好きか？

4. all of them
   5種のサイのうち絶滅の危機にさらされているのは何種か？

5. 1976
   何年にサイの狩猟と諸器官の商取引が違法になったか？

6. 2010
   何年にサイの密猟がピークを迎えたか？

7. rhino horn
   サイの角と金では，時にはどちらがより価値があるか？

8. only an inch or two
   密猟者はどれくらいの長さの角のためにサイを殺すか？

9. GPS transmitters
   最近では何のおかげでサイの追跡が楽になったか？
   * make it C to *do*「～することを C にする」

10. helicopters
    どこから鎮静剤付きの矢を撃つか？

11. with chainsaws
    野生動物「警備隊」はどのようにしてサイの角を切除するか？

12. No, it doesn't.
    角を切除する方法はサイに痛みを感じさせるか？

13. "disfigured, but alive"
    ある当局者は角を切除されたサイをどのように描写しているか？

Listening for Ideas:

選択疑問文を聞き取り，下の答えを完成させなさい。

1. They have been used for <u>medical purposes</u>.
   医療の目的で使用されてきた。

2. They have killed them <u>as trophies</u>.
   狩猟記念品としてサイを殺してきた。

3. It made <u>the situation worse</u>.
   禁止令によってさらに状況が悪化した。

4. They are <u>professionals</u>.
   密猟者たちはプロである。

5. <u>Law enforcement officials</u> have been killed as well.
   同様に法執行官も殺されている。

6. They <u>carry rifles, too</u>.
   警備隊もライフル銃を持ち歩く。

7. They say <u>it is necessary</u>.
   専門家たちは切除は必要だと言う。

8. It costs <u>a lot of time and money</u>.
   その計画はかなりの時間とお金を要する。

Listening Script

1. In Asia, have rhino horns been used for medical or magical purposes?
   アジアではサイの角は医療の目的で、それとも魔法の目的で使用されてきたか？

2. Have safari hunters killed rhinos for their horns or as trophies?
   狩猟旅行のハンターたちはその角のために、それとも狩猟記念品としてサイを殺してきたか？

3. Did the international ban on rhino hunting save the rhino, or did it make the situation worse?
   サイ狩猟の国際禁止令はサイを救ったか、それとも状況をさらに悪化させたか？

4. Are today's rhino poachers professionals or just poor locals?
   今日のサイ密猟者はプロか、それともただの貧しい地元の人か？

5. Who has been killed in the battle over the rhino, only poachers or law enforcement officials as well?
   サイをめぐる争いで殺されたのは密猟者だけか、それとも法執行官も巻き込まれているか？

6. Are anti-poaching police unarmed, or do they carry rifles, too?
   反密猟警備隊は非武装か，それとも同様にライフル銃を持ち歩くか？

7. Do experts say removing the rhinoceros's horns is necessary, or do they say it is too extreme?
   専門家たちはサイの角を切除することは必要だと言っているか，それともやり過ぎだと言っているか？

8. Is the scheme to save the rhinos quite quick and cheap to carry out, or does it cost a lot of time and money?
   サイを救う計画はすぐ実行できてお金もかからないか，それともかなりの時間とお金を要するか？

● ● ● **EXERCISES 2: COMPOSITION** ● ● ●

Making Questions:

下の ANSWER が答えとなる疑問文を完成させなさい。音声で疑問文をチェックしなさい。

1. Q. 大物狙いのハンターたちはどれくらいの間，サイを殺してきたか？
   A. ほぼ 200 年間。

   解答 have big-game hunters been killing rhinos

2. Q. サイ狩猟の国際禁止令が出されて何が起きたか？
   A. アフリカのサイ総数の約 90 パーセントが殺された。

   解答 after an international ban was placed on rhino hunting

3. Q. サイの角の値段はいくらに達したか？
   A. 1 キロ 2 万ドルまで。

   解答 can rhinoceros horn fetch

4. Q. 歩兵は 1 日 24 時間何をするか？
   A. 密猟者を警戒してパトロールする。

   解答 What do foot soldiers do 24 hours a day

Writing with Idioms:

下線部の代用として下の語句を使い，文を書き換えなさい。語形を変える必要があることもある。音声で答えをチェックしなさい。

1. As <u>a case in point</u>, let me tell you about my own experience.
   適当な例として，私自身の経験を話させてください。

2. Don't <u>get in my way</u>! I'm doing what I have to do!
   邪魔しないで! やらなきゃいけないことがあるんだから。

3. Raising university tuition <u>gave rise to</u> student demonstrations.
   大学授業料の値上げのために学生デモが起きた。

4. Make sure you <u>keep track of</u> where you've filed these papers.
   書類をファイルした場所をきちんと覚えておいて。

Word Forms:

カッコの単語を適当な形に直しなさい。

1. predicted
   ラムズ [ロサンゼルスを本拠地とする全米フットボールリーグのチーム] が勝つと予想し，当たった。

2. embarking
   その船は明日の午前6時に出航することになっている。

3. covetous
   ジョーンズ氏は，金持ちでハンサムな隣人が持っているすべてのものを欲しがる。

4. vulnerability
   主力選手の何人かがケガをし，チームは攻撃されやすい状態にあった。

5. aggressively
   その候補者は，女性有権者を引きつけるために積極的にキャンペーンを行った。

● ● ● EXERCISES 3: CHALLENGE ● ● ●

Using Key Concepts:

Aの文と意味が同じになるように，Bの文の空所を埋めなさい。KEY CONCEPTSの語句を使いなさい。

1. international ban
   奴隷制度には国際禁止令が適用されるべきだ。

2. law enforcement officials
   まもなく法執行官が姿を見せた。
   ＊ It was not long before .... 「まもなく…した」

3. endangered species
   法により絶滅危惧種が守られる。

4. GPS transmitter
   私たちはGPS送信機を容疑者の車に取り付けた。

Vocabulary Expansion:

いろいろな種類の「殺すこと」を表した動詞の辞書定義を読み，それぞれの文の下線部の動詞の代わりにこれらの動詞を使い，文を書き換えなさい。正しい語形にすること。

1. Police stopped the planned <u>assassination</u> of the Pope.
   警察はローマ法王の暗殺計画を阻止した。

2. Raskolnikov <u>murdered</u> the old woman and stole her money.
   ラスコーリニコフ［ドストエフスキーの小説『罪と罰』に出てくる架空の人物］は老女を殺害し，お金を奪った。

3. The <u>execution</u> of the condemned man was carried out at dawn.
   死刑宣告された男の処刑が明け方に執行された。

4. Hundreds of "mad cows" had to be <u>euthanized</u>.
   何百頭もの「発狂した牛」が安楽死されなければならなかった。

5. During Rwanda's civil war, thousands of people were <u>massacred</u>.
   ルワンダの内戦の間，何千人もが大量虐殺された。

辞書定義

murder: たいていは怒りや敵意から不法に殺す（〜を殺害する）
execute: 死刑を執行するために殺す（〜に死刑を執行する）
assassinate: 不意の攻撃で有名人や重要人物を殺す（〜を暗殺する）
massacre: 団体・集団などを全員殺す（〜を大量虐殺する）
euthanize: 苦痛をなくすために瀕死の人を殺す（〜を安楽死させる）

Listening Activity:

ショートトークとそれに続く質問を聞きなさい。それぞれの質問に対する下の答えを完成させなさい。

1. a conservation organization
   世界野生動物基金は保護団体と呼ばれている。

2. the Houston Zoo
   その計画はヒューストン動物園で始まった。

3. to donate just $5.00
   1人5ドルの寄付が求められる。

4. gunshot wounds
   そのお金は銃撃による傷の治療に使われる。

5. their parents to poaching
   サイの赤ちゃんは密猟によって両親を奪われた。
   ＊ lose A to B「AをBによって奪われる」

6. moved to safer areas
   何頭かのサイはより安全な地域へ移動させられている。

Questions

1. What kind of organization is the WWF described as?
   世界野生動物基金はどのような団体であると呼ばれているか？

2. Who launched the new program to save rhinos in Zimbabwe?
   ジンバブエのサイを救うその計画は誰が始めたか？

3. How much is each person asked to donate to the program?
   その計画に対する寄付は1人いくらか？

4. What kind of injuries will the money be used to treat?
   そのお金はどのような種類の傷を治療するために使われるか？

5. What has happened to some baby rhinos?
   何頭かのサイの赤ちゃんに何が起きたか？

6. Where are some rhinos being moved to?
   何頭かのサイはどこに移動されられているか？

Listening Script

　Zoos, conservation organizations like the WWF, and field researchers have been fighting for decades to save the rhino from extinction. Now you can help, too, thanks to a wonderful new program launched by the Houston Zoo to protect rhinos in Zimbabwe from poachers and other threats. Here's how the program works. A one-time donation of just $5.00—that's right, only $5.00—will be added to your next mobile phone bill. All the proceeds collected will be sent to the International Rhinoceros Foundation. The money will be used to treat rhinos with injuries like gunshot wounds, to help care for baby rhinos that have lost their parents to poachers, to move rhinos to safer areas, and to capture poachers and put them in jail. If you would like to help save the rhino, just text the Houston Zoo today.

　動物園，世界野生動物基金のような保護団体，野外研究者たちは何十年もの間，サイを絶滅から救うために闘ってきた。ジンバブエのサイを，密猟者やその他の脅威から保護するためにヒューストン動物園が始めた素晴らしい新計画のおかげで，今ではあなたも手助けができる。その計画の仕組みはこうだ。1回たった5ドル—その通り，たった5ドル—の寄付が次回の携帯電話の請求書に加算される。集まったすべての収益は国際サイ財団に届けられる。そのお金は，銃撃による傷のような負傷をおったサイの治療，密猟者に両親を奪われたサイの赤ちゃんの世話の援助，より安全な地域へのサイの移動，密猟者の逮捕と投獄に使用される。もしあなたがサイを救う手助けがしたいなら，今日にでもヒューストン動物園に携帯メールを送ってください。

　＊ put A in jail「Aを投獄する」

Lesson 3　Of Nukes and Minefields
核兵器と地雷原に関して

> **NOTES**
> follow suit「先例にならう」　Russian President Dmitry Medvedev「ロシアのドミトリー・メドベージェフ大統領」　African pouched rat「アフリカオニネズミ」　sniff out A「Aをかぎつける」

● ● ● GETTING READY TO READ ● ● ●

Key Concepts:

リーディングの重要語句と下の定義や説明を結びつけなさい。定義や説明の文字を空所に書きなさい。

1. d　アメリカ合衆国上院＝アメリカ国家の立法組織の半分
2. e　核兵器＝大量殺人と大量破壊を引き起こす爆弾
3. a　国家院＝ロシアの国会
4. g　兵器削減条約＝兵器の数を減らすための協定・条約
5. c　弾頭＝ミサイルの先に装着されている爆弾
6. h　兵器の貯蔵量＝ある国の銃，戦車，爆弾の貯蔵量
7. i　軍備縮小＝銃，戦車，爆弾などを減らすこと
8. b　ユニセフ＝子どもの利益を守るための国連の機関
9. f　読み書きができない人々＝読んだり書いたりできない人々
10. j　ロイター通信社＝国際的な通信社

Active Reading:

リーディングを読み，質問の答えをさがしなさい。答えが見つかった文をマークしなさい。

1. ロシアとアメリカの間の協定は何をしたか？

　　解答　The arms-control pact places a limit on the number of nuclear warheads each side can possess and, to prevent cheating, allows mutual inspection of nuclear bases and missile arsenals.

2. それについて両国のリーダーは何と言わなければならなかったか？

   解答 While reducing the world's stockpile of nuclear weapons is a vital step towards "making us all safer," other more conventional weapons call for urgent disarmament as well.

3. 地雷とは何か？ また，なぜ地雷は残酷なのか？

   解答 Landmines are explosive devices designed to go off when stepped on or run over. What makes mines so inhuman is that their purpose is not just to take lives, but to maim and cause terrible pain and suffering.

4. なぜ地雷は特に子どもにとって危険なのか？

   解答 Even when a minefield is discovered, it poses an especially persistent danger to children and the illiterate, who can't read signs warning them to keep away.

5. なぜネズミが即戦力の対地雷兵器になるのか？

   解答 Rats have an acute sense of smell and, more crucially, are too small and lightweight to trigger mine, making them much more effective than dogs.

Words in Context:

文の一部の下線部に最も意味が近い語句を選びなさい。

1. (A)　アメリカ合衆国上院は「新戦略的兵器削減条約」を批准した
   - (A) ～に署名した
   - (B) ～を創造した
   - (C) ～を拒絶した

2. (B)　相互の監査を許す
   - (A) 秘密の
   - (B) 両者間の
   - (C) 最後の

3. (A)　他のより通常な兵器
   - (A) ありきたりの
   - (B) 危険な
   - (C) 高価な

4. (C)　敵の兵士や乗り物
   - (A) 機械
   - (B) 兵器
   - (C) 車やトラック

Lesson 3　Of Nukes and Minefields　25

5. (A)　障害者にしたり，ひどい痛みを引き起こすこと
　　　(A) 〜を不自由にする　　(B) 〜を殺す　　(C) 〜を爆発させる

6. (C)　引き金を引かれるのを待っている命にかかわる遺産
　　　(A) 特に危険な兵器　　(B) 消極的な考え　　(C) 過去から受け継いだもの

7. (A)　無知な者によって引き金を引かれるのを待っている
　　　(A) 爆発させられる　　(B) 組み立てられる　　(C) 攻撃される

8. (B)　気づいていない人々や疑いのない人々によって
　　　(A) 若者
　　　(B) その状況にかかわっていない人々
　　　(C) それほど知能が高くない人々

9. (B)　子どもに対して特にいつまでも続く危険性
　　　(A) 残虐な　　(B) 頑固な　　(C) 危険な

10. (C)　鋭い嗅覚
　　　(A) 普通でない　　(B) 役に立つ　　(C) 鋭い

11. (A)　さらに，もっと決定的なことに，小さすぎる
　　　(A) さらに重要なことに　　(B) 面白いことに　　(C) 紛らわしいことに

12. (B)　都市部で爆弾をかぎつけること
　　　(A) 戦争で荒れた　　(B) 都会の　　(C) 未開発の

● ● ● TODAY'S READING ● ● ●

エッセイを注意深く読み，それに続く練習問題を解きなさい。

試訳

① 2010年12月22日に，アメリカ合衆国上院は「新START」を批准した。STARTは「戦略的兵器削減条約」を意味し，ロシアとアメリカの核兵器の制限に対する協定である。ロシアの国会である国家院はすぐにアメリカにならうことが期待されている。（これら2か国は世界の核兵器の90パーセントを保有している。）兵器削減条約は，それぞれが保有できる核弾頭の個数を制限し，不正を防ぐために，核兵器の基地やミサイルの兵器工場へのお互いの査察を認めている。

② オバマ大統領とロシアのドミトリー・メドベージェフ大統領が述べたように「私たちみ

んなをより安全にすること」に向かって，世界の核兵器の備蓄を削減することは不可欠なステップである一方，他の多くの通常兵器にも同様に緊急の軍備縮小が必要となる。これらの兵器の中で，地雷は最も残酷なものに違いない。地雷は，踏んだり車で上を走ったりすると爆発するようにつくられた爆発性装置である。典型的なものは，地表の少し下の地雷原に「植えられて」いる地雷だが，350以上もの異なった種類があり，接触した敵の兵士を障害者にしたり，接触した乗り物を運転不能にすることを目標としている。地雷を非常に残酷なものしているのは，その目的がただ命を奪うだけではなく，障害者にしたり，ひどい痛みや苦痛を引き起こすことである。国際法で禁止されているが，地雷は価格が低く，製造が容易であり，依然として広い範囲で使用されている。一度置かれると，地雷は50年間効力がある。1億以上の不発地雷が依然として70か国以上に存在しており，ユニセフは「それに気づいていない疑いのない人々によって，引き金を引かれるのを待っている命にかかわる遺産」である，と言う。地雷が発見された後でさえ，その地雷は近づくなという警告標識を読むことができない，特に子どもたちや読み書きができない人々にとっては危険な状態を持続させるのである。

③ この不発地雷を取り除くには費用も時間もかかり，言うまでもなく非常に危険な工程である。最初の，そして最も難しい段階は地雷を探知することで，通常は地雷中の爆発物をかぎつける訓練を受けた犬が行う。軍事用ロボットも使用されてきた。（地雷を見つけるとすぐに，専門家は周りの地面にある化学物質を撃ち込むことによって「安全に取り除く」のである。）しかし今では，いくつかのアフリカ諸国では，新たな「兵器」が対地雷戦で従事している，とロイター通信社は報じている。それはネズミである。アフリカオニネズミは非常に知能が高いため，学習するのが早く，調教もしやすい。ネズミは嗅覚が鋭く，さらに決定的なことに，小さくて軽いため地雷の引き金にならず，犬よりもずっと即戦力となる。さらに，ネズミは作業が速い。ヒモをつけられ，調教を受けたネズミは，たった30分でサッカー場の大きさの地域をカバーすることができる。それは「犬の爆弾探知チーム」では，少なくとも2日間はかかる任務である。爆発物探知器として，ネズミを利用することがうまくいくと証明されたので，ネズミが都市部でテロの爆弾をかぎつけるような，様々な他の危険な任務でも使用されるだろう。

● ● ● EXERCISES 1：COMPREHENSION ● ● ●

Reading for Information:

下の文を読みなさい。文がリーディングの内容と合っていればTに，合っていなければFに○をつけなさい。

1. F　STARTは核兵器を保有している諸国の間の協定である。
2. F　ロシアはアメリカが批准する前にSTARTを批准した。
3. T　世界の核兵器の10分の9はアメリカかロシアのものだ。
4. F　ユニセフはSTARTが世界をより安全にしている，と言う。

5. T　地雷が置かれている地帯は地雷原として知られている。
6. F　世界中には今でも使用されている1億の違ったタイプの地雷がある。
7. T　地雷は疑いをもっていない子供を殺傷することがある。
8. F　ネズミが使用されるまで，犬だけが地雷を探知するのに使用されてきた。
9. T　ネズミが非常に有用な点は，体重が軽く作業がすばやいことだ。
10. F　ネズミはヒモなしで，単独で自由に作業できる。

Listening for Ideas:

音声の質問を聞き，最も適当な答えを選びなさい。

1. (A)　お互いの兵器を調べられるようにすることで。
   (B) お互いの兵器の個数を減らすことで。
   (C) オバマ大統領とメドベージェフ大統領の二人に協定に署名してもらうことで。

2. (C)　永久的に続く痛い傷を負わせることを目的にしているから。
   (A) 人々だけでなく乗り物も破壊できるから。
   (B) 地表の少し下に埋められているから。
   ＊ A as well as B「Aだけでなく B もまた」

3. (B)　いいえ，国際法がその使用を禁止している。
   (A) いいえ，まだ使用されている。
   (C) いいえ，まだ多くの不発地雷がある。

4. (B)　ネズミはこれまでよく任務を果たしてきたから。
   (A) はい，かなりよく活躍している。
   (C) 主に都市部である。

Listening Script

1. How does START try to keep the two sides from cheating?
   どのようにして START は両陣営の不正を回避しているか？

2. What makes a landmine so cruel and inhuman?
   なぜ地雷は残酷で無慈悲なのか？

3. Is it still legal to use landmines?
   地雷の使用は今でも合法的か？

4. Why will rats soon be used for other explosive-device detection purposes?
なぜすぐにネズミは他の爆発物探知の目的で使用されるか？

● ● ● EXERCISES 2: COMPOSITION ● ● ●

Making Questions:

下の ANSWER が答えとなる疑問文を完成させなさい。音声で疑問文をチェックしなさい。

1. Q. 何に START は上限を置いているか？
   A. 1 国が保有できる兵器の個数。

   解答 What does START place

2. Q. いつ地雷は爆発するか？
   A. 踏んだり，車で上を走ると。

   解答 do landmines go off

3. Q. なぜ地雷は今でも使用されているか？
   A. たぶん価格が低く，製造するのが容易だから。

   解答 landmines still being used

4. Q. 地雷を発見するとすぐに，専門家はどのように地雷を安全に取り除くのか？
   A. その周りの地面にある化学物質を撃ち込むことで。

   解答 disarm a landmine once it is found

Writing with Idioms:

下線部の代用として下の語句を使い，文を書き換えなさい。語形を変える必要があることがある。音声で答えをチェックしなさい。

1. The alarm clock is set to go off at 5:30.
   目覚まし時計は 5 時 30 分に鳴るようにセットされている。

2. The board of directors called for the CEO's resignation.
   取締役会は最高経営責任者の辞任を要求した。

Lesson 3 Of Nukes and Minefields 29

3. Everyone agrees. We expect you to <u>follow suit</u>.
   全員同意しています。あなたもみんなと同じようにしてください。

4. To many, Kennedy <u>stood for</u> youth and a better future.
   多くの人にとって，ケネディーは若さと明るい未来の象徴だった。

Word Forms:

カッコから正しい語を選びなさい。

1. crucial
   さらに重大なことは淡水の不足である。

2. convention
   意外な結末はオー・ヘンリー［「最後の一葉」や「賢者の贈りもの」などの短編で有名なアメリカの短編小説家］の短編小説の伝統的な手法である。

3. mutually
   その計画はお互いに有益のようだ。

4. acutely
   私は必要なものを鋭く意識している。
   ＊ be aware of A 「A に気づいている」

5. inherited
   大金を相続して，レナは仕事を辞めかかり切りで油絵を始めた。

6. persistence
   彼女の我慢と粘り強さがとうとう実を結んだ。

● ● ● **EXERCISES 3: CHALLENGE** ● ● ●

Using Key Concepts:

Aの文と意味が同じになるように，Bの文の空所を埋めなさい。KEY CONCEPTSの語句を使いなさい。適当な形に直しなさい。

1. arsenal

   その国が兵器貯蔵庫にどのくらいの個数の核兵器を保有しているか，誰もはっきりとは知らない。

2. warheads

   それぞれのミサイルにはいくつかの弾頭が装着されている。

3. UNICEF

   ユニセフは「国際連合児童緊急基金」の頭文字である。

4. United States Senate

   議会は2つに分かれている。上院と下院である。

5. illiterate

   その図書館では，読み書きができない人々に読み書きを教えるための特別クラスを毎週，いくつか開講している。

Vocabulary Expansion:

形容詞 "innocent" の辞書定義を見て，下の文を読みなさい。それぞれの innocent がどの意味かを判断し，辞書定義の番号を空所に書きなさい。

a. 3　悪意のない冗談のつもりで言ったことが多くの人を傷つける結果となった。
   * end up *do*ing「最後には〜することになる」
b. 2　その囚人は死刑が執行される直前まで無罪を主張した。
   * up until A「Aまで」
c. 6　無関係な見物人が何人かその襲撃で殺された。
d. 1　子どものように純真で，彼はハエ1匹も殺せない。
e. 5　習慣を知らずに，ムーア夫人は靴を履いたまま寺に入った。
f. 4　貪欲でインチキな人に利用されるのは君のような世慣れていない人だ。
   * It is A who ....「…なのはAだ」

Lesson 3　Of Nukes and Minefields　31

辞書定義

1. 邪悪によって堕落していない；罪がない
2. ある特定の罪から無罪である
3. 悪意のない
4. 経験がなく世慣れていない；未熟な
5. 精通してなく，触れさせられていない；知らない
6. 関わりを避けた，その一員ではない

Listening Activity:

ショートトークを聞き，その主旨に最も合う文を選びなさい。

Answer: (C)

(A) アメリカ人は昔より敵意をもつことが少なくなった。
(B) ますます多くのアメリカ人がより厳しい銃規制を求めている。
(C) 銃の数が増えることで，怒りや憎しみが，将来ますます多くの暴力を引き起こすことになる。
(D) アリゾナ銃撃事件は最終的により厳しい銃規制につながった。

Listening Script

   Will last January's shootings in Arizona lead to stricter gun-control laws in the United States? In my opinion, the answer is a resounding no. Just look at the statistics. A poll taken in 2010 shows that only 44% of Americans say gun-control laws should be made tougher. Back in 2000, 62% of Americans called for making laws stricter. And way back in 1990, nearly 80% of the people were in favor of stricter laws. In other words, each year, fewer and fewer Americans want gun-control laws to be made tougher. In the meantime, America has become a much angrier place. Hatred and hostility among racial and ethnic groups has increased. Political speeches have become more antagonistic. So what this means to me is that America is becoming more divided and violent than ever. And that guns will become even more numerous in the years ahead.

   この前の1月に起きたアリゾナでの銃撃事件によって，アメリカ合衆国での銃規制法がより厳しくなるだろうか？私の意見では，答えは断定的にノーだ。ちょっと統計を見

てみよう。2010年に行われた世論調査では、アメリカ人のたった44パーセントが銃規制法をより厳しくすべきと答えている。2000年にさかのぼると、アメリカ人の62パーセントが銃規制法を厳しくすることを求めていた。そして、さらに1990年にさかのぼると、アメリカ人のほぼ80パーセントが厳しい規制法を支持していた。言い換えれば、銃規制法をより厳しくすべきだというアメリカ人が年々減少しているのである。一方では、アメリカは人々がみんな腹を立てているところとなってきた。人種間・民族間の憎しみや敵意が大きくなってきている。政治のスピーチはより敵意のあるものになった。そして、これがアメリカを今までより分裂させ、暴力的にしているのではないか、と私には思える。それなのに、その銃の数はこれから年々、ますます増えていくのである。

* in favor of A「Aを支持して」
* in other words「言い換えれば」
* in the meantime「一方では」

Lesson 4 Languages Lost and Found
消滅した言語と発見された言語

> **NOTES**
> Koro「コロ語」インド北東部における少数派言語　different A to B「Bとは違ったA」　the Kallawaya「カラワヤ族」ボリビアのアンデス山麓に住んでいる巡回治療者たち

● ● ● **GETTING READY TO READ** ● ● ●

Key Concepts:

リーディングの重要語句と下の定義や説明を結びつけなさい。定義や説明の文字を空所に書きなさい。

1. d　フィールド言語学者＝その母語を研究するため，地元の人たちと生活する科学者
2. f　方言＝多数派言語と関係のある少数派言語
3. h　［人・言語などが］その土地に固有の＝土着の，またはその土地の
4. i　神話＝神や起源についての伝説
5. b　生態系＝自然環境や周囲の状況
6. g　薬草医＝薬草を薬として使う人々
7. c　インカ帝国＝古代南アメリカ文明社会
8. e　ケチュア語＝アンデス山脈で話されている母語
9. a　先史時代＝人間の文明が出現する前の時代

Active Reading:

リーディングを読み，質問の答えをさがしなさい。答えが見つかった文をマークしなさい。

1. K・デイビッド・ハリソン博士は誰か？

    解答 Dr. K. David Harrison, the team leader and a well-known activist for the preservation of the world's indigenous languages.

2. コロ語として知られている独立言語を発見した時，研究者たちは何をしていたか？

    解答 The researchers thought they were documenting a minor dialect of another language.

3. 自然界に関するほとんどの人間の知識はどこにあるか？

   解答 Most of what we know about the natural world is not written down anywhere. It's only in people's heads.

4. ハリソン博士は，カラワヤ族の人たちは私たちに何を教えるべきだと考えているか？

   解答 But they also use an ancient secret language, now vulnerable, to encode information about thousands of medicinal plants that the tribe uses as remedies for afflictions of all kinds.

5. オーストラリアのアボリジニ語はなぜとても重要なのか？

   解答 Aborigines represent an unbroken link with the past that people in other places on Earth don't.

Words in Context:

文の一部の下線部に最も意味が近い語句を選びなさい。

1. (A)　山麓の丘の<u>独立した</u>地区
   (A) へんぴな　　　　(B) 無名の　　　　(C) 古代の

2. (A)　研究員たちは少数派方言を詳細に<u>記録していた</u>
   (A) 〜を記録する　　(B) 〜を発見する　　(C) 〜を学ぶ

3. (B)　独自の言語<u>構造</u>や語彙
   (A) 音　　　　　　　(B) 型　　　　　　　(C) 歴史

4. (B)　まったく違った<u>観点</u>
   (A) 知識　　　　　　(B) 見地　　　　　　(C) 細部

5. (B)　<u>差し迫った</u>消滅に直面している
   (A) 危険な　　　　　(B) 近づいている　　(C) 自然な

6. (A)　人間知識の土台の<u>崩壊</u>
   (A) 破壊　　　　　　(B) 構成　　　　　　(C) 拡大

7. (B)　種の生態系を<u>深く</u>知っている
   (A) ひそかに　　　　(B) とてもよく　　　(C) 偶然に

Lesson 4　Languages Lost and Found

8. (C)　より洗練された分類法をもっている
　　(A) 難しい　　　　　　(B) 敬意を払われた　　　(C) 進歩した

9. (A)　いろいろな種類の苦悩の治療薬として使用する
　　(A) 薬　　　　　　　　(B) 研究　　　　　　　　(C) 情報源

10. (C)　いろいろな種類の苦悩の治療薬として
　　(A) けが　　　　　　　(B) 傷　　　　　　　　　(C) 心の病

11. (A)　そこで実際にあなたは人間の先史時代を垣間見ることができる
　　(A) 〜をちらっと見る　 (B) 〜を深く研究する　　(C) 〜でわくわくする

● ● ● **TODAY'S READING** ● ● ●

エッセイを注意深く読み，それに続く練習問題を解きなさい。

試訳
① インド北東部，ヒマラヤ山脈の山麓の丘にある孤立した地区で調査しているフィールド言語学者たちが，以前には知られていない「隠れた」言語を最近，たまたま発見した。コロ語として知られているその言語は，1,000人足らずの人々によって話されている。研究員たちは，別の言語の少数派方言を記録していると勘違いしていた。しかし，コロ語が独自の言語構造と語彙をもっていることがすぐにわかった。そのチームリーダーで，世界の現地語保護で有名な活動家，K・ディビッド・ハリソン博士にとって，この発見は特に興味をそそるものだった。コロ語は，今までわかっている言語とはまったく異なったものの見方，歴史，神話，科学技術，文法をもたらしている，と彼は言う。

② しかし悲しいことに，コロ語は，差し迫った消滅に直面している世界中の何百という言語の中のほんの1言語にすぎない。実際に，2週間ごとに1言語が消滅している。この調子では，世界の約7,000言語の半分以上が今世紀末までには消滅することになる。ハリソン博士は『ナショナル ジオグラフック』誌で，1言語が滅びると自然界に関する「かけがえのない知識」も失ってしまうことになる，と述べている。「私たちが自然界について知っている大部分がどこにも書き記されていない。人々の頭の中だけにある。」植物と動物の種の約80パーセントが，組織的な科学ではなく，原住民によって発見されてきた，とハリソン博士は指摘する。こうした人々は，種の生態系に精通していて，「科学よりも種を分類するより洗練された方法」をもっていることもある。

③ ハリソン博士は，ボリビアの1部族であるカラワヤ族とオーストラリア原住民のアボリジニを例に挙げている。カラワヤ族は，インカ帝国の時代から伝統的に薬草医だった。カラワヤ族のほとんどが，現在ではより共通語であるケチュア語を話す。しかし，彼らは，その部族がいろいろな苦痛のための治療薬として用いる何千もの薬草植物についての情報を符号化するのに，今では消滅寸前の古代秘語も使う。その秘語が消滅すると，たぶん，

ガンやエイズのための治療法といった―きわめて貴重な情報が―その秘語とともに消えてしまうのである。

④ 世界で最も消滅の危機にさらされている言語の中で，オーストラリアのアボリジニ語の消滅は，人間が有する別の種類の知識が近いうちになくなってしまうことを意味する，とハリソン博士は信じている。「オーストラリアは，人間が5万年間もそこに住んできたという点で驚くべき場所である。アボリジニは，地球の他の場所にいる人々ではなれない，過去から脈々と続くきずなの代表者なのだ。そこで実際に，あなたは人間の先史時代を垣間見ることができる。どんな種類の文書にも頼ることなしに―あなたは人々がそこで生み出し，口述で伝えてきた神話信仰や体系に触れられるのだ。」

● ● ● EXERCISES 1：COMPREHENSION ● ● ●

Reading for Information:

下の質問に対して簡潔に答えなさい。

1. 1,000
   今日，約何人の人がコロ語を話すか？

2. a dialect of another language
   最初，研究員たちはコロ語を何だと思ったか？

3. every two weeks
   今日，どれくらいの頻度で1言語が消滅するか？

4. in people's heads
   私たちの自然界に関する知識のほとんどはどこにあるとハリソン博士は考えているか？

5. Kallawaya and Australia's aboriginal languages
   ハリソン博士が挙げた消滅の危機に瀕している言語の2例は何か？

6. Quechua
   ほとんどのカラワヤ族は何語を話すか？

7. a cure for cancer or AIDS
   カラワヤ族がもっている薬草や医療に使える植物に関する情報にはどんなものがあるか？

Lesson 4　Languages Lost and Found　37

8. orally—without recourse to written language
   アボリジニの間ではどのように伝統的知識が継承されるか？
   * without recourse to A「A に頼らずに」

Listening for Ideas:

音声を聞き，文の空所を埋めなさい。その文がリーディングの内容に合っていれば T に，合っていなければ F に○をつけなさい。

1. F　[they had heard it spoken before]
   研究員たちは今まで耳にしたことがなかったため，コロ語を個別言語であると考えた。

2. T　[only 3,500 or so languages remaining around the globe]
   2100 年まで地球上に残っている言語はたった約 3,500 言語だろう。

3. T　[more sophisticated ways of classifying species]
   ハリソン博士によると，組織的な科学ではなく，原住民が種を分類する洗練された方法をもっていることがあるという。

● ● ● EXERCISES 2: COMPOSITION ● ● ●

Making Questions:

下の ANSWER が答えとなる疑問文を完成させなさい。音声で疑問文をチェックしなさい。

1. Q. コロ語はどこで発見されたか？
   A. ヒマラヤ山脈の山麓の丘。

   解答　Where was Koro

2. Q. なぜハリソン博士はその発見を興奮させるものだと思ったか？
   A. コロ語は私たちにいろいろな種類の新しい知識をもたらしてくれるから。

   解答　Dr. Harrison find the discovery so exciting

3. Q. どれくらいの間，人間はオーストラリアに住んできたか？
   A. 5 万年以上もの間。

   解答　How long have humans been living

4.　Q. アボリジニは何の代表者か？
　　A. ハリソン博士によると，過去から脈々と続くきずな。

解答　Aborigines represent

Writing with Idioms:

下線部の代用として下の語句を使い，文を書き換えなさい。語形を変える必要があることもある。音声で答えをチェックしなさい。

1. If you <u>come into contact with</u> [chance upon も可] any famous people, get their autographs.
   もしあなたが有名人と出会ったら，サインをもらいなさい。

2. The lecturer <u>pointed out</u> ten simple steps to save the planet.
   講演者は地球を救うための 10 の簡単なステップを指摘した。

3. Would you kindly <u>pass on</u> this updated information to the staff?
   この最新情報をスタッフに伝えていただけますか？

4. I <u>chanced upon</u> this first edition of Middlemarch in Jimbocho.
   私は『ミドルマーチ』［イギリスの女性小説家 George Eliot の小説］の初版を神保町で偶然見つけた。

Word Forms:

それぞれの単語を適当な形に直して，文の空所を埋めなさい。

1. intimate
   この秘密は君のような親しい友だちにしか言えない。

2. isolation
   動物は空港では隔離病棟で保護される。

3. eroding
   海岸は波によって徐々に侵食される。
   ＊ erode A away「A を侵食する」

4. structural

　エンジニアたちはその橋の構造的欠陥に気づいた。

5. documents

　財務文書すべてが火事で燃えてしまった。

6. Sophistication

　教養は知識と経験からくる。

● ● ● EXERCISES 3: CHALLENGE ● ● ●

Using Key Concepts:

Aの文と意味が同じになるように，Bの文の空所を埋めなさい。KEY CONCEPTSの語句を使いなさい。

1. Field linguists

　フィールド言語学者たちは，「テ・レオ」として知られるマオリ語を研究・記録するためにニュージーランドにいる。

2. indigenous

　アイヌは日本の先住民である。

3. ecosystems

　森林伐採はアマゾン川流域の生態系を破壊している。

4. dialect

　広東語[中国南部・香港・マカオで話されている中国語]は1方言か，それとも個別言語か？
　＊ in *one's* own right「他に依存せずに」

5. mythology

　ジョイスの『ユリシーズ』[アイルランドの作家 James Joyce の小説]はギリシャ神話やローマ神話に基づいている。

Vocabulary Expansion:

紛らわしい3つの単語の辞書定義を読みなさい。下の文の空所を選んだ1語で埋めなさい。

1. eminent

   天文学の分野で最も有名な人たちの何人かがその会議に出席した。

2. immanent

   貪欲は資本主義制度に内在している。

3. imminent

   患者は今のところ差し迫って危険な状態ではないが，彼の状況をまだ見守っていく必要がある。

辞書定義

imminent: すぐにやってくる；近づいている；不可避の（差し迫った）
immanent: 内に存在・残存する；本来備わっている（内在する）
eminent: 地位の高い；目立った；優れた（著名な）

Listening Activity:

ショートトークを聞き，下の質問に対して簡潔に答えなさい。

1. ここで触れられている2つの主要言語は何ですか？

   解答 Spanish and English

2. 2か国語が話されている環境で一方が他方より重要でないことを最もよく理解しているのは誰か？

   解答 children

3. ある固有言語が経済的・社会的進歩を妨げるとその地域社会が判断するとどうなるか？

   解答 The language becomes endangered.

4. ハリソン博士によると，ある言語が生き残れると確信できる唯一の方法は何か？

   解答 We must make sure that six-year-olds value and use it.

Lesson 4　Languages Lost and Found

Listening Script

What is the biggest threat or danger to the world's most endangered indigenous languages? The answer is simple. Dominant major languages like Spanish and English are replacing them. It is children, says Dr. Harrison, who most often stop using a native language. Children naturally understand that if they live in an environment where two languages are spoken, one of the languages is less important than the other. So children will speak the more important language. When a community decides that their native language prevents or gets in the way of social or economic progress, that language becomes endangered. The only way to ensure that a language survives is to make sure that six-year-olds value and use it. Thus, it is not the parents but the children who have the power to decide whether a language will continue to be spoken, according to Dr. Harrison.

　世界のほとんどの消滅危機に瀕した現地語にとって，最も大きな脅威や危険は何か？答えは簡単だ。スペイン語や英語のような最も有力な主要言語がその現地語に代わりつつあるということである。ハリソン博士によると，最もよく母国語を使用しなくなるのは子どもであるという。2つの言語が話されている環境で生活すると，どちらか一方が他方より重要でないことを子どもは自然に理解する。その通り，子どもはより重要な言語を話すのである。母国語が社会的・経済的発展を妨げたり邪魔になると，地域社会が判断すると，その言語は消滅の危機にさらされる。ある言語が生き残れると確信できる唯一の方法は，6歳児たちにその言語を尊重し，使用してもらうことである。このように，ある言語が話され続けられるかどうかを決定する力があるのは親ではなく子どもなのだ，とハリソン博士は語る。

＊ get in the way of A「Aの邪魔をする」

Lesson 5　It's About Time
もう女性が自由になってもいいころだ

> **NOTES**
> on the way out「廃れかかって」 stand up for A「Aを支持する」 Mark my words.「私の言うことを注意して聞きなさい」

● ● ● GETTING READY TO READ ● ● ●

Key Concepts:

リーディングの重要語句と下の定義や説明を結びつけなさい。定義や説明の文字を空所に書きなさい。

1. b　ジェンダーギャップ＝男性と女性の間の地位の違い
2. d　進歩的社会＝個人の自由について進歩的な考え方をもった国々
3. f　二流市民＝政治的な力や影響力がほとんどない人
4. g　中東＝南西アジアから北アフリカに広がった地域
5. e　奴隷制度＝ある人が別の人を所有する制度
6. i　コーラン＝イスラム教の教典
7. a　原告＝裁判所で要求を提起する人
8. h　公平な裁判＝要求を告発された人が弁護され，偏見なしに証拠が判断される訴訟
9. c　民主主義＝自由な選挙で市民が投票する政治形態
10. j　弾圧的な政権＝市民の自由を厳しく支配する政府

Active Reading:

リーディングを読み，質問の答えをさがしなさい。答えが見つかった文をマークしなさい。

1. 『ニューヨークタイムズ』紙は女性の増大する力を何と呼んでいるか？

    解答　"The Female Factor," as the *New York Times* calls it, is playing an increasingly important role in the Arab world.

2. なぜ中東の女性は二流市民か？

    解答　Nowhere is this gap more visible than in the countries of the Middle East, where tradition and religion have long relegated women to the status of second-class citizen.

3. 「アドフル」とは何か？またどのように行われるか？

   【解答】 In Saudi Arabia, for example, there is an age-old practice known as "adhl." This allows male guardians, most often girls' fathers, to make all the decisions about how their single daughters conduct their lives—particularly whom they can marry and how they can spend the money they earn. Under adhl, women cannot travel, enter hospitals, or live independently without a male guardian, who is entitled by custom to beat any woman who disobeys him.

4. 何人かのサウジの女性はどのようにアドフルに挑んでいるか？

   【解答】 But thanks to this discrepancy between law and practice, many single Saudi women are now suing their guardians in courts of law and demanding the right to make their own decisions.

5. 「ムハラベー」で有罪とされた女性はどうなるか？

   【解答】 A woman convicted of this crime can be sentenced to death by stoning with nothing even resembling a fair trial.

Words in Context:

文の一部の下線部に最も意味が近い語句を選びなさい。

1. (C)　過去の歓迎すべき進歩にもかかわらず
   (A) 変化　　　　　　　(B) 相違　　　　　　　(C) 進歩

2. (B)　女性が同じ権利を否定されていること
   (A) 〜を提供される　　(B) 〜を拒否される　　(C) 〜を罰せられる

3. (C)　この格差がそれらの国々よりも顕著な
   (A) ひどい　　　　　　(B) 頻繁に起こる　　　(C) 明らかな

4. (A)　伝統や宗教が長い間〜に女性を追いやってきた
   (A) 〜を低い地位にしてきた　(B) 〜を奨励してきた　(C) 〜に挑戦してきた

5. (C)　公平な社会をつくろうと努力している
　　　(A) 〜と望んでいる　　　(B) 〜と計画している　　　(C) 〜と熱心に努力している

6. (B)　公平な社会をつくること
　　　(A) 普通の　　　　　　　(B) 公正な　　　　　　　　(C) 現代的な

7. (A)　慣習によってたたく権利を与えられている
　　　(A) 〜ことを許されている　(B) 〜ことを禁じられている　(C) 〜ことを要求されている

8. (A)　この法律と習慣の不一致のおかげで
　　　(A) 相違　　　　　　　　(B) 線　　　　　　　　　　(C) 貿易

9. (A)　彼女らはメディアで自分たちの訴訟を弁護している
　　　(A) 〜を論争して　　　　(B) 〜について書いて　　　(C) 〜から隠して

10. (C)　原告に保護者と和解するように
　　　(A) 抗議する　　　　　　(B) 議論する　　　　　　　(C) 仲直りする

11. (A)　政権は悪名高く弾圧的だ
　　　(A) 道理が通っていないことで有名で
　　　(B) 悲劇的に
　　　(C) 危険なほどに

12. (B)　この罪で有罪とされた女性
　　　(A) 訴えられた　　　　　(B) 有罪とわかった　　　　(C) 無罪とわかった

● ● ● TODAY'S READING ● ● ●

エッセイを注意深く読み，それに続く練習問題を解きなさい。

試訳
① 過去50年以上の歓迎すべき進歩にもかかわらず，ジェンダーギャップ，つまり女性が仕事，学校，政治，結婚と離婚，活動の自由という点で，男性と同じ権利や機会をもつことが否定されていることは依然として世界中の現実である。北アメリカやヨーロッパのような比較的進歩した社会でさえ，女性は依然として賃金，給与，管理職，政府の代表といった点で男性に後れをとっている。
② 伝統や宗教が長い間女性を二流市民としてきた中東ほど，この格差が目に見えるところはない。しかし，この傾向は変わりつつある。『ニューヨークタイムズ』紙がいう「女性的要素」はアラブ世界でますます重要な役割を果たしている。女性は，昔からの規則

や考え方に挑んでいる。彼女らは，独立と平等に向かう大きな一歩を踏み出し，より公平な社会をつくる努力をしているのである。
③ 例えば，サウジアラビアでは「アドフル」という古くからの習慣がある。これにより男性の保護者は，ほとんどがその父親であるが，独身の娘がどのように生活するか，特に誰と結婚するか，稼いだお金をどのように使うかについて，すべての決断を下すことができるのである。アドフルのもとでは，女性は旅行もできず，入院することもできず，男性の保護者なしに独立して生活することができないのである。保護者は，服従しない女性をたたくことを習慣によって許されている。「サウジ女性は，保護者の許可なしに電話を買うことすらできない」とある女性権利の活動家は，『タイムズ』紙で述べている。「それは一種の奴隷制度のようなものだ。」
④ アドフルは違法であり，コーランで規定されているようにイスラムの法律では禁止されているが，そのことで広く実行されるのを防いではいない。しかし，この法律と習慣の不一致のおかげで，多くのサウジの独身女性が，法廷で自分の保護者を告訴しており，自分自身で決断を下す権利を要求している。さらに，彼女らはメディアで訴訟を主張することで，この習慣の不公平さは世界中の注目を集めている。しかし予期されるように，このような訴訟の判決には時間がかかる。裁判官は主に男性であり，ふつうは原告に保護者と和解するように強く勧める。しかし，これは時間の問題であり，アドフルは廃れかかっている。
⑤ 一方，そのイスラム政権が悪名高く弾圧的なイランでは，ムハラベー（神に対する憎しみ）として知られている告訴が，しばしば女性反政府抗議者に対して行われる。この罪で有罪判決を受けた女性は，公正な裁判とは似ても似つかない，石を当てて殺すという死刑宣告を受けることもある。しかし，死の恐れにもかかわらず，ますます多くのイラン女性が自分たちの権利を主張しており，女性法律家たちが彼女らを弁護している。ある弁護士が『タイムズ』紙で，「今に私の正しさがわかります。イランに民主主義をもたらすのは女性である」と誇らしげに述べている。

● ● ● EXERCISES 1：COMPREHENSION ● ● ●

Reading for Information:

下の質問に対して簡潔に答えなさい。

1. wages / male
   女性労働者は，男性労働者ほど賃金や給与を稼げないことがよくある。

2. management
   ほとんどの会社では，管理職の女性は男性ほどいない。

3. government
   ほとんどの国では，女性は政府や政治において男性ほど影響力がない。

4. tradition / religion

   中東では，女性は伝統や宗教によって抑圧されることもよくある。

5. rules / ideas

   中東では女性は昔からの規則や観念に挑んでいる，と『ニューヨークタイムズ』紙は報じている。

6. fathers

   サウジアラビアでは，ほとんどの少女の保護者は父親だ。

7. custom / obey

   サウジの習慣によると，保護者は服従しない女性をたたくことができる。

8. law

   実は，アドフルはイスラムの法律に反している。

9. media

   メディアに暴露されたおかげで，世界中の人々がアドフルがどんなに不公平かがわかった。

10. stones

    ムハラベーの有罪判決を受けると，女性に石が投げられる刑が行われることがある。

Listening for Ideas:

音声の質問を聞き，最も適当な答えを選びなさい。

1. (B)　いいえ，違います。いまだに格差がある。

   (A) はい，みんなそうである。
   (C) はい，北アメリカとヨーロッパでは。

2. (C)　そうではない。女性も働いている。

   (A) はい，イスラムの法律が禁止している。
   (B) いいえ，さもないと保護者にたたかれる。

3. (C)　いいえ，彼らは少女たちに保護者に従うように強く勧める。

   (A) はい，裁判官はふつう男性だから。
   (B) そうすることが求められている。

4. (A) はい，そうです。
   (B) いいえ，違います。
   (C) 私は反対する。

5. (C) はい，そうでしょう。
   (A) 彼女にははっきりわからない。
   (B) それは彼女の意見である。

Listening Script

1. In all progressive societies, all women have equal rights and opportunities, don't they?
   進歩したすべての社会では，すべての女性は同等の権利と機会をもっていますよね?

2. Saudi women aren't allowed to work at all, are they?
   サウジの女性は働くことはまったく許されていないですよね?

3. Most Saudi judges give single women the right to do as they please, don't they?
   ほとんどのサウジの裁判官は独身女性に好きなように行動する権利を与えますよね?

4. Fair trials are rare in Iran, aren't they?
   イランでは公正な裁判はまれですよね?

5. According to one lawyer, it will be women who make democracy a reality in Iran, won't it?
   ある弁護士によると，イランで民主主義を実現させるのは女性ですよね?

● ● ● EXERCISES 2: COMPOSITION ● ● ●

Making Questions:

下の ANSWER が答えとなる疑問文を完成させなさい。音声で疑問文をチェックしなさい。

1. Q. 過去 50 年に何が起きたか?
   A. 女性の権利や機会が進歩した。

   解答 happened over the last fifty years

2. Q. 中東の女性は何をつくろうと努力しているか？
   A. より公平な社会。

   解答 What are women in the Middle East

3. Q. 何人かのサウジの女性は自分の保護者に何をしているか？
   A. 彼女らは裁判所に告訴している。

   解答 some Saudi women doing to their guardians

4. Q. 権利を支持するイランの女性を弁護しているのは誰か？
   A. 女性弁護士。

   解答 defending Irani women who stand up for their rights

Writing with Idioms:

下線部の代用として下の語句を使い，文を書き換えなさい。

1. Printed books are <u>on the way out</u>.

   印刷された本は廃れかかっている。

2. Our students <u>lag behind</u> those in other schools.

   うちの生徒は他校の生徒に後れをとっている。

3. I don't need you to <u>stand up for</u> me. I can take care of myself.

   守ってもらわなくていいよ。自分のことは自分でできるから。
   * take care of *oneself*「自分のことは自分でする」

4. Making a decision is one thing; <u>carrying</u> it <u>out</u> is another.

   やろうと決めることと実際に実行することは別のことだ。
   * A is one thing; B is another.「AとBとは別のことだ」

Word Forms:

カッコから正しい語を選びなさい。

1. plea

   容疑者は無罪の申し立てをした。
   * enter a plea of not guilty「無罪の申し立てをする」

Lesson 5　It's About Time　49

2. notoriety

   女優はその政治的活動で悪評を得た。

3. denying

   その歌手は声が出なくなったということは否定できない。
   * There is no *do*ing. 「～することはできない」

4. endeavors

   あなたたちの努力のおかげで，これまでで最も成功した慈善運動を行うことができた。

5. visibly

   繰り返される乱気流で乗客はみんな明らかに怖がっていた。

6. convicts

   昨日，2人の囚人が脱獄した。

● ● ● EXERCISES 3: CHALLENGE ● ● ●

Using Key Concepts:

KEY CONCEPTS の語句を使って，下の文の空所を埋めなさい。

1. plaintiff

   その裁判の原告は，誤った薬を処方したことで医師を訴えている患者だ。

2. a fair trial

   裁判官がイスラム教徒に対して偏見をもっていたために，公平な裁判を受けられなかった，と彼は主張した。

3. democracy

   民主主義では，問題に関する自由な公開討論が不可欠だ。

4. repressive regime

   彼は国の弾圧的な政権に反対したとされ，30年以上も刑務所で過ごした。

5. progressive societies

   スウェーデンやベルギーのような，いわゆる進歩的な社会でさえ最近では保守的になっている。

6. gender gap
   ジェンダーギャップを埋めることが国連の最も優先的な目標の1つだ。

Vocabulary Expansion:

政府のタイプを下の「政府」の辞書定義と結びつけなさい。下線に定義の文字を書きなさい。

1. d 無政府状態   2. g 貴族社会   3. c 独裁国家   4. b 官僚政治
5. h 君主政治   6. a 実力主義社会 7. e 金権政治   8. f 神政国家

辞書定義

a. 技術者や専門家による政府
b. 公務員（政府に勤めている人）による政府
c. 1人（独裁者）による政府
d. だれもいない政府
e. 金持ちたちによる政府
f. 宗教指導者による政府
g. 上位階級（貴族階級）による政府
h. 王や女王（または天皇や皇后）による政府

Listening Activity:

ショートトークを聞き，空所を埋めなさい。

The Grameen Bank is a <u>financial</u> institution in <u>Bangladesh</u>. To fight <u>poverty</u>, the bank loans money to poor people to allow them to start up small <u>businesses</u>. Over <u>98%</u> of its <u>borrowers</u> are women. The bank also gives loans to women to buy a <u>cellphone</u>. Each woman then <u>charges</u> others in her village to use the phone. This gives the "village phone lady" a small <u>income</u> and puts the <u>community</u> on the telephone <u>network</u>.

　グラミン銀行は，バングラディシュにある金融機関である。貧困と闘うために，グラミン銀行は，ちょっとした商売を始められるように貧困層にお金を融資している。借り手の98パーセント以上が女性である。グラミン銀行はまた，携帯電話を買えるように女性にローンを組ませている。村の他の人たちにその携帯電話を使用させることで，持ち主の女性は電話代を請求できる。これにより「村の電話レディー」にわずかだが収入が入り，その地域社会に電話ネットワークをつくることができる。

Lesson 6   Where Would We Be Without It?
もし国連がなかったら

> **NOTES**
> be much worse off「もっと生活が苦しくなる」 President Hamid Karzai「ハミド・カルザイ大統領」 the UN Security Council「国連安全保障理事会」 UN Secretary-General Ban Ki-moon「パン・ギムン国連事務総長」

● ● ● GETTING READY TO READ ● ● ●

Key Concepts:

リーディングの重要語句と下の定義や説明を結びつけなさい。定義や説明の文字を空所に書きなさい。

1. f 　人権侵害＝市民を不公平に，残酷に扱うこと；人の自由を奪うこと
2. b 　福祉＝健康と幸福
3. g 　生活水準＝生活の快適さの水準
4. i 　人道的援助＝人々が自然災害から復興するための手助け
5. c 　紛争解決＝争いを防止したり，終結させること
6. h 　法による統治＝社会を安全・公平にするため法的手段を利用すること
7. a 　三権分立＝政府の1部門が権力をもちすぎるのを防ぐこと
8. d 　肥満の＝ひどく太りすぎの
9. e 　非伝染病＝ガン，心臓病，肺病，糖尿病のように人に伝染しない病気

Active Reading:

リーディングを読み，質問の答えをさがしなさい。答えが見つかった文をマークしなさい。

1. 国連は人間の裏表どちらの面を代表しているか？

   解答 The UN represents the other side of the human coin. It's the side of us that yearns for peace, seeks the health and well-being of every individual, deplores racial and gender inequality, and understands the importance of creating a sustainable environment.

2. 国際連合はいつ，誰によって，何のために設立したか？

   解答 The UN's official website informs us that the United Nations was set up in 1945 by 51countries "committed to maintaining international peace and security, developing friendly relations among nations, and promoting social progress, better living standards, and human rights."

3. 最近，国連はアフガニスタンに対して何と言ったか？

   解答 "Afghanistan's peaceful future lies in the building up of robust democratic institutions based on the rule of law and clear respect for the separation of powers," the UN said.

4. 国連は平和協定が機能しなくなるのをどのように防げるか？

   解答 The UN, he said, is determined to help such nations create institutions that will strengthen their economies and allow non-violent management of political disputes.

5. 何が子供たちの食べ物の好みに影響を与えるか？

   解答 TV advertising is largely responsible for influencing children's food choices.

Words in Context:

文の一部の下線部に最も意味が近い語句を選びなさい。

1. (B)　問題が私たちを困らせ続けている
    (A) 〜を助け　　　　(B) 〜を悩ませ　　　　(C) 〜を励まし

2. (A)　最も弱く最も絶望的な状態の
    (A) 見込みがない　　(B) 暴力的な　　　　　(C) 興奮させる

3. (B)　平和を切望する人間の側面
    (A) 演じる　　　　　(B) 〜を願う　　　　　(C) 〜に反対する

Lesson 6　Where Would We Be Without It?　53

4. (B)　人種と男女の不平等を遺憾に思う
　　　(A) ～を保護する　　　(B) ～を嫌悪する　　　(C) ～を防ぐ

5. (A)　つくり出す重要性を理解する
　　　(A) ～を把握する　　　(B) ～を否定する　　　(C) ～を提案する

6. (C)　国会を開くように
　　　(A) ～を選ぶ　　　　　(B) ～を変える　　　　(C) ～を始める

7. (C)　健全な民主主義の強化
　　　(A) 普通の　　　　　　(B) 完全な　　　　　　(C) 強い

8. (B)　平和をもたらす役割を拡大させる方法
　　　(A) ～を変える　　　　(B) ～を高める　　　　(C) ～を減らす

9. (A)　彼は～の重要性を強調した
　　　(A) ～を力説した　　　(B) ～を減らした　　　(C) ～を説明した

10. (C)　紛争から抜け出している国々
　　　(A) ～に入っている　　(B) ～で苦しんでいる　(C) ～から出ている

11. (A)　流血に逆戻りする
　　　(A) 以前の状態に戻る　(B) ～を引き起こす　　(C) ～の犠牲者となる

12. (B)　政治論争の非暴力的な管理
　　　(A) 解決法　　　　　　(B) 言い争い　　　　　(C) 選挙

13. (C)　若年死の主要な原因
　　　(A) 暴力の　　　　　　(B) 病気の　　　　　　(C) 早い

● ● ● **TODAY'S READING** ● ● ●

エッセイを注意深く読み，それに続く練習問題を解きなさい。

試訳

① 記事の見出しをちらっと見ても，世界が困惑している場所であることが十分にわかる。戦争や暴力行為，貧困や飢え，人種差別や人権侵害，気候変化や地球温暖化―こうしたことや他の問題が私たちをしつこく悩まし続けている。それらは最も弱く，最も絶望的な状態の人間を明らかにしている。しかし，毎日のニュースをちらっと見るだけで，あ

る団体がなかったら，私たちはもっと生活が苦しくなっていたであろうということもわかる：「国際連合」である。国連は人間のコインの別の面を代表している。それは，平和を切望し，あらゆる個人の健康と福祉を追い求め，人種や男女の不平等を遺憾に思い，生態系を破壊しない将来の環境をつくる重要性を理解するという私たち人間の側面だ。

② 国際連合が「国際平和と国際安全の維持，国家間の友好関係の進展，さらに社会的進歩，より高い生活水準，人権の促進をゆだねられ」，51か国によって1945年に設立されたことが国連の公式ホームページでわかる。国連は平和維持，紛争解決，人道的援助でよく知られている。しかし，下記の最近のマスコミ記事でもわかるように，他の様々な方法で，「国連とその専門機関は，私たちの生活に影響を及ぼして，世界をよりよい場所にしている」。

③ 先週，アフガニスタンのハミド・カルザイ大統領が，国民に新しく選出された国会を議席に就かせなかった時，国際連合はカルザイ大統領にできるだけ早く国会を正式に開くように促す強い声明を発表した。「アフガニスタンの平和な未来は法の規律や三権分立に対するはっきりした尊重に基づいた確固たる民主主義制度の強化にある」と国連は語った。

④ その一方では，1月11日に，国連安全保障理事会は，平和を構築するという国連の役割を拡大させるいろいろな方法を見つけ出すのにまる1日かけた。残念ながら，すべての和平協定の半分が5年以内に機能しなくなる，パン・ギムン国連事務総長は述べた。事務総長は「紛争から抜け出しかけている」国々を「流血にまた逆戻り」させないことの重要性を強調した。国連はそのような国々が自国の経済を強化し，政治紛争の非暴力的な管理を許可するような制度をつくる手助けをすると固く決めている，と彼は言う。

⑤ さらに，国連の保健機関である世界保健機関は，今日では，脂肪，糖分，塩分を多く含む食べ物のテレビコマーシャルから世界中の子どもたちが悪い影響を受けないようにする行動が必要だとしている。テレビ広告は子どもたちの食べ物の選択に影響を与えていることで大いに責任がある。粗末な食事のため，世界中で約4,300万人の学齢に達していない子どもたちが肥満になったり，とても太りすぎたりしている，と世界保健機関は述べている。そして，粗末な食事は非伝染病の危険にさらされる重大な要因であり，世界中の若年死の主要な原因でもある。

⑥ 本当に，もし国際連合がなかったら，私たちはどこで生きていけるだろうか。

● ● ● EXERCISES 1：COMPREHENSION ● ● ●

Reading for Information:

それぞれの文の続きになる正しい選択肢を選びなさい。

1. (B) 世界を絶えず悩ませ続けているものとして挙げられていない問題は［悲観的なニュースの見出し］である。
 (A) 地球温暖化 　　 (C) 人種差別 　　 (D) 飢え

Lesson 6 　Where Would We Be Without It? 　55

2. (D) ［男女不平等を促進すること］以外の次に述べることはすべて国連の公式ホームページに載っている。
   (A) 地震，洪水などの犠牲者に援助を提供すること
   (B) 国々が仲良くやっていく手助けをすること
   (C) 人々の生活をより快適なものにすること

3. (B) ［国際連合はアフガニスタンの政治問題に関与するのを避けた］以外の次に述べることはすべて本当である。
   (A) アフガニスタンの国民は国会議員を選出するため選挙を行った
   (C) パン・ギムン事務総長は，平和協定が維持されていることを確実にしたい
   (D) 粗末な食事は過多の脂肪，砂糖，塩から成っている

4. (C) このエッセイで断言されている唯一の情報は［粗末な食事につながる子どもたちの食べ物の選択に影響を与えるもの］である。
   (A) 今日，国際連合に加盟している国の数
   (B) 1月11日に国連安全保障理事会が開催された都市名
   (D) 毎年，非伝染病で亡くなる人の数

Listening for Ideas:

音声で文を聞き，その内容に合っていればTに，合っていなければFに○をつけなさい。

1. T   2. T   3. F   4. T   5. F

Listening Script

1. According to today's reading, mankind has a good and bad side, both of which are reflected in the news.
   今日のリーディングによると，人間には良い面と悪い面があり，その両方がニュースに反映されている。

2. The UN believes in progress as a way to make the world a better place.
   国連は世界をよりよい場所にする1つの方法として前進することはよいことだと信じている。

3. The UN wants Afghanistan to elect a new Parliament.
   国連はアフガニスタンに新しい国会を選出してほしい。

4. The UN's Secretary-General says that a country cannot keep a peace agreement if its economy is weak.
   国連事務総長は，経済が弱いと平和協定を存続できなくなる，と述べている。

5. The UN recommends that children stop watching TV altogether.
   子どもたちはテレビを見るのを完全にやめるべきだと国連は推奨する。

● ● ● EXERCISES 2: COMPOSITION ● ● ●

Making Questions:

下の ANSWER が答えとなる疑問文を完成させなさい。音声で疑問文をチェックしなさい。

1. Q. 戦争と暴力行為，貧困と飢え，人種差別と人権侵害，気候変化と地球温暖化は何を明らかにしているか？
   A. 最も弱く，最も絶望的な状態の人間。

   解答 war and violence, poverty and hunger, racism and human rights violations, and climate change and global warming

2. Q. 国連は何で有名か？
   A. 平和維持や紛争解決。

   解答 the UN best known for

3. Q. アフガニスタンの平和な未来はどこにあるか？
   A. 法の規律と三権分立の尊重。

   解答 Where does / lie

4. Q. すべての平和協定の半分が機能しなくなるのはいつか？
   A. 5 年以内。

   解答 When do half of all / fall through

Writing with Idioms:

下線部の代用として下の語句を使い，文を書き換えなさい。語形を変える必要があることもある。音声で答えをチェックしなさい。

1. The student newspaper is put out three times a year.
   その学生新聞は年 3 回発行される。

Lesson 6   Where Would We Be Without It?   57

2. The elderly are often <u>taken in</u> by Internet scam artists.
   お年寄りはインターネット詐欺名人によくだまされる。

3. We <u>set up</u> a committee to look into the rising drop-out rate.
   私たちは上昇する途中退学者率を調査するための委員会を設けた。

4. The project <u>fell through</u> because of a lack of funds.
   その計画は資金不足のため失敗に終わった。

Word Forms:

左の語を適当な形に直して，文の空所を埋めなさい。

1. desperately

   私たちは極度に出費を減らす必要がある。

2. disputed

   島の獲得をめぐって戦争が起きた。

3. inauguration

   就任式は 1 月に行われる。

4. deplorable

   何と嘆かわしい事態だろう！

5. prematurely

   私は彼を早まって上流気取りのやつだと判断したようだ。

6. augmenting

   株に投資することで収入を増やそうとすべきだ，と私の計理士は言った。

● ● ● **EXERCISES 3: CHALLENGE** ● ● ●

Using Key Concepts:

文の下線部の代わりに KEY CONCEPTS の語句を使って，文を書き換えなさい。

1. Without the rule of law, the country fell into chaos.
   法の規律がなく，その国は大混乱に陥った。

2. The man was so obese that he could barely walk.
   その男性は非常に肥満なので，何とかかろうじて歩くことができるくらいだ。

3. The government was criticized for human rights violations.
   その政府は人権侵害で批判された。

4. Raising living standards makes for a stronger society.
   生活水準を上げることはより強い社会をつくるのに役立つ。

5. The university now offers a course in conflict resolution.
   その大学は紛争解決に関する講座を開講している。

Vocabulary Expansion:

接頭語 "under-" で始まる動詞の辞書定義を読みなさい。動詞を正しい形にして，下の文の空所を埋めなさい。

a. undermined
   私たちの平和への努力は欲と憎しみによって徐々に弱くなってきた。

b. underestimated
   こんな大事な任務を担当できるなんて君の能力を過小評価していた。

c. underachieving
   意欲の欠如のため，うちの生徒たちは能力を発揮できていない。

d. underpinned
   環境問題を人々が意識することで環境保護が支持されなければならない。

e. undergo
   もうあんな怖い経験はしたくない。

辞書定義

1. underachieve: 期待ほど成功しない（能力を発揮できていない）
2. underestimate: 〜を低く推測・予測しすぎる（〜を過小評価する）
3. undergo: 〜を経験する；〜を経る（〜を受ける）
4. undermine: 〜を弱くする；〜を傷つける（〜を徐々に弱める）
5. underpin: 〜に支援や力を与える（〜を支持する）

Listening Activity:

4つの意見を聞き，TODAY'S READING の主旨に最も合う意見の番号に○をつけなさい。

Answer: 3

Listening Script

1. 国連の保健機関である世界保健機関によると，世界中の子どもたちがテレビのジャンクフードの広告に影響を受ければ受けるほど，より肥満になり，より不健康になるという。

   The more children around the world are affected by junk-food advertising on TV, the more obese and less healthy they become, says WHO, the UN's health agency.

2. 国際連合は第2次世界大戦後すぐの1945年に設立され，その当時は世界が戦争に飽き飽きして，平和と安全を切望していた。

   The United Nations was set up in 1945 just after World War II, at a time when the world had had enough of war and yearned for peace and security.

3. 人間性において最も望ましい状況は，それを表現する機会があることだということを確実にするために，国際連合が存在しなければ，世界がどんなに恐ろしい場所になるかを想像することはほとんど不可能だ。

   It is almost impossible to imagine what a frightening place the world would be if the United Nations didn't exist to ensure that the best in human nature has a chance to express itself.

4. 国際連合とその専門機関の活動がどんなに多様であるかを把握する最善の方法は，毎日，新聞を読んだりテレビでニュースを見ることだ。

   The best way to grasp how varied the activities of the United Nations and its specialized agencies are is to read the newspaper or to watch the news on TV every day.

Lesson 7　　Virtually Better
ゲームで築くよりよい世界

> **NOTES**
> First Things First「『重要なことをまず第一に』」実験的カリキュラムの名称　PTSD「心的外傷後ストレス障害」

● ● ● GETTING READY TO READ ● ● ●

Key Concepts:

リーディングの重要語句と下の定義や説明を結びつけなさい。定義や説明の文字を空所に書きなさい。

1. d 　常習性の＝人が何かをやめることができないようにする
2. e 　仮想世界＝テレビゲームやコンピューターゲームの中の世界
3. a 　行動上の問題＝精神的な病気
4. b 　社会からの引きこもり＝友だちや他の関係を避けること
5. h 　中毒＝何かをやめることができない状態
6. c 　攻撃性＝怒りや敵意のある行動
7. f 　精神衛生の分野＝精神的な問題をかかえた患者に取り組む医学の領域
8. g 　PTSD＝心的外傷後ストレス障害。戦争，自然災害，臨死体験のような激しい恐怖やショック［心的障害］を体験した人に起こる精神的苦痛。患者は悪い思い出［フラッシュバック］や悪い夢［悪夢］を体験する

Active Reading:

リーディングを読み，質問の答えをさがしなさい。答えが見つかった文をマークしなさい。

1. テレビゲームやコンピューターゲームに対する議論はどんなものか？

　　解答 Playing them constantly can cause a variety of behavioral problems.

2. ゲームはどのように教育や治療に利用されるか？

   解答 For instance, First Things First, an experimental curriculum being tried out in several schools in the United States, presents high-school math as a series of levels that encourage students to master basic concepts, as they would in a game, before advancing to the next level. And in the field of mental health, game-playing is effective in decreasing the symptoms of PTSD.

3. 『ニューヨークタイムズ』紙によると，ゲームは何をするためにデザインされているか？

   解答 Games are designed to provide instantaneous feedback and continual encouragement.

4. どんな転換や大きな変化が必要か？

   解答 "One of the most profound transformations we can learn from games is how to turn the sense that someone has 'failed' into the sense that he or she 'hasn't succeeded yet.'"

5. ジェーン・マゴニガルは，ゲームがどんなことができると言っているか？

   解答 Used effectively, she said, games can instill a "sense of productivity and purpose" in our lives. Games can work to build a strong "social fabric" and create a sense of "epic meaning" in society, making each member feel like part of a much bigger picture.

Words in Context:

文の一部の下線部に最も意味が近い語句を選びなさい。

1. (A)　～と空想を区別することができないこと
   - (A) あるものと別のものを区別する
   - (B) 真実として受け入れる
   - (C) ～から逃れる

2. (B)　いくつかの研究はプレーすることは～と強く主張する
   - (A) ～に反対する
   - (B) ～を主張する
   - (C) ～と望む

3. (A)　ゲームは学習として高い潜在能力がある
　　(A) 可能性　　　　　　(B) 理由　　　　　　　(C) 困難

4. (C)　実地で試されている実験的カリキュラム
　　(A) 方法　　　　　　　(B) 治療　　　　　　　(C) 教育課程

5. (C)　心的外傷後ストレス障害の症状を減らす効果がある
　　(A) 患者　　　　　　　(B) 苦しみ　　　　　　(C) 兆候

6. (C)　全体的に心配を感じることが断然少なくなる
　　(A) 痛み　　　　　　　(B) 快適さ　　　　　　(C) 不安

7. (C)　技術，決断力，楽観性，自信
　　(A) 決定　　　　　　　(B) 信念　　　　　　　(C) 意志

8. (A)　彼らはやり続ける意欲をもち続けたままである
　　(A) 奮い立たされた　　(B) 打ち負かされた　　(C) 決心していない

9. (A)　単に成功というわけではなく，努力は報われるのだ
　　(A) ほめられる　　　　(B) 強調される　　　　(C) しかられる

10. (B)　これらの基本的なゲームの長所を見習う必要がある
　　(A) 〜を増やす　　　　(B) 〜をまねる　　　　(C) 〜を実行する

11. (A)　これらの基本的なゲームの長所を見習う必要がある
　　(A) 恩恵　　　　　　　(B) 考え　　　　　　　(C) 状況

12. (C)　私たちが学べる最も深遠な転換の1つ
　　(A) 難しい　　　　　　(B) 不運な　　　　　　(C) 深い

13. (A)　ゲームは「生産性の感覚」を徐々に浸透させることができる
　　(A) 〜を導入する　　　(B) 〜を増やす　　　　(C) 〜を巻き込む

Lesson 7　Virtually Better　63

TODAY'S READING

エッセイを注意深く読み，それに続く練習問題を解きなさい。

試訳

① 私たちはみんな，ビデオゲームやコンピューターゲームに対する議論を聞いたことがある。ギャンブル，麻薬，アルコールのように，ゲームは常習的になることがある。絶えずゲームをすることで（先進国の平均的な人は21歳までに，仮想世界で10,000時間以上も過ごすことになる），様々な行動上の問題を引き起こすことがある。これらは自己管理の喪失，社会からの引きこもり，不正直（家族や友だちたちに嘘をつくこと），空想を現実と区別できなくことである。ゲーム中毒の人はその常習壁を維持するために，犯罪行動に頼ることさえある。攻撃性という問題もある：暴力的なビデオゲームをすることは現実世界での暴力行為に直接結びつく，と主張する研究がいくつかある。

② しかし，この話には別の側面もある。ゲームは学習や治療の道具としての大きな可能性がある。例えば，『重要なことをまず第一に』というアメリカのいくつかの学校で試されている実験的カリキュラムは，次のレベルに進む前に，ゲームで行われているように，生徒を励まして基本的な概念をマスターさせる一連のレベルがある「高校数学」を提供する。そのプログラムはとても成功している：参加している生徒たちは州全体のテストで驚くほど得点が上昇しており，40パーセントも向上している生徒たちがいるくらいだ。また，精神衛生の分野では，ゲームをすることは（特に「テトリス」のようなパズル式ゲームでは）心的外傷後ストレス障害の症状を減らす効果がある。患者は，フラッシュバックや悪夢の経験が減り，全体的に心配を感じることが少なくなったのである。

③ 『ニューヨークタイムズ』紙の最近の記事で，ゲームにその他の機能もないだろうか，と問いかけている。ゲームがもたらす技術，決断力，楽観性，自信が，私たちをよりよい人間にして，現実社会の問題を解決してくれるような方法はないだろうか？ ゲームは瞬間的なフィードバックや，継続的な励ましを与えるように設計されている。何度も失敗するかもしれないが（失敗はゲームのプレー時間の80パーセントを占める），プレーヤーはやり続ける意欲をもち続けたままでいる。ただ単なる成功だけでなく，努力も報われる。短期目標は長期達成につながる。仕事，学校，他の社会的施設をゲームと同じくらい魅力的にするために，『タイムズ』紙が提案するように，私たちはこれらの基本的なゲームの長所を見習う必要がある：「私たちがゲームから学ぶことができる最も深遠な転換の1つは，だれかが『失敗した』という感覚を，その人が『まだ成功していない』という感覚にどのように変えるかということである」。

④ 「ロンドン・ノキア国際フォーラム」でスピーチしたように，尊敬すべきゲームデザイナーであり，未来派のジェーン・マゴニガルはこの考えを支持している。彼女が言うには，効果的に使用されれば，ゲームは私たちの生活に，「生産性や目的の感覚」を浸透させることができる。ゲームは社会の一員に大きな絵の一部であるという感覚を与え，強い「社会構造」をつくるために機能し，社会において「壮大な価値」という感覚をつくり出すことができるのである。

● ● ● EXERCISES 1 : COMPREHENSION ● ● ●

Reading for Information:

下の指示に従い，簡潔に答えを書きなさい。

1. ゲームの他に常習的なものを3つ挙げなさい。

   解答 Gambling, drugs, and alcohol.
   ギャンブル，麻薬，アルコール

2. リーディング中の「不正直」を定義しなさい。

   解答 Lying to family and friends.
   家族や友だちたちに嘘をつくこと

3. アメリカで使用中の実験的カリキュラムの名称を挙げなさい。

   解答 First Things First.
   『重要なことをまず第一に』

4. そのカリキュラムはなぜ成功だといえるか説明しなさい。

   解答 Participating students have scored impressive increases in statewide tests, with some improving by as much as 40%.
   参加している生徒たちは州全体のテストで驚くほど得点が上昇しており，40パーセントも向上している生徒たちがいるくらいだ。

5. 「テトリス」はどんなゲームか言いなさい。

   解答 It's a puzzle-solving game.
   パズル式ゲーム

6. 『ニューヨークタイムズ』紙が指摘する，ゲームがプレーヤーを発達させるものを4つ挙げなさい。

   解答 Skills, determination, optimism, and confidence.
   技術，決断力，楽観性，自信

Lesson 7 Virtually Better 65

7. 何を提供するためにゲームはデザインされているか言いなさい。

    解答 Instantaneous feedback and continual encouragement.
    瞬間的なフィードバックや継続的な励まし

8. 短期目標は何につながることがあるか明らかにしなさい。

    解答 Long-term achievement.
    長期達成

9. 『ニューヨークタイムズ』紙が指摘する，私たちがゲームから学べる大変化，または転換は何か明らかにしなさい。

    解答 How to turn the sense that someone has "failed" into the sense that he or she "hasn't succeeded yet."
    だれかが「失敗した」という感覚を，その人が「まだ成功していない」という感覚にどのように変えるか。

Listening for Ideas:

音声を聞き，文の空所を埋めなさい。

1. having personal goals and working hard
   ジェーン・マゴニガルの「生産性は目的の感覚」は，個人的な目標をもち熱心に働くことを意味する。

2. a feeling of community and common purpose in society
   ジェーン・マゴニガルによって使用された「社会構造」という用語は，地域社会や社会の共通目的という意味である。

3. giving people the feeling that their society is working toward an important goal
   「社会において『壮大な価値』をつくること」は自分たちの社会はある重要な目標に向かって努力しているという感覚を人々に与えることである。

● ● ● **EXERCISES 2: COMPOSITION** ● ● ●

Making Questions:

下の ANSWER が答えとなる疑問文を完成させなさい。音声で疑問文をチェックしなさい。

1. Q. 21 歳までに，先進国の平均的な人が仮想世界で過ごす時間は？
   A. 1 万時間以上。

   解答 hours will the average person in a developed country spend in virtual worlds

2. Q. いくつかの研究は何と主張しているか？
   A. 攻撃的なゲームをすることで人々は現実世界で暴力になる。

   解答 do some studies

3. Q. アメリカのいくつかの学校で高校数学はどのように提供されるか？
   A. ゲームのような一連のレベルとして。

   解答 How is / presented in several schools in the United States

4. Q. 失敗はゲームのプレー時間の何パーセントを占めるか？
   A. 80 パーセント。

   解答 of game-playing time is taken up by failing

Writing with Idioms:

下線部の代用として下の語句を使い，文を書き換えなさい。語句や直後の語の語形や語順を変える必要があることもある。音声で答えをチェックしなさい。

1. We may have to <u>resort to</u> suing the polluters in court.

   私たちは公害の原因となる人たちを告訴しなければならなだろう。

2. How many hours did you <u>put in</u> writing this report?

   このレポートを書くのに何時間かかりましたか？
   ＊ How many hours did writing this report *take up*? とも表現できる。

3. If you complain to the teacher, I'll <u>back</u> you <u>up</u>.

   もし君が先生に不満を言うなら，ぼくが支援するよ。
   ＊ back A up「A を支援する」＜動詞＋代名詞＋副詞＞の語順に注意。

Lesson 7　Virtually Better

4. Making calls to clients <u>takes up</u> half my day.
   顧客に電話をかけるのに半日かかる。
   * I *put in* half my day making calls to clients. とも表現できる。

Word Forms:

カッコ内の語を適当な形に直しなさい。

1. potentially
   正しく服用しなければ，その薬は命取りになる可能性がある。

2. contention
   死刑は禁止すべきだというのが私の主張だ。

3. rewarding
   やりがいがあり，私が役立っていると感じさせる仕事がやりたい。

4. distinguishing
   その容疑者は，左のほおに特徴的な傷跡がある。

5. determined
   彼女はどんなに費用がかかっても，成功させると心に決めている。

6. anxious
   私は面接の前にとても不安になり，呼吸ができなくなるほどだった。

7. motivational
   刺激を与える講演者として，彼は多くの聴衆を魅了する。

● ● ● EXERCISES 3: CHALLENGE ● ● ●

Using Key Concepts:

次の語句が KEY CONCEPTS のどの語句を説明したものかを答えなさい。

1. field of mental health
   心理学者，精神病医，カウンセラー

2. addiction [habit-forming]

   アルコール中毒，仕事中毒の人，やめられないギャンブラー

3. social withdrawal

   孤独と隔離

4. behavioral problems

   恐れ，うつ病，摂食障害

5. aggression

   抑えられない怒り

Vocabulary Expansion:

動詞 "copy" に関係がある動詞の辞書定義を読み，下の文を読みなさい。それぞれの動詞を正しい形にして，文の空所を埋めなさい。

1. mimicked

   彼らはひどいことに，外国人の新入生の下手な英語をまねた。

2. emulating

   負けまいとジャックの有機や決意に張り合うことは君にはできない。

3. simulates

   この機械は，宇宙飛行士を訓練するために宇宙飛行を模擬的に行う。

4. impersonated

   泥棒たちは美術館に侵入するために，清掃員に扮した。

5. duplicate

   誰も王選手のホームラン生涯記録を繰り返すことはできないだろう。

6. imitation

   このダイヤモンドは本物のように見えるが，実は偽物だ。

辞書定義

imitate: 　　　見本として〜を使ったり従う（〜を模造する）
emulate: 　　　〜に負けまいと努力する（〜と張り合う）
mimic: 　　　　〜のまねをする，ふつうからかうために（〜をまねる）
impersonate: 　別人である〜になりすます（〜に扮する）
simulate: 　　 何かの見本として〜の役に立つ（〜を模擬的に行う）
duplicate: 　　〜を正確にコピーする（〜を繰り返す）

Listening Activity:

未来派のジェーン・マゴニガルが「ゲームが人の生活を向上させることができる」と考える4つの方法を音声で聞き，彼女の言うことに賛成ならAに，反対ならDに○をつけなさい。

Answer: 個人的な意見なので答えなし。

Listening Script

1. Games can bring out the best in people. If we play games where we do good things like clean up litter, help people, or fight pollution, we will want to do good things in real life.

   ゲームは人々の善良な部分を引き出すことができる。ゴミを拾ったり，人々を助けたり，公害と闘ったりするゲームをやれば，実生活でもいいことをしたくなるだろう。

2. Games can change the way people see themselves. Having an attractive avatar or character in a virtual world can give us more confidence and self-respect in real life.

   ゲームは自分に対する見方を変えることができる。仮想世界で魅力的なアイコンや登場人物になることで実生活での自信や自尊心が生まれる。

3. Games can keep people mentally healthy. Studies have shown that when we are in stressful or dangerous situations, we can cope better by playing games 3-4 hours a day. Games are the best way to take our minds off our troubles and prevent emotional problems caused by stress.

   ゲームは人々を精神的に健康にすることができる。いくつかの研究によると，私たちがストレスの多い危険な状態にあるとき，1日3,4時間ゲームをすることでなんとか対処できる。ゲームは悩みから心を解放し，ストレスによる感情的な問題を防ぐ最善の方法である。

4. Games can inspire people to live a fuller life. For example, if we play a musical, literary, or art-related game, we are more

likely to want to play a musical instrument, read good books, or do something creative and artistic in real life.

ゲームはより充実した生活を送るように人々に奮起させることができる。例えば，音楽的，文学的，芸術的なゲームをやれば，私たちは実生活で楽器を演奏したり，よい本を読んだり，何か創造的なことや芸術的なことをしたいという気持ちになるだろう。

＊ be likely to *do*「たぶん〜するだろう」

Lesson 8 　It's Never Too Late
謝るのに遅すぎることはない

> **NOTES**
> Metis「メティス」ヨーロッパ人と北米先住民の混血児　ship off to A「Aへ送り込む」　POW「捕虜」Prisoner Of War の略

● ● ● **GETTING READY TO READ** ● ● ●

Key Concepts:

リーディングの重要語句と下の定義や説明を結びつけなさい。定義や説明の文字を空所に書きなさい。

1. b 　イヌイット，インディアン，メティス＝カナダの土着民・先住民
2. h 　精神的・肉体的虐待＝残酷に，そして不公平に人々を扱うこと
3. a 　バターン半島＝第2次世界大戦の最も痛ましい事件の1つが起きたフィリピンの一地域
4. d 　捕虜＝戦争の人質；捕らえられた，または投獄された敵の兵士
5. g 　満州＝20世紀前半のほとんど日本の植民地だった中国の一地域
6. f 　強制労働者＝奴隷労働者
7. e 　アパルトヘイト時代＝南アフリカの歴史において，支配層の白人が黒人南アフリカ人のすべての権利と自由を否定した時代〔1948年から1980年代初頭〕
8. c 　人種差別主義＝ある人種が別の人種より優れているとする信念

Active Reading:

リーディングを読み，質問の答えをさがしなさい。答えが見つかった文をマークしなさい。

1. カナダのスティーヴン・ハーパー首相は，一般的に何に対して，そして誰に対して謝罪したか？

    解答 In June 2008, Canadian Prime Minister Stephen Harper, standing humbly before Inuit, Indian, and Metis representatives, apologized for Canada's past treatment of its indigenous children.

2. 寄宿学校に強制的に行かされたカナダの先住民の子どもたちはどうなったか？

   解答 All were deprived of the care and nurturing of parents, grandparents, and communities. Native languages and cultural practices were prohibited. Tragically, some of these children died.

3. 「バターンの死の行進」とは何か？

   解答 The incident occurred in April 1942, after Japanese military forces took over the Bataan Peninsula in Philippines. Some 80,000 American and Filipino soldiers were captured and made to walk 80 kilometers in intense heat without food or water. Thousands perished.

4. 南アフリカとマオリ族のラグビー選手は何の犠牲者だったか？

   解答 South African Rugby president Oregan Hoskins apologized to the "innocent victims of the racist ideology of our former government."

Words in Context:

文の一部の下線部に最も意味が近い語句を選びなさい。

1. (B)　イヌイット，インディアン，メティスの代表者たちの前で謙虚に立って
   (A) 誇らしげに　　　　(B) 控えめに　　　　(C) 悲しげに

2. (A)　多くは不十分に食べ物，着る物，住む場所が与えられた
   (A) 乏しく　　　　　　(B) 突然　　　　　　(C) 怒って

3. (B)　すべての者が保護を奪われた
   (A) 〜を提供された
   (B) 〜なしで済ますようにさせられた
   (C) 〜を強制的に他人に与えさせた

4. (C)　両親の保護や養育
   (A) 食べ物を与えること　(B) 教育　　　　　　(C) かわいがること

Lesson 8　It's Never Too Late　73

5. (C)　何千もの人が<u>亡くなった</u>
    (A) 姿を消した　　　　(B) 生き残った　　　　(C) 死んだ

6. (B)　後になって～によって<u>謝罪が繰り返された</u>
    (A) 否定された　　　　(B) 繰り返された　　　(C) 議論された

7. (A)　除外したことに対する心からの<u>自責の念</u>
    (A) 後悔　　　　　　　(B) 責任　　　　　　　(C) 混乱

8. (C)　間違いを<u>認めること</u>
    (A) 知識　　　　　　　(B) 現実　　　　　　　(C) 承認

9. (B)　<u>前任者たち</u>の間違い
    (A) 目上の人たち　　　(B) 前任者たち　　　　(C) 敵対者たち

10. (B)　私たちのスポーツへの<u>非難</u>に対する謝罪
    (A) 歴史　　　　　　　(B) 非難　　　　　　　(C) 過失

11. (C)　そのような謝罪は<u>うわべだけで誠意がない</u>
    (A) 一時的で　　　　　(B) 事実に反して　　　(C) 薄っぺらで

12. (A)　<u>犯されてしまった</u>ひどい不正
    (A) 犯されてしまった　(B) 発見されてしまった (C) 報告されてしまった

13. (A)　過去に対する<u>憤慨した</u>感情
    (A) 怒った　　　　　　(B) 永久的な　　　　　(C) 悲しい

● ● ● ● **TODAY'S READING** ● ● ● ●

エッセイを注意深く読み，それに続く練習問題を解きなさい。

試訳

① 公式の謝罪が最近，見出しになってきた。2008年6月に，カナダのスティーヴン・ハーパー首相が，イヌイット，インディアン，メティスの代表者たちの前に謙虚に立って，カナダ先住民の子どもたちの過去の待遇に対して謝罪した。カナダには、1800年代の後半に始めた「インディアンを子どものうちに殺す」という政府公認の政策があった。数千の先住民の子どもたちが家族から引き離され，はるか遠くの寄宿学校へ送り込まれた。そして，そこでは多くの子どもたちが厳しい精神的・肉体的な虐待を受けた。「多くの子どもたちは衣，食，住が不十分だった」とハーパー首相は言う。「すべての子ど

もが両親，祖父母や地域社会による保護や養育を奪われた。母語や文化的習慣が禁止された。痛ましいことに，これらの子どもたちの何人かが亡くなってしまった。」首相はさらに続ける。「カナダ政府がこの国の先住民の人々をまったく見捨ててきたことを許してもらいたい。」

② 2009年5月，日本の藤崎一郎駐米大使は「バターンの死の行進」の73人のアメリカの生存者に直接謝罪した。日本が引き起こしてしまった「非常に大きな損害と苦難」に対して心から謝罪する，と藤崎は言った。その事件は日本軍がフィリピンのバターン半島を占領した後，1942年4月に起こった。約8万人のアメリカ兵とフィリピン兵が捕虜になり，食べ物も水もなしで，猛烈な暑さの中を80キロ歩かされた。数千人が亡くなった。生存した捕虜たちは，強制労働者として働くために日本や満州に送り込まれた。藤崎大使の謝罪は，後になって当時の岡田克也外務大臣によって何度も繰り返された。「日本政府を代表して，あなた方が体験した非人道的な扱いと苦難に対して心から謝罪する。」

③ 2010年5月，ニュージーランドと南アフリカのラグビー協会が，アパルトヘイト時代にチームからマオリ族や黒人の選手を除外したことに対する心からの自責の念を公表声明文で述べた。南アフリカ・ラグビー協会のオレガン・ホスキンス会長は「かつての協会による人種的イデオロギーの巻き添えとなった犠牲者たち」に謝罪した。彼はあの長く暗い年月の間，自国を代表する機会を拒否された，南アフリカの黒人に謝罪する重要性を強調した。私たちの前任者たちの愚行とラグビーに対する非難への謝罪を認めることが，あの暗い影を取り除くための新たな一歩である。

④ 謝罪を酷評する人たちは，このような謝罪がうわべだけで誠意がないものである，と不平を言うだろう。犯されたひどい不正を簡単に「ごめんなさい」と言われて，どうして償うことができようか。たぶんできない。しかし，私たちが自らの過ちから学ぶ能力をもっていること，そして，私たちが過去の憤慨した感情を和らげることが歴史を繰り返さないようにする最善の方法であるとわかっていること，を少なくとも謝罪は明らかにしている。

● ● ● EXERCISES 1：COMPREHENSION ● ● ●

Reading for Information:

下の質問に対して簡潔に答えなさい。

1. スティーヴン・ハーパー首相は謝罪したとき，どこに立っていたか？

    解答 Before [In front of] Inuit, Indian, and Metis representatives.

2. 当時のカナダ政府公認の政策は，何をすることを目指していたか？

    解答 Kill the Indian in the child.

3. 寄宿学校の子どもたちは，何をすることを認められなかったか？

    解答 Speak their native languages or practice native culture.

4. 藤崎一郎大使は，日本が何を引き起こしたと発言したか？

    解答 Tremendous damage and suffering.

5. 藤崎大使が謝罪したとき，「バターン死の行進」から何年たっていたか？

    解答 Sixty-seven years.

6. その行進の生存者たちは日本や満州で何をしたか？

    解答 Worked as forced laborers.

7. オレガン・ホスキンス会長は南アフリカの黒人選手は何のとばっちりを食った犠牲者だと発言したか？

    解答 The racist ideology of South Africa's former government.

8. 公的な謝罪を酷評する人たちは，その謝罪についてしばしば何だと発言するか？

    解答 That they are superficial and insincere.

Listening for Ideas:

音声を聞き，文の空所を埋めなさい。その文がリーディングの内容に合っていればTに，合っていなければFに○をつけなさい。

1. T   2. T   3. F   4. F   5. F

Listening Script

1. Not all the children in Canada's boarding schools survived.
    カナダの寄宿学校の子どもたち全員が生き残ったわけではない。

2. Harper asked indigenous peoples to forgive his country.
    ハーパー首相は，先住民たちにカナダを許してほしいと言った。

3. All of the Death March POWs are now dead.
    「死の行進」の捕虜全員が今では亡くなっている。

4. Katsuya Okada is still Japan's foreign minister.
   岡田克也は今でも日本の外務大臣である。

5. The South African Rugby president apologized on TV.
   南アフリカのラグビー協会会長はテレビで謝罪した。

● ● ● EXERCISES 2: COMPOSITION ● ● ●

Making Questions:

下の ANSWER が答えをなる疑問文を完成させなさい。音声で疑問文をチェックしなさい。

1. Q. (「インディアンを子どものうちに殺す」という) カナダ政府公認の政策はいつ始まったか?
   A. 1800 年代後半。

   解答 Canada's official government policy (to "kill the Indian in the child") start?

2. Q. スティーヴン・ハーパー首相は寄宿学校の子どもたちは何を奪われたと発言したか?
   A. 両親による保護と養育。

   解答 What did Stephen Harper say the children in the schools

3. Q. 捕虜たち[アメリカとフィルピンの捕らえられた兵士たち]は強制的に何をさせられたか?
   A. 猛烈な暑さの中, 80 キロ歩かされた。

   解答 What were the POWs [captured American and Filipino soldiers]

4. Q. オレガン・ホスキンス会長はアパルトヘイト時代を何と呼んだか?
   A. あの長く暗い年月。

   解答 What did Oregan Hoskins call

Writing with Idioms:

下線部の代用として下の語句を使い, 文を書き換えなさい。語形を変える必要があることもある。
音声で答えをチェックしなさい。

1. Are you speaking <u>on behalf of</u> all the class members?
   君はクラスのみんなを代表して話しているのか?

2. In June 1940, Nazi troops <u>took over</u> Paris.
   1940 年 6 月に，ナチス軍はパリを占領した。

3. How can I ever <u>make up for</u> what I said?
   自分の発言をどのように償うことができるか？

4. He's much shorter <u>in person</u> than he looks on the screen.
   彼は画面で見るよりも実物はずっと背が低い。

Word Forms:

カッコ内の語を適当な形に直しなさい。

1. humble
   ほらを吹いたり自慢したりしない人は謙虚な人である。

2. perpetrator
   犯罪を犯す人は加害者である。

3. perishable
   果物や野菜はすぐに腐るから腐りやすい食品として知られている。

4. remorseful
   後悔している人は何か悪いことをしたため気分が悪い。

5. deprivation
   睡眠なしでやっていくことは睡眠遮断として知られている。

6. resents
   あなたを好きでない人はあなたに憤慨する。

● ● ● EXERCISES 3: CHALLENGE ● ● ●

Using Key Concepts:

Aの文と意味が同じになるように，Bの文の空所を埋めなさい。KEY CONCEPTSの語句を使いなさい。

1. forced laborers

   強制労働者たちがあの運河を掘ったそうだ。

2. mental and physical abuse

   新聞によると，そこで捕虜にされている人々は精神的・肉体的な虐待の犠牲者だという。
   ＊ hold A prisoner「Aを捕虜にしている」

3. racist ideology

   あの政党には人種的イデオロギーがある。

Vocabulary Expansion:

"ability" に関係した語とその辞書定義を読みなさい。下の文の空所を選んだ1語で埋めなさい。

1. competence

   単なる技術はほしくない；私は最高の能力がほしいのだ。

2. talent

   ええ，確かに君には才能があるが，プロの音楽家になるのに必要なものをもっていると約束することはできない

3. capacity

   人間には過ちを犯すと同様に謝る能力もある。

4. skill

   気難しい顧客を扱う技術があるので，彼女は会社で欠かせない人になっている。

5. faculty

   彼は自己批判の能力をもたずに生れてきた。

Lesson 8　It's Never Too Late

辞書定義

capacity: 精神的・肉体的に発達する能力（才能）
faculty: 一般的な天性の能力（手腕）
talent: 天性の能力，特に芸術におけるもの（天分）
skill: 訓練で身についた能力（技術）
competence: 満足できるが，優秀ではない能力（技能）

Listening Activity:

自由を求めて闘ったインドのマハトマ・ガンディーとイギリスの詩人アレキサンダー・ポープの引用を聞き，書き取りなさい。2人の作者がお互いに賛成しているならAに，反対しているならDに○をしなさい。

Answer: A

Listening Script

" The week can never forgive. Forgiveness is the attribute of the strong." —Mahatma Gandhi.

「弱い者は許すことができない。許すとは強い者の性質なのだ。」
　　　　　　　　　　　　　　　　　　　　—マハトマ・ガンディー

" To err is human; to forgive divine." —Alexander Pope

「過つは人の常，許すは神の性。」　　　　　　—アレキサンダー・ポープ

Lesson 9   Global Concepts 1: People
グローバル社会の潮流：人々

NOTES

to his horror「彼にとって恐ろしいことに」　put A right「Aを正常な状態に戻す」
the U.K.'s Royal Botanic Gardens at Kew「キュー地区にある英国王立植物園」
stave off A「Aを食い止める」　vault「地下貯蔵庫」

● ● ● GETTING READY TO READ ● ● ●

Key Concepts:

リーディングの重要語句と下の定義や説明を結びつけなさい。定義や説明の文字を空所に書きなさい。

1. e　婦人科医＝女性の健康問題を専門にしている医師
2. b　戦車の砲弾＝大きな軍事車両から発射された爆破装置
3. d　ガザ地区＝エジプトとイスラエル間の地中海沿岸西部に沿った細長い土地；イスラエルが1948年に建国したとき，その地域の住人である何千ものパレスチナ人がこの狭いガザ地区に強制移動させられた。そこは目下継続中のイスラエル・パレスチナ紛争の中心地となってきた；ガザ地区は高い失業率と政治不安を抱えている；イスラエルの統治の下，好戦的な人々が反イスラエルの暴力行為を行い，それに対してイスラエルが独自の暴力行為で応戦している状態で，その地区は独立を要求している
4. g　接着双生児＝体の一部がつながって生まれた2人の赤ちゃん
5. f　慈善基金＝善行を施す機関
6. h　植物園＝多種多様な植物や花々を展示している公園
7. a　生物多様性＝特定の生態系や地球全体の多種多様な植物種・動物種
8. c　地球滅亡の日＝私たちが予想する世界の終わり

Active Reading:

リーディングを読み，質問の答えをさがしなさい。答えが見つかった文をマークしなさい。

1. イゼルディーン・アブルアイシュ医師は誰か？ また，彼の悲劇とは何か？

   解答　Izzeldin Abuelaish is a Palestinian gynecologist. On January 16, 2009, a series of Israeli tank shells exploded in his Gaza Strip home. Sifting through the rubble, Dr. Abuelaish discovered to his horrow that three of his daughters had been killed outright.

Lesson 9   Blobal Concepts 1: People   81

2. アブルアイシュ医師はその悲劇にどのように反応してきたか？

   解答 But instead of allowing his grief to torment him, Dr. Abuelaish has transformed the tragedy into a quest for peace.

3. スティブン・ポッパー教授は誰か？また，彼の目標は何か？

   解答 According to the BBC and Professor Stephen Hopper, director of the U.K.'s Royal Botanic Gardens at Kew, one-fifth of the world's plants could soon die out. To help stave off such an eventuality, Hopper oversees Kew's Millennium Seed Bank. This is a "doomsday" vault where 1.8 billion samples of plant and crop seeds from around the world are stored in deep, underground, refrigerated rooms to keep them safe from natural and manmade disasters.

Words in Context:

文の一部の下線部に最も意味が近い語句を選びなさい。

1. (A)　悲嘆が彼をひどく苦しめるのを許すこと
   (A) 〜に痛みを与える　　(B) 〜をなだめる　　(C) 〜を興奮させる

2. (B)　苦しみに対する免疫を与えた
   (A) 〜を納得させた　　(B) 〜を保護した　　(C) 抗議した

3. (C)　共有した不安で危うい人間性
   (A) 価値の高い　　(B) 永久的な　　(C) 確実でない

4. (C)　『平和と人間尊厳への道〜』
   (A) 自己意識　　(B) 自信喪失　　(C) 自尊

5. (C)　死や歴史や復讐について
   (A) 誰かにお金を返す
   (B) 誰かに親切な行為でこたえる
   (C) 残酷な，または危険な行為で誰かに報復すること

6. (A)　復讐によって台無しにされてはいけない
   (A) 損害を与えられて　　(B) 覚えられて　　(C) 忘れられて

82

7. (C) それらは施設のドアを飾る
　　(A) 〜を閉める　　　　(B) 〜を開ける　　　　(C) 〜を飾る

8. (C) この貴重な生物の多様性を保護する
　　(A) 〜を研究する　　　(B) 〜を楽しむ　　　　(C) 〜を維持する

9. (B) この貴重な生物の多様性
　　(A) 古代の　　　　　　(B) 大切な　　　　　　(C) 脅された

10. (B) 植物と相互に影響し合うことを必要とする
　　(A) 〜と交換すること　(B) 一緒に作用すること (C) 成長すること

11. (B) これらの植物を死滅させれば大惨事となるだろう
　　(A) 危険な　　　　　　(B) 悲惨な　　　　　　(C) まぬけな

12. (A) そのような不測の事態を食い止める
　　(A) 結果　　　　　　　(B) 悲劇　　　　　　　(C) 概念

● ● ● TODAY'S READING ● ● ●

エッセイを注意深く読み，それに続く練習問題を解きなさい。

試訳

① イゼルディーン・アブルアイシュはパレスチナ人の婦人科医である。2009年1月16日，連発されたイスラエル軍戦車の砲弾が，ガザ地区の彼の自宅に炸裂した。がれきの中を調べると，アブルアイシュ医師は，彼にとって恐ろしいことに，3人の娘が即死しているのに気づいた。もう1人の娘は片目の視力を失った。だが，アブルアイシュ医師は悲嘆にくれることなく，その悲劇を平和の探求へと変えていった。娘たちの死は「苦しみに対する免疫を私にくれた」，と『ニューヨークタイムズ』紙のジョゼフ・バーガーに彼は語った。数十年間にわたって長引いている，イスラエル・パレスチナ紛争は「双方が共有している，不安定な人間性」を認め合うときにだけ，正常な状態に戻せると彼は信じる。「私たちは1つの心と1つの頭脳をもった接着双生児のようだ」と彼は語る。「片方の何らかの生涯がもう片方に影響を与える。」アブルアイシュ医師は『我，憎むことなかれ：ガザの医師の平和と人間尊厳への旅の途中』という自伝を執筆し終えた。その本の中で，彼が世界中に広めてきた，そして，彼をノーベル平和賞候補にさせているメッセージ「憎しみは病気である」をもう一度断言している。死や歴史や復讐をくよくよ考えることは，時間の浪費である。「復讐によって私の娘たちは戻らない」と彼は書いている。「娘たちの純真さは復讐によって台無しにされてはならない。私がよい行いをすることで，娘たちの思い出をもち続けられる。」そして，そのよい行いこそが，ア

ブルアイシュ医師がこれまで行ってきたことである。2009年から，医師と彼の生き残った子どもたちはカナダに住み，彼はトロント大学で「国際保健」を教えている。医師はまた，女子教育を支援する「命を引き換えにした娘たち」と呼ばれる慈善基金を設立した。自分の娘たちの「名前が墓石に銘記されるだけでなく」，いろいろな施設のドアや他の「素敵な場所」に飾られるようにしようと彼は心に決めている。

② BBC 放送や，(ロンドン郊外の) キュー地区にある英国王立植物園の責任者であるスティブン・ホッパー教授によると，世界の植物の5分の1はまもなく絶滅するという。地球は約8万の植物種の生息地であり，その中で熱帯雨林の植物種が最も危険にさらされている。未来の世代のために，この貴重な生物の多様性を保護することは絶対に必要である，とポッパー教授は言う。「私たちは植物種が消滅するのを何もしないで傍観していることはできない。植物は，きれいな空気，水，食べ物，燃料を供給し，地球上のあらゆる生命のもとである。私たちが呼吸するには植物と相互に影響し合わなければならない。世界の最も貧しい国々では，植物療法が健康管理の唯一の供給源であり；これらの植物を消滅させれば大惨事につながる」と教授はつけ加える。そのような不測の事態を食い止める援助をするため，ホッパー教授は「キューのミレニアム種子銀行」の監視者となっている。これが，天災や人災から種子を守るために，世界中の18億の植物や農作物の種子の標本が深い地下の冷凍庫に貯蔵されている「地球滅亡の日」貯蔵庫である。

● ● ● EXERCISES 1：COMPREHENSION ● ● ●

Reading for Information:

下の文を読みなさい。文がリーディングの内容に合っていればT，合っていなければFに○をつけなさい。

1. F　アブルアイシュ医師のすべての子どもたちは爆発で死傷した。
2. F　イスラエル・パレスチナ紛争は，イスラエル戦車がガザ地区を攻撃した2009年に始まった。
3. F　アブルアイシュ医師の体験に関する本は『ニューヨークタイムズ』紙のジョゼフ・バーガーによって書かれた。
4. F　アブルアイシュ医師は今，カナダに住み，そこでガザ紛争史のクラスを教えている。
5. T　「命を引き換えにした娘たち」は若い女性の教育機会の改善に取り組んでいる。
6. T　ほぼ8万の植物種が絶滅の危機に瀕している。
7. F　植物は薬や薬剤以外のすべてのものを私たちに供給してくれる，とスティブン・ホッパー教授は言う。
8. F　ミレニアム種子銀行は，キュー植物園の来園者に開放されている。
  ＊ be open to A「Aに公開されている」

Listening for Ideas:

音声の質問を聞き，最も適当な答えを選びなさい。

1. **(A)** よい行いをすることで
   (B) カナダに移り住むことで　　(C) ノーベル平和賞の候補となることで

2. **(C)** 病気
   (A) 死　　(B) 復讐

3. **(B)** 新しい種類の種子を開発することで世界の農作物や植物の蓄えを増やすこと
   (A) 未来のために生物の多様性を保護すること
   (C) もし地震や，例えば核戦争が起きても種子を安全にしておくこと

Listening Script

1. In what way is Dr. Abuelaish keeping alive the memory of his daughters who died in the attack?
   アブルアイシュ医師は，どのようにして攻撃で亡くなった娘たちの思い出をもち続けているか？

2. What does Dr. Abuelaish compare hate to?
   アブルアイシュ医師は憎しみを何にたとえているか？

3. Which of these is not mentioned as a goal of the Millennium Seed Bank?
   ミレニアム種子銀行の目標として挙げられていないものはどれか？

● ● ● EXERCISES 2: COMPOSITION ● ● ●

Making Questions:

下の ANSWER が答えとなる疑問文を完成させなさい。音声で疑問文をチェックしなさい。

1. **Q.** アブルアイシュ医師の娘の1人はどうしたか？
   A. 片目の視力を失った。

   解答　to one of Dr. Abuelaish's daughters

Lesson 9　Blobal Concepts 1: People　85

2. Q. パレスチナ・イスラエル紛争はどれくらい続いているか？
   A. 何十年もの間。

   解答 How long has the Palestinian-Israeli conflict

3. Q. アブルアイシュ医師は，娘たちの名前がどこを飾ればいいと思っているか？
   A. 施設のドアや他の素敵な場所。

   解答 Dr. Abuelaish like his daughters' names to adorn

4. Q. ミレニアム種子貯蔵庫の種子はどこにあるか？
   A. 深い地下の冷凍庫。

   解答 Where are the seeds in the Millennium Seed Vault

Writing with Idioms:

下線部の代用として下の語句を使い，文を書き換えなさい。語形を変える必要があることもある。音声で答えをチェックしなさい。

1. Perhaps apologizing will help <u>put</u> the situation <u>right</u>.
   たぶん謝ることで，状況は正常化するだろう。

2. Japanese baseball games would often <u>drag on</u> for four hours.
   日本の野球の試合は4時間続くこともよくある。

3. Some say it may be too late to <u>stave off</u> further global warming.
   さらなる地球温暖化を食い止めるにはもう遅すぎる，という人もいる。

4. Don't <u>dwell on</u> what happened.
   起こってしまったことをくよくよ考えるな

Word Forms:

カッコから正しい語を選びなさい。

1. eventual
   新しい証拠は最終的に容疑者逮捕をもたらした。

2. catastrophes
   私たちは，洪水，地震，その他の自然災害にもっと素早く対応する必要がある。

3. tormentor

   映画の中で，その男の子を悩ますのはペスターという名のちっちゃなグレムリン［想像上の小悪魔で，機械などに入り込んで不調をもたらすとされる］だった。

4. adorned

   通りに並んだ建物には，国旗，横断幕，一連の万国旗が飾られていた。

● ● ● EXERCISES 3: CHALLENGE ● ● ●

Using Key Concepts:

Aの文と意味が同じになるように，Bの文の空所を埋めなさい。KEY CONCEPTSの語句を使いなさい。

1. conjoined twins

   接着双生児を引き離す手術は，14時間以上も続いた。

2. charitable organization

   世界をよりよい場所にする手助けをしていると自覚できるので，私は慈善団体で働きたい。

3. doomsday

   その小説では，巨大隕石が地球に衝突し，地球上のすべての生物を死滅させ，地球滅亡の日がくる。

4. biodiversity

   植物の自生地，動物の生息地，および生態系の破壊は生物の多様性が失われる主な原因である。

5. Gaza Strip

   ガザ地区では貧困が広がり，多くの居住者はそこをイスラエルに監視されている刑務所にたとえている。

Vocabulary Expansion:

"artificial"に似た意味の形容詞をどのように用いるかの説明を読みなさい。下の文の空所を選んだ1語で埋めなさい。

1. sham

   それは妻がアメリカ永住権を得られるように行った，見せかけの結婚だった。

2. forged

   その偽造の手紙は，ライバルの 1 人をからかういたずらとして，文芸評論家によって書かれた。

3. ersatz

   みんなが本物ではないとわかる偽のミンクコートを着て，彼女は入ってきた。

4. Synthetic

   合成ゴムは実質的には本物のゴムにとって代わっている。
   * take the place of A「A にとって代わる」

5. counterfeit

   店員は偽の 20 ドル札に注意しなければならない。

説明

synthetic:	「合成の」は，現物のように見えたり，感じたり，味わったりするために化学的につくり出された物質を指している。
counterfeit:	「偽の」は，偽って本物として流通させるように，プロの犯罪者によってつくられたお金を指している。
forged:	「偽造の」は，本物をまねた印刷物，文書，署名を指している。
sham:	「見せかけの」は，人々がしたり，言ったりすることで，ただ正直に，本物に見えるだけの何かを指している。
ersatz:	「人工の」は，本物より明らかに劣る偽物を指している。

Listening Activity:

ショートトークを聞き，その答えを下線に書きなさい。

1. It's a symbolic clock.

   それは象徴的な時計である。

2. It was six minutes to twelve.

   12 時 6 分前だった。

3. Its warnings are based on environmental dangers.

   それらの警告は環境危機に基づいている。

4. It is set back or ahead by atomic scientists at the University of Chicago in the United States.

その時計は，アメリカのシカゴ大学の原子力科学者たちによって戻されたり，進ませたりされる。

Listening Script

Perhaps you've heard of the Doomsday Clock. It isn't a real clock, however; it's a symbolic one. What the clock tries to show us is how close the world is coming to doomsday, or the end of the world. The closer the clock comes to midnight, the closer the world is estimated to be approaching global catastrophe. For example, as of January 2010, the clock stood at only six minutes to twelve. During the era of the Cold War between Russia and the United States, doomsday meant worldwide nuclear war, so the clock was very close to midnight. But today, the Doomsday Clock's warnings have more to do with potential disaster resulting from climate change and environmental destruction. The clock started "ticking" in 1947 and is set back or ahead by atomic scientists at the University of Chicago in the United States.

「地球最後の日の終末時計」のことをたぶん聞いたことがあるだろう。しかし，それは本物の時計ではなく，象徴的な時計である。終末時計が私たちに示そうとしているのは，世界が人類滅亡の日，つまり世界の終わりにどれくらい近づいているかだ。時計が真夜中の12時に近づけば近づくほど，世界が地球の悲劇的な破局に近づいていると判断される。例えば，2010年1月現在で，時計は12時6分前を指していた。ロシアとアメリカの冷戦時代には，地球滅亡の日は世界中での核戦争を意味し，時計は真夜中の12時に限りなく近かった。しかし今日では，「地球最後の日の終末時計」の警告は，気候変化や環境破壊によって生じる，将来大惨事になりうる事態により関係がある。終末時計は，1947年にカチカチと音をたて始め，アメリカのシカゴ大学の原子科学者たちによって，戻したり進められている。

* estimate A to be *do*ing「Aが〜していると見積もる」
* as of A「A現在で」
* have more to do with A「よりAに関係がある」
* set ahead A「Aを進める」

Questions

1. What kind of clock is the Doomsday Clock?
「地球最後の日の終末時計」はどんな時計か？

2. What time was it on the Doomsday Clock in January 2010?
2010 年 1 月に，「地球最後の日の終末時計」は何時だったか？

3. Today, are the Doomsday Clock's warnings based more on the threat of nuclear war or on environmental dangers?
今日，「地球最後の日の終末時計」は核戦争の脅威により基づいているか，それとも環境危機により基づいているか？

4. Who decides when the Doomsday Clock should be moved back or ahead?
「地球最後の日の終末時計」を戻したり，進ませたりしているのは誰か？

Lesson 10 　　Global Concept 2: Trends
グローバル社会の潮流：流行

> **NOTES**
>
> Esther Koplowitx「エステル・コオプロヴィッチ」 George Soros「ジョージ・ソロス」 twenty-something「20代の」 Mark Zuckerberg「マーク・ザッカーバーグ」アメリカ「フェイスブック」の創設者　Bill Gates「ビル・ゲイツ」アメリカ・マイクロソフト社の共同創業者　Warren Buffet「ウォーレン・バフェット」アメリカの投資家・経営者　Chen Guangbiao「陳光標［チェン・グアンビャオ］」中国の慈善家　David Blanchflower「デービッド・ブランチフラワー」

● ● ● **GETTING READY TO READ** ● ● ●

Key Concepts:

リーディングの重要語句と下の定義や説明を結びつけなさい。定義や説明の文字を空所に書きなさい。

1. b 　慈善活動＝多額のお金を慈善事業団体に寄付すること
2. c 　複合企業＝多くの会社から成る大会社　＊ be made up of A「Aで構成される」
3. f 　多発性硬化症＝神経や筋肉がだんだん弱くなる病気
4. g 　投資家＝大規模にお金を稼ぎ出す仕事に関係した人
5. d 　自由主義運動＝人権，男女平等，社会福祉といったもの
6. i 　AP通信社＝有名な国際的な通信社
7. j 　控えめに振る舞うこと＝世間の目から逃れること；注目を避けること
8. h 　にわか成金＝最近，金持ちになった人，または人々
9. a 　景気下降＝景気後退；働きが遅い，またはにぶい経済
10. e 　公的信頼の喪失＝人々が将来について悲観的で，政府の国家運営に不満足なこと

Active Reading:

リーディングを読み，質問の答えをさがしなさい。答えが見つかった文をマークしなさい。

1. 最近，いろいろな運動に多額のお金を寄付した3人の慈善家は誰か？

解答 The reclusive billionaire Esther Koplowitz, head of a Spanish construction conglomerate, recently donated $21 million to a Barcelona biomedical research center that seeks treatments for cancer and multiple sclerosis.

Last year, billionaire financier and philanthropist George Soros, known for his contributions to liberal causes, donated $100 million to Human Rights Watch. Mark Zuckerberg, the twenty-something founder of Facebook, gave $100 million to Newark, New Jersey, to help it revamp its struggling school system.

2. 億万長者であるビル・ゲイツとウォーレン・バフェットは中国で何をしたか？

   解答 Not too long ago, Bill Gates and Warren Buffet, two of America's richest men and most generous donors, called on Beijing to try to convince their Chinese counterparts to give most of their fortunes to charity.

3. いろいろな政府が行っている「緊縮政策」とは何か？

   解答 In fact, Merriam-Webster Dictionary named "austerity," defined as "enforced or extreme economy," as its 2010 Word of the Year.

4. ある経済学者が「緊縮政策」がうまく機能しないと考えるのはなぜか？

   解答 In short, austerity means a loss of public confidence. Businesses and consumers see what is coming and cut back on spending and investing accordingly, Blanchflower says. Shops and factories go out of business. Schools close. Unemployment goes up, real estate prices come down. The result? Deeper and deeper recession and mounting citizens' anger and unrest.

Words in Context:

文の一部の下線部に最も意味が近い語句を選びなさい。

1. (A) 　多額の，ある人たちの見方では「モラルの低下した」財産
    (A) 不道徳な　　　　　(B) うらやましい　　　　(C) 賞賛すべき

2. (B) 　他人との交際を拒む億万長者エステル・コオプロヴィッチ
    (A) 有名な　　　　　　(B) 人前にあまり出ない　(C) 気難しい

3. (C)　学校制度を改造する援助をするために
   (A) ～を取り戻す　　　(B) ～を逆にする　　　(C) ～を作り直す

4. (B)　成長で多くの億万長者を生んでいる
   (A) ～を配達している　(B) ～をつくり出している　(C) ～を受け入れている

5. (A)　不法な～で財を獲得したと信じている
   (A) ～を集めた　　　　(B) ～を盗んだ　　　　(C) ～をだました

6. (A)　にわか成金たちは注目を浴びすぎることに対して慎重である
   (A) 注意を払う　　　　(B) 熱心な　　　　　　(C) 傷ついた

7. (C)　全財産を慈善事業に寄付することを誓う
   (A) ～を相続する　　　(B) ～を貸す　　　　　(C) ～を約束する

8. (C)　けちん坊にはなりたくない
   (A) 貧乏人　　　　　　(B) 有名人　　　　　　(C) 卑しくけちな人

9. (C)　イギリスはすべての政府支出を徹底的に切り詰めている
   (A) 即座に　　　　　　(B) 最後には　　　　　(C) 劇的に

10. (A)　公的な借金を減らそうと努力して
    (A) お金を借りている状態；借りているお金
    (B) 働いて得た収入
    (C) 安全・安心

11. (B)　そして，だんだん高まる市民の怒りと不安
    (A) 睡眠不足　　　　　(B) 心配；抗議　　　　(C) 意見

● ● ● TODAY'S READING ● ● ●

エッセイを注意深く読み，それに続く練習問題を解きなさい。

試訳

① 最近，慈善活動が流行している。世界最高の金持ちたちが多額の，ある人たちの見方では「モラルが低下した」財産を寄付したことが新聞の見出しになっている。スペインの建設複合企業の会長であり，他人との交際を拒む億万長者エステル・コオプロヴィッチは最近，ガンや多様な硬化症の治療法を研究しているバルセロナ生物医学研究所に，2,100万ドル寄付した。昨年，自由主義運動への貢献で知られている億万長者の投資家

Lesson 10　Global Concept 2: Trends　93

であり慈善家でもあるジョージ・ソロスが「ヒューマン・ライツ・ウォッチ」に1億ドル寄付した。「フェイスブック」の創設者である20代のマーク・ザッカーバーグは，なんとかして学校制度を改造する援助をするために，ニュージャージー州のニューアークに1億ドル寄付した。急激な経済成長をしている中国は，独自にたくさんの億万長者を出している。つい最近，アメリカで最高の金持ちの2人で，最高多額寄贈者でもあるビル・ゲイツとウォーレン・バフェットは，中国の寄贈者たちに財産のほとんどを慈善団体に寄付するように納得させるために，北京に立ち寄った。多くの中国人の金持ちは控えめに振る舞うのが好きである，とAP通信社は伝えている。貧富の差が大きくなったために，「不法手段で財を獲得したと信じられている人々に対して憤りの念がある」と記事にある。これらのにわか成金たちは，注目を浴びすぎることに対して慎重である。それにもかかわらず，ゲイツとバフェットの「宣伝」によって，大富豪でリサイクル大会社の会長であるチェン・グアンビャオ（陳光標）は奮起して，自分の死後，全財産を慈善団体に寄付すると誓約した。「私は金持ちだが，けちん坊にはなりたくない」，とチェンはAP通信社に語った。

② お金と言えば，もう1つの流行が最近，見出しになっている：緊縮政策である。事実，『メリアム・ウェブスター』辞典が，2010年の「年間を代表する言葉」として，「強制された，または極度の節約」と定義し，「緊縮政策」と命名した。なぜだかわかりやすい。どこの政府も，特にヨーロッパでは，現在の世界的な景気下降をなんとか切り抜けるために，厳しい緊縮政策を発表してきた。ギリシャ，アイルランド，ポルトガル，イギリスは各国とも公債を減らそうと努力し，政府支出を徹底的に切り詰めている。これが意味することは教育，生活保護手当，保健医療や他の社会改善計画に利用できるお金が少なくなるということである。そして，最も苦しむのはたいてい最も貧しく，貧乏な人々である。しかし，緊縮政策はうまくいかない，と少なくとも経済学者デービッド・ブランチフラワーは言う。商店や工場が倒産する。学校が閉校となる。失業率が上がり，不動産の価格は下がる。その結果は？ますます深まる不景気やだんだん高まる市民の怒りと不安。最近のロンドンでの暴動からもわかるように。

● ● ● ● EXERCISES 1：COMPREHENSION ● ● ● ●

Reading for Information:

それぞれの文の続きになる正しい選択肢を選びなさい。

1. (A)　　［ビル・ゲイツ］以外の次のすべての人は，特定の慈善団体にお金を寄付したと書かれている。
   (B) エステル・コオプロヴィッチ
   (C) ジョージ・ソロス
   (D) マーク・ザッカーバーグ

2. (B) その意見が事実でなく，ただの意見である主張は［中国人の億万長者たちは不正にお金を稼いだ］である。
   (A) ニューアークの学校は本当に寄付金を必要としている
   (C) 陳はゲイツとバフェットの意見に感銘を受けた
   (D) ジョージ・ソロスは人権運動に興味がある

3. (D) リーディングではっきり言っていない情報は［デービッド・ブランチフラワーが意見を述べたところ］である。
   (A) 『メリアム・ウェブスター』辞書による「緊縮政策」の意味
   (B) 緊縮政策をとっている国々
   (C) 支出削減で最も苦しんでいる人

4. (C) デービッド・ブランチフラワーが述べていない，政府緊縮政策によって起こる問題は［公衆衛生の悪化］である。
   (A) 失業　　　　　　(B) 会社投資の削減　　　　　(D) 教育機会の喪失

Listening for Ideas:

それぞれの質問に対する答えを聞き，正しい選択肢に○をつけなさい。

1. (B)
   ある人たちは世界最高の金持ちたちの財産をどのように思っているか？

2. (A)
   最近，中国の金持ちたちに対する怒りが大きくなっているのはなぜか？

3. (C)
   政府が緊縮政策をとっている理由として挙げられていないものはどれか？

Listening Script

1. (A) They think rich people should give all their money to charity.
   金持ちたちはすべての財産を慈善事業に寄付すべきだと考えている。

   (B) They think having so much money is selfish and a little disgusting.
   多額のお金を所有することは利己的で，少し嫌悪を感じている。

Lesson 10　Global Concept 2: Trends　95

(C) They wish they were super-rich themselves.
自分も大金持ちになりたいと思っている。

2. (A) Because of the widening gap between rich and poor.
貧富の差が大きくなっているため。

(B) Because of the country's explosive economic growth.
中国の急激な経済成長のため。

(C) Because rich people attract too much attention.
金持ちたちが注目を浴びすぎているため。

3. (A) They want to reduce public debt.
政府は公債を削減したい。

(B) They are trying to deal with the present global economic downturn.
政府は現在の世界的な景気下降に対処しようとしている。

(C) They want poor, needy people to suffer.
政府は，貧しく貧乏な人々を苦しめたい。

● ● ● EXERCISES 2: COMPOSITION ● ● ●

Making Questions:

下の ANSWER が答えとなる疑問文を完成させなさい。音声で疑問文をチェックしなさい。

1. Q. バルセロナ生物医学研究所がその治療法をさがし求めている2つの病気は何か?
   A. ガンと多様な硬化症。

   解答 is the Barcelona biomedical research center seeking treatments for

2. Q. ビル・ゲイツとウォーレン・バフェットが北京に立ち寄ったのはなぜか?
   A. (つい最近) 中国人の富裕層に財産のほとんどを慈善団体に寄付するように勧めるため。

   解答 Bill Gates and Warren Buffet call on Beijing (not too long ago)

3. Q. 陳光標は何になりたくないか？
   A. けちん坊。

   解答 Chen Guangbiao want to be

4. Q. デービッド・ブランチフラワーは緊縮政策に関して何と言っているか？
   A. うまく機能しない。

   解答 David Blanchflower say about austerity

Writing with Idioms:

下線部の代用として下の語句を使い，文を書き換えなさい。語形を変える必要があることもある。音声で答えをチェックしなさい。

1. Donna seems to be <u>coping with</u> her new duties very well.
   ドナは新しい任務にとてもうまく対処しているようだ。

2. Many small companies have <u>gone out of business</u> recently.
   最近，多くの小企業が倒産している。

3. <u>More often than not</u>, Ian is practicing the piano at this time of day.
   この時間にはイアンはたいていピアノの練習をしている。

4. Thanks for <u>calling on</u> my mother in the hospital yesterday.
   昨日，入院中の母を見舞ってくれてありがとう。

Word Forms:

カッコ内の語を適当な形に直して，文の空所を埋めなさい。

1. debtor
   多額のお金を借りている人は債務者と呼ばれる。

2. miserly
   けちな人はお金を内緒にしておく。

3. warily

そこに何があるか，誰がいるかわからないため，暗い部屋に注意深く入ることを「その部屋に慎重に入る」と表現できる。

4. drastic

問題解決のために思い切った行動をとることは，これがその解決のための最後のチャンスだと信じることだ。

5. decadence

人々が自分に甘く，愚かにお金を浪費する歴史上の時期はよく「モラルの低い時代」と呼ばれる。

● ● ● EXERCISES 3: CHALLENGE ● ● ●

Using Key Concepts:

Aの文と意味が同じになるように，Bの文の空所を埋めなさい。KEY CONCEPTSの語句を使いなさい。

1. Associated Press [AP]

AP通信社をチェックすれば，最新の見出しを読むことができる。

2. conglomerate

「三菱」のような大会社は複合企業と呼ばれる。

3. loss of public confidence

市民がリーダーを信頼できないと，リーダーは「公的信頼の喪失」に苦しむ。

4. economic downturn

財政危機はよく景気下降につながる。

5. low profile

プライバシーを守る人々は世間の注目から逃れている。

6. liberal causes

革新的な政治家は自由主義運動を促進しようとする。

Vocabulary Expansion:

形容詞 "generous" と同じような意味の形容詞のリストを見なさい。その形容詞を正しい名詞形にして，下の文の空所を埋めなさい。

1. munificence

   大学はその裕福な寄付者にその気前の良さに対して感謝した。

2. lavishness

   その映画スターは，主催するパーティーの豪華さで有名だ。

3. tolerance

   そのキャンプで子どもたちは，他の宗教や文化的習慣に対する忍耐を学ぶ。

4. magnanimity

   その医者が，自分の深い悲しみをもたらした人々を憎まないことで示した寛大さは私たちみんなの模範となる。

5. altruism

   自分たちが危険なのにもかかわらず，仲間のけが人や病人を助け，その大隊は利他主義を見せた。

辞書定義

lavish:	寛大な，でもたまに見せびらかすためだけに（気前のよい）
	＊ for show 「見えで；見せびらかすために」
magnanimous:	他人を許すことに寛大な（度量が大きい）
munificent:	お金を贈ることに寛大な（非常に気前がよい）
altruistic:	自分に関心がなく寛大な（利他的な）
tolerant:	他人の信念や意見を理解することに寛大な（寛容な）

Listening Activity:

ショートトークを聞き，その主旨に最も合う文を選びなさい。

Answer: 2

1. ピッツバーグ大学は最近，巨大総合金融サービス機関から多額の寄付を受けた。
2. ピッツバーグ大学の「企業の社会的責任（CSR）」プロジェクトは，学生たちによりよい徳育と相互連結した世界の必要性に対するより深い理解を提供する。

Lesson 10　Global Concept 2: Trends

3. ピッツバーグ大学の学生たちは，きれいな水を提供し，豊富な電力を生産し，雇用機会をつくり出すために科学技術を利用する方法を学ぶ。

Listening Script

　According to Yahoo News, the University of Pittsburgh has just received a one-million-dollar donation from a major financial conglomerate. The money is to be used to set up programs and education for corporate social responsibility, or CSR. The new curriculum will mix socially responsible ideas and principles into students' business and leadership training. One university official said that in our increasingly interconnected world, students need to focus more on ethical issues. They need to think about what good they can do as well as what money they can make. By developing a keen understanding of corporate social responsibility, students will be better prepared for future leadership opportunities. The university's new program will include courses on how to use technology and research to solve such pressing world problems as providing clean water, making electricity universally available, and creating work opportunities.

　ヤフーニュースによると，ピッツバーグ大学は巨大総合金融サービス機関から100万ドルの寄付を受けたという。そのお金は企業の社会的責任，つまりCSRに関するプログラムと教育を始めるために使われる。新しいカリキュラムは社会的責任という考え方と基本方針を学生の実務教育と幹部訓練に加えたものになる。ある大学当局者によると，ますます相互連結していく世界では，学生はもっと倫理問題に関心を向けるべきだという。学生はどれくらいお金を稼ぐかだけでなく，どんなよいことをできるかについても考えなければならない。企業の社会的責任に対して鋭い理解を伸ばすことで，学生は将来の幹部になる機会に対してきちんと準備しておくことができる。ピッツバーグ大学の新しいプログラムには，きれいな水を供給し，世界のいたるところで手に入る電力を生産し，雇用機会をつくり出すといった世界的な緊急問題を解決するために，どのように科学技術や研究を利用するかに関する講座もある。

＊ according to A 「Aによると」

＊ focus on A 「Aに関心を向ける」

＊ A as well as B 「BだけでなくAもまた」

＊ such A as B 「BのようなA」

Lesson 11　　Psychology
心理学

> **NOTES**
> PET「陽電子放射断層撮影（=Position Emission Tomography）」ガンを検査する方法の１つ　fMRI「機能的磁気共鳴断層撮影装置（=functional magnetic resonance imaging）」脳が機能しているときの血流の変化などを画像化する方法　frontal lobe「前頭葉」　familial vulnerability「遺伝的脆弱性」

● ● ● **READY TO READ** ● ● ●

下の練習問題はリーディングから最大限のものを得るのに役立ちます。

I. KEY VOCABULARY:

左の単語と右の定義／同義語を結びつけなさい。適切な下線に，a～jを書き入れなさい。

1. c　　乱用；虐待＝物や人を悪用すること
2. h　　確定的な＝信頼できる；明らかに証明された
　　　　＊ beyond a doubt「疑いなく」
3. b　　無能な＝技術に欠ける；判断力に欠ける；不器用な
4. e　　避けられない＝必ず起こる，または起こる運命である；不可避の
　　　　＊ be bound to do「きっと～する」
　　　　＊ be destined to do「～する運命である」
5. a　　受け継がれた＝親から子へ伝わった
6. j　　仲裁をする＝仲介者として行動する；交渉する
7. i　　悲観的な＝暗く絶望的な世界観を持っている
8. f　　特別の好み＝素質；ありうること
9. g　　～に抵抗する＝～したり，しようとする誘惑にかられていない；～を拒絶する
　　　　＊ be tempted to do「～したい誘惑にかられる」
10. d　　傷つきやすいこと＝弱いこと；攻撃されやすいこと

II. ACTIVE READING:

この課のエッセイを読んで，次の作業をしなさい。

(A) それぞれの番号のついたカッコから正しい語を選び，慣用表現を完成させなさい。

1. against   go against ~「~に反する」
2. ahead   ahead of time「前もって」
3. after   after all「結局は」
4. touch   keep in touch with ~「~と連絡を保つ」
5. from   stems from ~「~から起こる」
6. up   come up with ~「~を出す」
7. up   pick up「身につける」
8. about   bring about ~「~をもたらす」

(B) これらの詳しい説明をさがしなさい。見つけたら○で囲みなさい。

1. 「運命づけられた」人々がたとえられているもの

    解答 **machines or gadgets**
    機械や装置

2. 古代ギリシャの哲学者が提唱した思想

    解答 **A man's character is his fate.**
    「人間の性格は宿命である」

3. 2つの脳画像撮影技術

    解答 **PET scans and fMRI**
    陽電子放射断層撮影と機能的磁気共鳴断層撮影装置

4. フランシス・ベーコン卿が知識を呼んだもの

    解答 **power**
    力

5. 自己分析に関する研究を行った人たち

    解答 **University College London scientists [researchers]**
    ロンドン大学ユニバーシティカレッジの科学者[研究者]

6. 自己分析はどのように定義されているか

    解答　the ability to examine and judge your own thoughts and actions
    自分の考えや行動を考察し判断する能力

7. 脳の「タンパク質」の別称

    解答　prefrontal cortex
    前頭前皮質

8. 重い精神病

    解答　schizophrenia
    統合失調症

9. 麻薬中毒者が抑えられないもの

    解答　impulsive behavior
    衝撃的行動

10. 運動制御，認知，行動

    解答　motor control, cognition, and behavior
    脳の前頭葉が「仲裁する」もの

(C) これらの質問の答えをさがし，下線を引きなさい。下の READING COMPREHENSION 3 を見なさい。

● ● ● READING ● ● ●

宿命づけられた

[1] 自由意志，個人の選択，人格的変化の可能性といった人道主義的（さらに言えば，民主主義的）観念に反するように思われるが，「運命づけられた」という言葉が，最近ますます使われるようになっている。「人がある人格的特徴や欠陥や人生観『に運命づけられている』」と言うと，その人が生まれながらにそうした特別な好みを持っており，本人にはどうすることもできないということである。またそれは，その人の精神的性格や遺伝的性格のようなあるものによって，将来必然的に，アルコール中毒や麻薬中毒になったり，例えば，恋愛がうまくいかなかったり，常に引っ込み思案になったり社会的に不適格な人間になってしまうことを意味している。もっと遠慮なく言えば，人間は，ある1つのことを，たった1つのことだけをするように設計され組み立てられた（運命づけ

Lesson 11　Psychology　103

られた）機械や装置のようなものだ，ということだ。この考え方は，最初はかなり悲観的な見方であり，2,500年以上前にギリシャの哲学者ヘラクレイトスが初めて提唱した「人間の性格は宿命である」という思想の模倣に思えるかもしれない。しかし，もう少し詳しく見ていこう。

[2] 「運命づけられた」という専門用語は，神経科学や，PETあるいはfMRIといった脳画像撮影技術におけるこの頃の進歩のおかげで，最近広く使われている。この新しい技術は，もともとは，外科医が病気や卒中が原因で起きる脳障害を発見するために開発されたものだが，今ではこの技術のおかげで活動中の脳を観察し，その機能をより正確に理解し，さらに脳のどの部位がどういった活動や行動を制御しているのかをチェックできるようになった。この新しい知識によって，医療目的だけではなく，性格上の問題点を発見するための一種の早期警戒システムを手に入れることができる。例えば，いわゆる暴力的行動を制御する脳の部位がいわば制御不能になっていることが前もってわかれば，そうした行動を抑えるのに役立つのだ。イギリス人のもう一人の哲学者，フランシス・ベーコン卿がかつて述べたように，「知識は力」である。そのため，「運命づけられた」という用語は，結局，全面的に悪いものではなく，楽観的な側面も持ち合わせているようだ。

[3] 例を挙げてみよう。ロンドン大学ユニバーシティカレッジの科学者たちが（『サイエンス』誌で），自分の考えや行動を考察し判断する能力である，意識の本質的機能―「自己分析」が欠けている人たちに希望を与えてくれる脳スキャンの研究結果を発表した，とAP通信が報じた。「単に経験することから，その経験について考察することまで，意識にはさまざまな段階がある。自己分析はその最高領域にあり，そこまでの過程を測り，それを脳と関連づけることによって，意識的思考の実態への洞察が得られるかもしれない」とその研究の主筆者は述べている。研究チームは，任意の被験者たちにある質問をし，その答えの正しさにどれくらい自信があるかを評価してもらうことにより，自己認識度を測定した。研究者たちは脳スキャンを使って，被験者が回答し，それを弁護するときの脳を観察した。AP通信によれば，実験の背後にあった考え方は，自己分析力の強い人たちは，答えが正しいときにはより自信を持ち，「全く間違っているときは，自己批判する可能性が高い」というものだった。そして，これが事実であることがわかった。一方，ちょっと「軽率で自信過剰な」人たちは，「自分が正しいのだと部外の人に思わせようとするだろうと考えられたが，実際にはそのような関連性はなかった」とのことである。報告によれば，強い自己分析力は，脳の前頭前皮質，つまり，通常，自己分析のような「高度な思考力」をつかさどる「タンパク質」部分の大きさと関連があることが，この研究によって明らかにされた。言い換えれば，前頭前皮質が大きくなればなるほど，それだけ自己分析力も高まるのである。脳スキャンによって，自己分析力はまた「より強力な白質の機能」，すなわち，脳細胞をお互いに結びつけている神経繊維によっても強化されていることがわかった。いつの日か，この研究結果は「脳の損傷や自己認識を奪ってしまう病気―例えば，自分が病気だということを認識せず，したがって，薬物治療も受けない統合失調症患者など―への取り組み」において助力となることが期待されている。関連した研究によれば，統合失調症は，少なくともその一部は，「タンパク質」機能の損傷が原因であることが判明している。

[4] 実験結果に励まされながらも，この研究によって重要な問題点が提起され，明確な答え

を出すにはさらなる研究が必要だ，と研究チームのリーダーは結論づけている。脳の大きさと機能におけるこうした違いは生来的なものなのか，あるいは，人がより多くの時間と労力をかけて「鍛えた」結果として，前頭前皮質が強くなるのか？また，自己分析力の向上は，訓練によって身につけることができる能力なのか？もし，後者の疑問に対する答えが「はい，そうです」なら，それは実に喜ばしいニュースである。

[5] 『サイエンス』誌に発表された脳スキャンを用いたもう1つの研究では，麻薬中毒者は衝動的行動を制御する脳の部位に「先天的異常」があることがケンブリッジ大学のイギリス人科学者たちによって明らかにされた。こうした脳の異常は，薬物により脳が損傷した結果なのか，それとも，すでに脳に存在しており，それが薬物乱用へと人を「宿命づけた」のかは，今まで不明確だった。研究を行うため，ケンブリッジ大学の研究者たちは，麻薬中毒とそうでない兄弟のペアをそれぞれ比較した。彼らは，運動制御，認知，行動をつかさどる部位である脳の前頭葉の構造に多くの欠陥を持っていた。したがって，中毒的行動は遺伝であることが明らかになった。中毒にかかっていない兄弟には，たぶん，「薬物依存に対する遺伝的脆弱性を中和する」何らかの「他の障害許容要因」—それが環境的なものであれ，あるいは，脳の構造における他の違いによって生じたものであれ—があるのだろうと，研究チームのリーダーは述べている。この研究結果は，薬物依存へ「宿命づけられた」人たちでも，その早期発見が可能であり，破壊的な薬物中毒になる前に助けることができるという希望を与えてくれる。

READING COMPREHENSION 1:

それぞれの文を正しい選択肢を選んで，完成させなさい。

1. (C)   著者は自由意志，個人の選択，人格的変化を民主社会に不可欠なものとみなしているようだ。
   - (A) ある個人的な態度に寄与する性格的特徴
   - (B) 私たちの精神的・遺伝的性格の側面
   - (C) 民主社会に不可欠なもの

2. (A)   PETスキャンやfMRIといった技術はもともと，脳手術をより信頼できて安心なものにするために使用されていたようだ。
   - (A) 脳手術をより信頼できて安心なものにするために
   - (B) 精神機能やその過程を研究する道具として
   - (C) 暴力行為や他の有害な行動を探知するために

3. (B)   第3パラグラフで用いられている下線部の表現「全く違っているときには，自己批判する可能性が高い」は被験者たちがなぜミスを犯したかを反省したという意味である。
   - (A) 自分のミスを認めるのを嫌がった
   - (B) なぜミスを犯したかを反省した
   - (C) 答えを変える許可を求めた

Lesson 11　Psychology　105

4. (B) 自己分析に対する強い好みが確かに先天的なものでないとしたら、それは「自分の考えを検討する」能力は学習し伸ばすことができるという意味である。
   (A) 家系に遺伝している
   (B) 学習し伸ばすことができる
   (C) ある人々は伸ばすことができない

5. (C) ケンブリッジ大学の研究によって、そうでないことが明らかになるまでは、ある科学者たちは麻薬中毒者の脳異常は麻薬それ自体が原因であると考えていた。
   (A) 脳の他の領域で発見された
   (B) 早期発見で克服できる
   (C) 麻薬それ自体が原因である

READING COMPREHENSION 2:

音声で文を聞き、文が合っていればTに、合っていなければFに○をつけなさい。

1. T 2. T 3. F 4. T 5. F

Listening sentences

1. To be unlucky in love means to have trouble maintaining romantic relationships.

   恋愛がうまくいかないというのは、恋愛関係をうまく続けられないという意味である。
   ＊ have trouble *do*ing「〜するのに苦労する」

2. Knowing more about how the brain works and what brain regions control what actions and behaviors can be used to warn people about possible future problems.

   脳がどのように機能するか、どの脳領域がどんな行動や態度をつかさどっているかをよりよく知ることで、将来起きそうな問題を人々に警告することができる。

3. Introspection, according to a University College London researcher, is one of the lower forms of conscious thought.

   ロンドン大学ユニバーシティカレッジの研究者によると、自己分析は意識的な思考の下位の形の1つである。

4. Subjects in the introspection experiment who came across as "brash and overconfident" were not able to reflect on or admit that they had been wrong.

   「性急で自信過剰で」あるという印象を与えた、内向性の実験の被験者たちは、自分たちが間違っていたことを熟考したり認めたりすることができなかった。

5. What made the University of Cambridge study definitive was that two addicted siblings were compared with non-addicted volunteers who were not related to the siblings.

ケンブリッジ大学の研究を完成させたのは，2人の中毒患者の兄弟を，その兄弟とは関係がない中毒でないボランティアたちと比較したことだった。

READING COMPREHENSION 3:

ACTIVE READING の質問に戻って，できるだけ自分の言葉を使い，完全な文で答えなさい。

解答例

1. 「運命づけられた」という用語はなぜ悲観的と見ることができるのか？また，なぜ楽観的と見ることができるのか？

    解答 The term can be seen as pessimistic because to say that a person is "wired" for a certain negative behavior, say, means that he or she has no hope of overcoming that behavior. It can be seen as optimistic in a way because new brain-scan techniques have made it possible to detect the predilection for negative behavior early, allowing the person to be aware of that predilection and to avoid such behavior.

    ある有害な行動にある人が「運命づけられた」ということは，その人にはその態度を克服する望みがないという意味になるため，その言葉は「悲観的」であると見ることができる。

2. ロンドン大学ユニバーシティカレッジの研究者たちは自分たちの発見がどのようなことにつながればいいと考えているか？

    解答 They hope that their discoveries will tackle or overcome brain injuries and diseases that make it difficult for victims to practice the self-reflection needed to live normal lives.

    自分たちの発見が，通常の生活をするのに必要な自己反省を患者が実行するのを困難にしている脳損傷や脳疾患に取り組んだり，克服できればいいと研究者たちは考えている。

3. 「遺伝的な脳の異常」をもった兄弟が薬物中毒にならないようにすることを可能にしているのは何か？

> **解答** The siblings who do not suffer from drug abuse may have been positively affected (made stronger) by their social environment or may have something about the structure of other parts of the brain that allows them to resist addiction.
>
> 薬物乱用にかかっていない兄弟は，社会環境に肯定的に影響を受けている（より強くなっている）かもしれないし，脳の他の部分の構造に，中毒に対抗する何かを持っているかもしれない。

Lesson 12　　The Environment
環境

> **NOTES**
> bring about A「Aを成し遂げる」　for lack of better words「他にいい言葉が見つからないが」　Human Rights Council「(国連の) 人権理事会」　Inter-American Commission on Human Rights「米州人権委員会」　Goldman Environmental Prize「ゴールドマン環境賞」　the Institute of Public and Environmental Affairs「公衆環境研究中心」

❋ ● ● ● READY TO READ ● ● ● ❋

下の練習問題はリーディングから最大限のものを得るのに役立ちます。

I. KEY VOCABULARY:

左の単語と右の定義／同義語を結びつけなさい。適切な下線に，a～jを書き入れなさい。

1. e　　鋭く＝鋭敏に；深く強く感じられた
2. h　　説得力のある＝賢い；説得力のある；知性に訴えた
3. f　　嘆かわしい＝悲しくみじめな；非常に残念な
4. i　　悲惨な＝ひどく悲惨な結果を招く
5. a　　怖がる＝楽しみにしない；これから起こることを恐れる
6. j　　～を犠牲にする＝～をあきらめたり，延期する；～を犠牲にする
7. c　　～を無効にする＝～を虚偽にさせる；～を無効にする
8. g　　不安定な＝安全でない；安定を欠く；すぐに影響を受ける
9. b　　持続可能（生態系環境を維持できる）＝続くことができる；安全な
10. d　　長い非難演説＝怒りの爆発；長く続く怒りの演説

II. ACTIVE READING:

この課のエッセイを読んで，次の作業をしなさい。

(A) それぞれの番号のついたカッコから正しい語を選び，慣用表現を完成させなさい。

1. at　　　　at times「たまに」
2. call　　　call attention to ~「～に対して注意を促す」
3. about　　go about ~「～に取りかかる」
4. about　　think about ~「～について考える」

5. do　　　　do without ~「~なしですます」
6. pitching　　pitch in「協力する」
7. look　　　look upon ~ as ...「~を…と考える」
8. fallen　　　fall through「失敗に終わる」

(B) これらの詳しい説明をさがしなさい。見つけたらそれぞれの説明に○をつけなさい。

1. 初めてアース・デーが催された年

    解答　1972
    1972 年

2. 「存在する理由」という意味の外国語

    解答　raison(s) d'etre
    存在理由

3. 「グリーン」とは何か？

    解答　an energy and environment blog
    エネルギーと環境に関するブログ

4. エリザベス・ローゼンタールがアース・デーをたとえたもの

    解答　Valentine's Day
    ヴァレンタイン・デー

5. 『ワン・デー・オン・アース』を何人の人が撮ったか？；何か国語になったか？；何時間の場面が撮影されたか？

    解答　19,000 professional and amateur photographers; 70 languages; 3,000 hours of footage
    19,000 人のプロ・アマチュアのカメラマン；70 の言語；3,000 時間の場面

6. 「気候の不正義」が意味するもの

    解答　the fact that nations that contribute the least to the greenhouse effect are the worst affected by global warming
    温室効果に最も寄与していない国々が地球温暖化に最も悪影響を受けているという事実

7. ダイナ・シェルトンは何の代表か？

   【解答】 the Inter-American Commission on Human Rights
   米州人権委員会

8. ディプー・モニはどこの出身か？

   【解答】 Bangladesh
   バングラディッシュ

9. どのくらいの頻度で誰にゴールドマン環境賞が授与されるか？

   【解答】 every year [annually] to six people who are "grassroots environmental heroes"
   毎年，「草の根環境運動のヒーロー」である6人に

10. マ・ジュンが「透明性」で意味していること

    【解答】 informing the Chinese people about who is fouling China's waters
    中国国民に誰が中国の水の汚染しているかを報せること

(C) これらの質問の答えをさがし，下線を引きなさい。下のREADING COMPREHENSION 3 を見なさい。

● ● ● READING ● ● ●

毎日がアース・デーであるべきだ

[1] 今日はアース・デー。175か国で何百万という人が，私たちの地球と，その地球を保護し守るために，（初めてアース・デーが開催された）1970年以来，収めてきた成果を祝福している。しかし，氾濫している毎日の記事が時に鋭く，時に憂鬱に私たちに知らせてくれるように，健全で思いやりがあり，安全で生態系を破壊しない環境と経済という私たちの目標を達成するには，未だ道のりは遠い。したがって，アース・デーの存在理由のもう1つは，二酸化炭素の放出と気候変動，生息地の破壊と絶滅危惧種，水質汚染や大気汚染といった差し迫った環境問題に注意を促し，それらの問題にいかに取り組んでいけるかを私たちに考えさせることである。

[2] 確かに，私たちはアース・デーに対してひねくれた態度をとり，『ニューヨーク・タイムズ』紙のエネルギーと環境に関するブログ「グリーン」の中で，エリザベス・ローゼンタールが述べているように，バレンタイン・デーのようなただの1日，つまり，「巨

大市場のチャンス―消費を促して物を売るという矛盾したやり方」と見なしている。環境問題を扱う記者として，ローゼンタールは，「オフィスや自宅のメールボックスに（あるいは，環境的に言えば，もっと悪い手段で）押し寄せるアース・デーのお買い得品や売り出し中の商品に恐怖を覚える」ようになったと述べている。アース・デーとは，ただ「環境にいい」お買い得品を求めて地元のショッピングセンターやスーパーマーケットに押しかけるための1日ではなく，購入をあきらめ，「環境的に問題がある，あるいはそれがなくても幸せに暮らしていける」習慣をやめることについて真剣に考える機会となるべきではないのか，と彼女は問いかけている。ローゼンタールは，「アース・デーは一時的なものだ。バレンタイン・デーの日にしか愛情を示さないのであれば，何の意味があるというのか？」という説得力があり，深く考えさせる意見でアース・デーに対する長い非難演説を締めくくっている。

[3] だが，私たちのひねくれた態度は少し後に回し，アース・デーをもっと前向きにとらえてみよう。それには，2010年10月10日のたった1日のみに，世界のすべての国で撮影された地球の素晴らしいビデオアルバム「ワン・デー・オン・アース」というタイトルの新作映画を見ることよりいい方法はないだろう。60の非営利団体および国連からの資金援助と技術援助を受けて（映画は現在ニューヨーク市の国連本部で上映されている），さらには，1万9千人のプロ並びにアマチュア映画製作者がそのプロジェクトに協力し，70以上の言語で累積3千時間以上の撮影フィルムから成るこの映画は，監督カイル・ラデックがロンドンの『テレグラフ』紙に語ったように，まさに「単純で偉大なアイデア」である。映画館，大学キャンパス，世界中の「間に合わせの野外会場」で見ることのできるこの映画が，「世界はこんなにも巨大で，力強く，そして時には危険で，また時には素晴らしい場所であること，さらに，自分たちの生活が他の人たちの生活と結びついていて，他にいい言葉が見つからないが，多かれ少なかれ，私たちはみんなこの同じ世界にいること」を人々が理解するのに役立ってくれること，をラデックは望んでいる。

[4] そして，アース・デーに浮かれながら，現在の進路を逆転させ，さらに，未来の生態系に関してされてきた深刻な災害が起こるという予測をすべて打ち消すことができる地球の能力を楽観視する一方で，環境問題の最前線に希望を与えてくれる新しい考えをいくつか見てみよう。

[5] スイスのジュネーブで開かれた国連人権理事会の最近の会議で，専門家たちは気候変動を人権問題と考え，気候変動を先進工業国が最も責任を負うべきであるという環境保護への斬新な取り組み方を提案した。この取り組み方は，嘆かわしい「気候の不正義」，つまり，温室効果に対して最も責任のない国々の多くが，地球温暖化の被害を最も受けているという事実に基づいている。オンラインのニュースサービスである「ワン・ワールド」ネットは，「気候変動の影響は，貧困者，移住者，障害者，原住民，女性を含め，その市民権保護がすでに不安定な者たちが最も敏感に感じているだろう」と説明している。ジュネーブでの会議参加者の1人，米州人権委員会の議長でもあるダイナ・シェルトンは，こうした考えを次のようにまとめている。「なぜ気候変動に対して人権的な取り組み方をするのか？第一に，とても皮肉なことに，他のやり方では効果がないのです」。「生態系を破壊しないことよりも発展すること」に重点が置かれてきたため，「環境に関

する法制度」と「生態系を破壊しない発展」の促進を通じて地球温暖化を制御しようとする努力の大部分は失敗に終わったと彼女は述べている。「人権に関する法が国際社会で占めている非常に高い地位」のために，人権が環境問題により効果的に取り組むことができる，とシェルトンは信じている。もう1人の会議参加者，バングラディッシュ外務大臣ディプー・モニも，「慣例的な国際法によると，自国が他国の人権に反する行為に利用されるのを故意に許してはいけないことはすべての国家の義務である。歴史的に責任を負う国々は，弱い国々で影響を受けている何百万という人たちの人権を認めていない現状に見て見ぬふりをしてはいけない。放出削減と資金調達が人権擁護義務となると断言できる根拠は十分にある」と同意している。

[6] 一方，「草の根環境運動のヒーロー」6人に毎年授与されるゴールドマン環境賞の2012年度受賞者の1人であるマ・ジュン（馬軍）は，中国の汚染された湖，小川，川をきれいにするための独自の斬新な取り組み方を提案している。マは，おそらく中国の最も有名な環境運動の闘士であるが，非営利団体「公衆環境研究中心」を設立し，現在，国内の汚染者を「恥じさせて」環境責任を取らせるためにこの組織を利用している。中国には汚染を規制する法律や規制はあるが「強制力が非常に弱い」，とマは『クリスチャン・サイエンス・モニター』誌に語っている。そこでマは，「透明性」―中国国民に対して，中国の水を汚染した責任が誰にあるのかを報せること―が大切だと判断した。もし国民が正しい情報を持っていれば，その情報を利用して汚染者に圧力をかけることができるだろう，とマは考えたが，彼は正しかった。すでに600ほどの企業が，汚染規制法に違反したとして処罰されており，中国でビジネスを行っている国際的大企業の多くは，公明正大に営業するため，現在では「マの違反者リストに照らし合わせて業者をチェック」している。

READING COMPREHENSION 1:

それぞれの文を正しい選択肢を選んで，完成させなさい。

1. (C) 著者によると，環境に関する毎日の見出しは，特にその見出しはその状況に希望がないように感じさせるために，時に暗い気持ちにさせる。
   (A) その見出しが多すぎて，遅れずについていくのが難しいために
   (B) その見出しを以前に何度も読み聞いているために
   (C) その見出しはその状況に希望がないように感じさせるために

2. (C) 第1パラグラフで触れられていない環境問題は他国に強制移住させられる人々である。
   (A) 地球の大気温度の上昇
   (B) 住む場所を追いやられて，その結果，死滅してしまう動物
   (C) 他国に強制移住させられる人々
   * as a result「結果として」

3. (B) エリザベス・ローゼンタールがアース・デーを「一時的」と呼ぶのは，人々はその日が終わるとすぐにその意味を忘れてしまうという意味である。
   - (A) その日が年に1度しかない
   - (B) 人々はその日が終わるとすぐにその意味を忘れてしまう
   - (C) その日が最近ではあまりにも商業的になっている

4. (A) 第5パラグラフで言いたいことは，ほとんどの国々では環境を守ることを目的としている法律よりも人権を守るための法律を守って施行しそうであるということである。
   - (A) ほとんどの国々では環境を守ることを目的としている法律よりも人権を守るための法律を守って施行しそうである
   - (B) 他国の人権を否定する責任がある国々はたいてい自分たちがそれを行っていることに気がついていない
   - (C) 温室効果はそれをつくり出している責任がある国々だけに影響があるべきだ

   * be likely to *do*「～しそうである」
   * be designed to *do*「～することを目的としている」
   * be responsible for *do*ing「～する責任がある」
   * be aware that ...「…であることに気づいている」

5. (B) 中国の人々が，何が起きているかを知れば知るほど，環境問題にかかわるようになるということが推測される。
   - (A) マ・ジュンは個人的に水質汚染の容疑をかけられているすべての会社を視察している
   - (B) 中国の人々が，何が起きているかを知れば知るほど，環境問題にかかわるようになる
   - (C) これまでは海外の国々だけが処罰されてきた

READING COMPREHENSION 2:

音声で文を聞き，文が合っていればTに，合っていなければFに○をつけなさい。

1. F   2. T   3. F   4. T   5. F

Listening sentences

1. This year, Earth Day is only focused on celebrating the earth and being optimistic about its future and is not concerned with calling attention to the serious environmental issues confronting the planet.

   今年，アース・デーは，地球を祝福し，その未来を楽観視することだけに集中していて，地球に立ちはだかる深刻な環境問題に対して注意を促すことには関心がない。
   * be optimistic about A「Aについて楽観的である」

114

* be focused on *do*ing「～することに集中する」
* be concerned with *do*ing「～することに関心がある」
* call attention to A「Aに対して注意を促す」

2. Elisabeth Rosenthal says e-mail makes more sense environmentally speaking than the avalanche of deals and promotions that arrive in her office or home mailbox.

   環境面から言うと，オフィスや自宅の郵便受けにどっとくるお買い得品や売り出し中の商品よりもメールのほうが道理にかなっている，とエリザベス・ローゼンタールは言う。

3. Kyle Ruddick's film aims to make audiences aware that people around the world are so different that it makes it very difficult for us to see how our lives are connected and that we are all part of "one big family," so to speak.

   カイル・ラディックの映画は，世界中の人々はそれぞれが違うので自分たちの生活がどのようにつながっているかを理解するのがとても難しく，私たちみんなが，いわば，「1つの大きな家族」の構成員であることを見ている観客にわからせることを目指している。
   * so to speak「いわば；まるで」

4. Climate change and global warming are likely to have direr consequences on people who are already suffering and whose lives are already threatened than they are on those who are well off and whose lives are more stable and secure.

   気候変動と地球温暖化は，裕福で生活がより安定し，より安全な人々に対してよりも，もうすでに苦しんでいる人々やすでに生活をおびやかされている人々により悲惨な結果をもたらしそうである。
   * be well off「生活が裕福である」

5. Because China has no laws and regulations against water pollution, Ma Jun has had to not only write and pass such laws but also to enforce them himself.

   中国には水質汚染に対する法律や規制がないので，マ・ジュンはそのような法律を作成し，可決するだけでなく，自分自身でその法律を守らせなければならない。

READING COMPREHENSION 3:

ACTIVE READING の質問に戻って，できるだけ自分の言葉を使い，完全な文で答えなさい。

解答例

1. このエッセイの著者は何が地球の目標であると述べているか？

    解答 He says that the goal is have a healthy and humane, secure and sustainable global environment and economy.

    その目標は，健全で思いやりのある，そして安全で生態系を破壊しない環境や経済を手に入れることである，と彼は言う。

2. カイル・ラディックによると，「ワン・デー・オン・アース」は世界がどのような場所であるかを示しているか？

    解答 He says it shows the world to be an enormous, powerful, sometimes dangerous, sometimes wonderful place.

    それは世界が巨大で力強く，時に危険で，時に素晴らしい場所であることを明らかにしている，と彼は言う。

3. 温室効果や地球温暖化の責任を負うべき先進国はどのような義務を負うべきだとディプー・モニは述べているか？

    解答 She says advanced countries are obligated to reduce their emissions (of greenhouse gases) and to pay compensation to countries that are affected by the global warming that the advanced countries are responsible for.

    先進国は（温室効果ガスの）排出量を減らし，先進国にその責任がある地球温暖化に影響を受けている国々に対して賠償金を払う義務がある，と彼女は言う。

Lesson 13　History
歴史

> **NOTES**
> worth a tinker's damn「わずかでも価値がある」　Holocaust「ホロコースト」ナチスによるユダヤ人の大量虐殺　Final Solution「最終的解決」ナチスのユダヤ人抹殺計画

● ● ● **READY TO READ** ● ● ●

下の練習問題はリーディングから最大限のものを得るのに役立ちます。

I. KEY VOCABULARY:

左の単語と右の定義／同義語を結びつけなさい。適切な下線に，a～jを書き入れなさい。

1. f　　逆境 = 苦難；不運；苦しみ
2. g　　支持者 = ある信条のために闘う人；活動家
3. j　　秘密の = 少数の人だけにしか知られていない；不思議な；秘義の
4. h　　保証できる = 本物の；証明できる
5. b　　年代順の = 時間の順序・順番で
6. i　　破壊的な = 大損害を与える；破壊を招く；荒廃した
7. e　　絶滅 = 大量殺人；全滅
8. a　　極悪非道な = 邪悪な；よこしまな；ふらちな
9. d　　簡潔に = 数語で表現された；そっけなく
10. c　　領域 = 地域；景色

II. ACTIVE READING:

この課のエッセイを読んで，次の作業をしなさい。

(A) それぞれの番号のついたカッコから正しい語を選び，慣用表現を完成させなさい。

1. dark　　　left in the dark「知らないままで」
2. miss　　　miss out on ~「~を見逃す」
3. familiar　be familiar with ~「~をよく知っている」
4. bother　　bother with ~「わざわざ~する」
5. worked　　work through ~「~にうまく対処する」

Lesson 13　History　117

6. keep　　　keep from ~ 「~を避ける」
7. putting　put on ~ 「~を催す」
8. tracked　track down ~ 「~を探し出す」

(B) これらの詳しい説明をさがしなさい。見つけたらそれぞれの説明に○をつけなさい。

1. 「教授」を意味する第1パラグラフの単語

    解答 fellow
    特別研究員

2. ロバート・トゥームが言う，イギリスの歴史授業で生徒たちが学ばされている話題

    解答 obscure topics in absurdly arcane detail
    ばかばかしいほど不可解で細かいあいまいな話題

3. イギリスの歴史で生徒がよく省いてしまう時代

    解答 the British Empire
    大英帝国

4. ヘンリー・フォードは誰か

    解答 an American automobile and industrial pioneer
    アメリカの自動車と自動車産業の先駆者

5. 「あまり受け入れられない」を意味する第2パラグラフの単語

    解答 heretical
    異端の

6. デビッド・ヒュームが言う歴史の3つの利点

    解答 It amuses the fancy, improves the understanding, and strengthens virtue.
    空想を楽しませてくれること，知識を増やしてくれること，徳性を強くしてくれること。

7. エドワード・ギボンが言う歴史が私たちに示してくれるもの

    解答 the crime, follies, and misfortunes of mankind
    人間の罪・愚かさ・不運

118

8. ノーマン・カズンズがそれに対して賛成の運動を起こしたもの

　　解答　world peace
　　　　　世界平和

9. マイケル・ベレンバームが専門にしていること

　　解答　the study of the Holocaust
　　　　　ホロコーストの研究

10. アドルフ・イッチマンが逮捕されたときにいた場所

　　解答　Argentina
　　　　　アルゼンチン

(C) これらの質問の答えをさがし，下線を引きなさい。
　　下の READING COMPREHENSION 3 を見なさい。

● ● ● READING ● ● ●

歴史の中の「物語」

[1] 痛烈な内容といわれている報告書の中で，ケンブリッジ大学の歴史学特別研究員ロバート・トゥーム教授は，イギリスの歴史教育は西洋世界の中で最悪の1つだと非難し，さらに，「大多数の卒業予定者が過去に繰り広げられた物語について何も知らないままでいるような」お粗末な教え方をしているヨーロッパの国名を（イギリス以外に）挙げるのは難しいとつけ加えた。生徒たちは「ばかばかしいほど不可解で細かいあいまいなテーマ」を学習することを要求されるので，イギリスの学校の歴史教育には「本物の歴史の学習と共通したものはほとんどない」，とトゥームは不平を言う。「支離滅裂な断片の寄せ集め」を教えられるため，生徒たちは，歴史の広大な断面，特に，「世界史において広域に影響を及ぼした」にもかかわらず，「わずかな注目」しか払われていない大英帝国の歴史を見逃してしまう，とトゥームは言う。この問題の多くは，歴史の物語を教えることではなく，「資料を判断するような人工的な歴史に関する技術」を身につけることに集中している歴史教師の責任である。さらに，もしそれがそれほど悪いものでないなら，ほとんどの教師には，自分たちが教えているテーマに関する真の知識がほとんどないのだ，とトゥームは言う。この報告書の中で，トゥームは，歴史教育の制度を「徹底的に見直すこと」を要求し，自身が言う，すべての中等学校が知っておくべきイギリス史における36の出来事から構成される代替カリキュラムを導入している。また，生徒たちに「世界史と自国の歴史を年代順に広く」学ばせている，フランス，ドイツ，オーストラリアといった国々の歴史教育をイギリスは規範として見習うべきだ，と彼は忠告

している。

[2] 明言されていないが，トゥームの報告書の行間にあるのは，歴史は重要であり，歴史学習は深い意味で私たちにとって不可欠であり，過去を学ぶのに費やされた時間は決して無駄ではないだろう，という推測である。しかし，歴史をそこまで重大にしているのは，歴史に関する何なのか？そもそもなぜ，私たちは歴史を学ぶ必要があるのか？アメリカの自動車と自動車産業の先駆者ヘンリー・フォードは，わざわざ歴史を学ぶ必要などまったくないと考えていた。「歴史など，多かれ少なかれ，くだらない話だ」と言い，さらに，「歴史は伝統だ。私たちは伝統など欲しくない。私たちは現在を生きたいのであり，わずかでも学ぶ価値のある歴史は，今私たちがつくっている歴史だ」と述べている。しかし，フォードの考えは異端であり，ほとんどの真面目な歴史家は（そして，ありがたいことに，ほとんどの一般の人々も），彼の考え方を，多少なりとも，くだらない話（フォードがつくりたい唯一の歴史は，歴史的に巨大な利益だけだ）として相手にしていない。18世紀イギリスの偉大な哲学者であり，歴史家であったデービッド・ヒュームは，「歴史は私たちをより賢明にしてくれる」という，今や歴史学習の重要性に関する通説となった考えをとても簡潔に述べている。「歴史の利点には3種類あるように思える。すなわち，空想を楽しませてくれること，知識を増やしてくれること，そして徳性を強めてくれることである。」

[3] ウエブサイト上でも，アメリカ歴史協会はヒュームの見解を支持し，「歴史は道徳的な瞑想の場を提供してくれる。過去の人間や状況がつむぐ物語を学ぶことによって，私たちは自分の道徳観を試すこと，つまり，個人が困難な環境の中で直面している現実の複雑さに対して，自分の道徳観に磨きをかけることができるのである。逆境に耐えた人たちからは，励ましを得ることができる。実例から学ぶ歴史教育とは，過去を学ぶことの特徴を述べてくれる1つの表現方法である。—それは本物の英雄，つまり，道徳的な窮地を見事に克服した人たちだけでなく，勇気，勤勉，建設的な抗議といった形で教訓を与えてくれる普通の人たちについて学ぶことだ。」しかし，不朽の書『ローマ帝国衰亡史』の著者，18世紀イギリスの歴史家エドワード・ギボンは，歴史は違った形で教訓的になることができると考えていた。「歴史とは，実際，人間の犯罪，愚行，不幸の記録にすぎない。」言い換えれば，歴史は同様にあらゆる種類の好ましくない手本を私たちに提供してくれる，つまり，それは，もし私たちが繰り返したくなければ，決して忘れてはならない歴史的な過ちや非難されるべき行為の実例である。こうした観点から見れば，20世紀アメリカのジャーナリストでもあり，教授でもあり，また世界平和主義者でもあったノーマン・カズンズが言うように，「歴史は広範囲の早期警戒システムだ」となる。

[4] 歴史を学ぶ理由を知った今，次の疑問は，「どのように歴史を学ぶか？」である。私たちの多くは，学校で歴史を「精を出して学ぶ」が，その学校では，しばしば歴史が最も退屈な科目である，つまり，歴史上の人物，場所，年月日—それらのテストが終わるとほとんど同時に忘れてしまう事実や数字—の丸暗記の退屈な作業だからだ。私たちは歴史の中の「物語」を教わることなどめったにない。そこで，どうすれば歴史を生き生きとしたものにし，私たち自身の生活にもっと関連づけることができるだろうか？ホロコーストの研究を専門とする著名な学者マイケル・ベレンバームによれば，1つの方法は，「本領を発揮した物語の力」を見せてくれる，彼が「語り手の施設」と呼ぶ，優れ

た歴史博物館を訪れることである。現在，悪名高きナチの戦争犯罪人アドルフ・アイヒマンを逮捕したモサド（イスラエルの「中央情報局」）の極秘作戦を記録した展示を行っている，イスラエルのテルアヴィヴ大学にあるユダヤ人博物館を例にとってみよう。アイヒマンは，ヨーロッパの全ユダヤ人の抹殺を求めたアドルフ・ヒトラーの「最終的解決」の立案者の1人だった。第二次世界大戦後，アイヒマンはアルゼンチンへ逃亡し，そこで身元を偽って働きながら生活していたが，ついに1960年モサドによって居所を突き止められ，内密にイスラエルへ飛行機で搬送された。世界中に放送され，20世紀最大のニュース記事の1つとなるイスラエルでの裁判において，アイヒマンは戦争犯罪および人類に対する極悪非道な罪によって有罪となり，絞首刑の宣告を受けた。『タイム』誌によると，博物館の展示は，「あらゆる点で満足のいく内容だ。そこでは正義が実践されたのを見るだけでなく，初期のスパイ技術の平凡な人造物」—AP通信の言葉を借りると，作戦を可能にした「ジェームズ・ボンド」のような道具—をすべて見ることができる。その展示は最もわくわくさせるスパイのスリラー物，つまり，来館者は館内を歩きながら，まるで歴史を学ぶと同時にその時代を生きているかのような感覚になれる物語であり，それは優れた歴史博物館にしかできないことだ，とマイケル・ベレンバームは言う。

READING COMPREHENSION 1:

それぞれの文を正しい選択肢を選んで，完成させなさい。

1. (B)　ロバート・トゥームは，イギリスの歴史教育には徹底的な変革が必要だと言う。
   (A) イギリスの生徒たちは西洋社会をよりよく理解するために，フランス・ドイツ・オーストラリアの歴史に関心を向けるべきだ
   (B) イギリスの歴史教育には徹底的な変革が必要だ
   (C) 彼が勧める36のイギリスの歴史的事件を学べば，世界史を学ぶ必要はないと言う
   ＊ from top to bottom「徹底的に」

2. (C)　トゥームの報告書がはっきりと言わずにほのめかしているのは，私たちは自分たちを知るために歴史について知る必要があるということだ。
   (A) 歴史は不可欠な科目なので小学校で教えられるべきではない
   (B) 今，教えられているような歴史教育は時間の無駄だ
   (C) 私たちは自分たちを知るために，歴史について知る必要がある

3. (B)　歴史が私たちに示してくれる実例に対するアメリカ歴史協会の見解とエドワード・ギボンの見解の違いは，前者は肯定的で後者は否定的である。
   (A) 前者は否定的で，後者は肯定的
   (B) 前者は肯定的で，後者は否定的
   (C) 前者は浅はかで，ギボンの見解は深い

4. (B)　ノーマン・カズンズは，歴史をそれ自身のために学ぶべきものと考えている。
   (A) それ自身のために学ぶべきもの
   (B) 現代の危険を避けるための実用的な入門書
   (C) 人間の最も輝かしい業績の記録
   ＊ for *one's* own sake「それ自身のために」

5. (C)　このエッセイから，イッヒマンは自分が戦争犯罪人として指名手配中であることを知っていたから戦争後アルゼンチンに逃亡した，と推論できる。
   (A) 著者は本人自らイッヒマンの展示を訪れた
   (B) 逮捕といったアイヒマンの裁判は内密に行われた
   (C) イッヒマンは自分が戦争犯罪人として指名手配中であることを知っていたから，戦争後アルゼンチンに逃亡した
   ＊ in person「本人自ら」
   ＊ in secret「内密に」

READING COMPREHENSION 2:

音声で文を聞き，文が合っていればTに，合っていなければFに○をつけなさい。

1. T　　　2. F　　　3. T　　　4. F　　　5. F

Listening sentences

1. Professor Tombs would rather that the U.K. taught a broad chronological sweep of world and national history in its history lessons.

   トゥーム教授は，イギリスの歴史授業で幅広く年代順に世界史とイギリス史を教えてもらいたいと思っている。

2. Henry Ford was just joking when he said that history was bunk and not worth a tinker's damn because he knew that making a profit depended on a broad knowledge of manufacturing history.

   ヘンリー・フォードは，利益を得ることは製造の歴史に関する幅広い知識に頼っていることを知っていたので，歴史はくだらない話でまったく価値がないと言ったのはただの冗談だった。
   ＊ not ~ a tinker's damn「まったく～ない」

3. Most historians think of David Hume's argument in favor of studying history as similar to their own view of the uses of learning about the past.

ほとんどの歴史家は，歴史教育を支持するデビッド・ヒュームの主張は過去について学ぶ効用という自分たちの見解に似ていると考えている。

＊in favor of A「Aを支持して」

4. The American Historical Association believes that we can only learn from the great women and men who have done great things and that the average person has little to teach us or inspire in us.

偉業を成し遂げた偉大な女性と男性からしか学ぶことができず，普通の人から学ぶことや奮起させられることはほとんどない，とアメリカ歴史協会は信じている。

5. *Time* magazine says the Eichmann exhibition places too much emphasis on the accomplishments of Israel's Mossad spy agency and not enough on the actual operation to capture and bring Eichmann to trial.

『タイム』誌によると，アイヒマンの展示は，イスラエルのモサド諜報局の業績に重点が置かれすぎていて，アイヒマンを逮捕したり，裁判にかけたりした実際の作戦に十分な重点が置かれていない。

READING COMPREHENSION 3:

ACTIVE READING の質問に戻って，できるだけ自分の言葉を使い，完全な文で答えなさい。

解答例

1. ロバート・トゥームはイギリスの歴史教師について何と言っているか？

   解答 He says that they focus too much on developing research skills that aren't really useful, and that teachers don't teach the actual story of history. Also, he says they don't really know much about the subject they teach.

   彼らはあまり役に立たない研究技術を伸ばすことに集中しすぎて，歴史の実話を教えていない，と彼は言う。さらに，彼らは自分が教えている科目についてあまりよく知らない，と彼は言う。

2. アメリカ歴史協会は，歴史の利用に関するデビッド・ヒュームの意見に特にどのように賛成しているか？

    解答 They both think that learning history is good for our moral or ethical education, that it teaches us how to be more virtuous and better people.

    > 歴史を学ぶことは道徳教育や倫理教育に適していて，どのようにより徳の高い，いい人になれるかを教えてくれる，と両者とも考えている。

3. このエッセイの著者は，歴史がほとんどの学校で教えられていることに関してどのように言っているか？

    解答 He says that in most schools history is taught by forcing students to memorize dry facts about people, places, and events. It is a rote chore that most students have to "slog through."

    > ほとんどの学校では，人・場所・事件に関する退屈な事実を学生に暗記させることによって歴史が教えられている，と彼は言う。ほとんどの学生が「精を出さなければ」ならないのは丸暗記の退屈な作業である。

Lesson 14　Space
宇宙

> **NOTES**
> HARPS「高精度視線速度系外惑星探査装置」　bio-engineered「生物工学による」
> the Red Planet「赤い惑星」火星の俗称　Lou Gehrig's disease「ルーゲーリッグ病」
> 筋委縮性側索硬化症の別名　droid「人造人間」　Outer Space Treaty「宇宙条約」

● ● ● READY TO READ ● ● ●

下の練習問題はリーディングから最大限のものを得るのに役立ちます。

I. KEY VOCABULARY:

左の単語と右の定義／同義語を結びつけなさい。適切な下線に，a〜jを書き入れなさい。

1. d　定評がある＝高く賞賛されている；評判のよい；賞賛された
2. i　苦痛＝精神的・肉体的健康問題
3. e　〜を編集する＝〜を集めたり，収集する；〜を蓄積する
4. f　〜から成る＝〜で構成されている；〜を含む；〜の一部を成す
5. b　減少＝少量まで減少すること；減少
6. h　命取りになる＝致命的な；死に至る
7. a　仮説上は＝理論上は；ひょっとすると；理論的には
8. j　貴重な＝とても大切な；かけがえのない
9. g　〜を突き止める＝〜を探検する；〜を調査する
10. c　主権＝国家の独立；自治

II. ACTIVE READING:

この課のエッセイを読んで，次の作業をしなさい。

(A) それぞれの番号のついたカッコから正しい語を選び，慣用表現を完成させなさい。

1. went　　go up「上がる」
2. makes　 make use of ~「〜を利用する」
3. hopes　 get our hopes up「希望をかきたてる」
4. may　　 be that as it may「それにもかかわらず」
5. doubt　 without a doubt「疑いもなく」

6. carry　　　carry on ~ 「~を続ける」
7. turned　　turn into ~ 「~に変わる」
8. go　　　　go into ~ 「~を詳細に論じる」

(B) これらの詳しい説明をさがしなさい。見つけたらそれぞれの説明に○をつけなさい。

1. 何倍まで私たちが地球外生物を発見する可能性が上がったか？

    解答　8 to 10 times
    8 倍から 10 倍

2. HARPS の A は何の意味か？

    解答　Accuracy
    精密さ

3. 私たちの銀河に赤色矮星がある見積もりの比率

    解答　80%
    80%

4. ダイアナ・アカーマンが恒星をたとえたもの

    解答　"distant campfires overhead"
    「頭上にある遠いキャンプファイア」

5. アカーマンは惑星をどのように利用すべきだと言っているか？

    解答　as stepping stones to the stars
    恒星への飛び石として

6. ステファン・ホーキンズの専門的知識の領域

    解答　theoretical physics
    理論物理

7. 激しい苦痛の名称

    解答　Lou Gehrig's disease
    リーゲーリック病

8. ホーキンズが言う，どんな天体環境の地球化が火星に行われるか？

    解答　"an analogue of Earth"
    「地球の類似体」

9. 億万長者たちがつくった新会社の名称

解答 Planetary Resources
惑星資源

10. 宇宙条約が施行された年

解答 in 1967
1967 年

(C) これらの質問の答えをさがし，下線を引きなさい。
下の READING COMPREHENSION 3 を見なさい。

● ● ● READING ● ● ●

銀河系探索

[1] 地球以外に私たちの銀河系のどこかに地球外生物がいる確率は，約「8 倍から 10 倍」と天文学的に上昇したことが，カリフォルニア州マウンテン・ビューの地球外知的生命体探査研究所が行った新たな研究によって明らかになった。この研究は，チリのラ・シラ天文台にあるヨーロッパ宇宙機関の HARPS（「高精度視線速度系外惑星探査装置」の略称だが，HARPS に短縮されて当然である！）分光写真機が集めたデータを利用している。HARPS はこの 10 年間，南の空を走査し，太陽系以外で生物が生息可能な惑星を探してきた（今までに，天文学者たちは，30 個以上の候補を見つけ出している）。この新しい研究によれば，太陽よりも小さくて，光が弱く，低温の恒星である赤色矮星の軌道を回る何百億という惑星には，液状水が存在している可能性があり，したがって，仮説上は生命を維持することができるとのことだ。これらの恒星は，太陽よりも寿命が長く，銀河の恒星の最大 80% を構成していると考えられている。しかし，このプロジェクトの参加者の 1 人は，希望を持ちすぎることは少し時期尚早かもしれないと警告している。「（[イギリスの昔話で，クマの家に入り込んで寝入ってしまう女の子]「ゴルディロックス」として知られる）これらの恒星の周囲にある生息可能地帯は極めて小さい。したがって，赤色矮星から適度な距離にあるどんな惑星も，実際は生物の生息に適している可能性は低いだろう」とセス・ショスタックはヤフーニュースに語っている。また，こうした恒星を取り巻く過酷で，おそらく致命的な環境，特に，高レベルの放射能のため，これらの恒星の惑星が生息可能かどうかという懸念が高まる，と彼は言う。それにもかかわらず，ショスタックは，たとえこうした障害があっても，「何百億という驚くほど多くの数の惑星が，生物の生息可能候補地として現れたことで，地球外生物が存在している確率が高まった」と確信し，探査を続けなければならない，と信じている。

[2] 現在最も読まれており，酷評されているアメリカの小説家兼ノンフィクション作家ダイアナ・アカーマンも，『ニューヨークタイムズ』紙の評論の中で（シャスロックの考えに）賛成し，「私たちは細胞にいたるまで目的を持った探検家であり，探求によって繁栄する。これらの恒星は，頭上にある遠いキャンプファイアのようにメラメラと燃えている。私たちは，私たちが住んでいるところと同じようなところが他の世界にあるだろうかと思いをめぐらす。それとも，ダイヤモンドでできているだろうか。NASAが必要な熱狂的な支持者を集め続けて，私たちの太陽系のあちこちにスカウト・ロケットを送り続け，惑星を飛び石にして恒星にたどり着くことを，私は望んでいる。」というのは，「それが私たちの羅針盤が指し示す方向だ」からだ，とアカーマンは結論づけている。

[3] 理論物理学界で間違いなく名前と顔が最も知られているステファン・ホーキンズもまた，宇宙空間の探検を続けなければならないと信じているが，それは単に私たちが「目的を持った探検家」だからではない。彼は，「宇宙の探査は，まさに私たちの生存にとって不可欠である」とし，「人類は危機に瀕している」と警告している。資源の枯渇，人口増加，気候変動，（ことによると生物工学による）世界的流行病，核による大破壊，さらには小惑星や彗星との衝突など—これらを人間にとっての「重大な脅威」と見なしている。「私たち人類が長期間生存できる可能性は，地球の中に目を向けたままでいることではなく，宇宙に拡張していくことだ。」彼は，これを，自身が意思の疎通のために使っているコンピューターを通じて最近行ったラジオインタビューで語った。その意味は，まず月を，そして火星を植民地化することだが，赤い惑星（火星）を「地球の類似体」に変えることのできる技術である「天体環境の地球化」を通じて，月や火星を生息可能な場所にできる，とホーキンズは主張する。今までほぼ全身が麻痺し，ふつうは早死の可能性が高い難病であるルーゲーリッグ病の犠牲者にもかかわらず，ホーキンズは最近70歳の誕生日を祝ったが，この点に，彼が依然楽観主義者でいられる理由があるかもしれない。「私たちは重大な脅威に直面しているが，もし今後2世紀の間，大惨事を避けることができれば，人類は宇宙へと拡張し，無事でいられるはずだ」と彼は述べている。

[4] 世界的に有名な億万長者たちの少人数の集まりが，人類の今後の生存も見込んで，宇宙に対しては他にもっと差し迫った目的があると発表した。鉱物やプラチナ，パラジウムといった貴金属を採掘して，それらを地球に持ち帰るために，小惑星に無人宇宙船を送ることを計画する「惑星資源」という会社を彼らは設立した。これによって世界経済に何兆ドルも加算されるだろう，と彼らは信じている。そうです，彼らはビジネスのことを言っているのだ。この点につき，その会社の共同設立者の1人，エリック・アンダーソンは，ABCニュースに，「将来の世代のために今後も繁栄を続けることが大切だと信じるならば，他の場所から資源を手に入れる必要がある。地球の近くにある小惑星たちが，私たちが探し回ることができる場所よりもはるかにずっと魅力がある」と語っている。ABC放送によると，アンダーソンは，「多数の『人造人間』宇宙船団が」地球の近くを通過する1,500個以上の「小惑星に近づき」，貴重資源を求めて「その表面を探査する」姿を心に描いている。

[5] しかし，この会社が計画していることは合法なのか？そうした貴重資源や潜在的な何兆ドルは，誰のものなのか？宇宙やその中のすべての物は，ここ地球上のすべての人，つまり，すべての国にとって平等な共有財産ではないのか？これらは多くの法律や国際関

係の大学教授たちが問うている疑問である。その答えは，宇宙を探査しているすべての国によって1967年に批准され，「月および他の天体を含めて」，宇宙空間は「いかなる国家主権の主張によっても，いかなる形の利用・占有によっても，またいかなる手段によっても，国家の私用に服従するものではない」ことを立証した宇宙条約にあるようだ。言い換えれば，宇宙空間はみんなの物なのだ。しかし，資源開発はどうなのか？宇宙の莫大な資源は誰のものなのか？不幸なことに，宇宙条約はこの疑問を詳細に論じていない。だが，『ワイアード』誌は，「この疑問は遠すぎる未来のことなので，今は答えを出すことはできない。しかし，その疑問に対する答えが出た日に，私たちはみんなでシャンパンのコルクを抜くことができる。そのとき人類は真に地球外で生活する種となる。私たちは宇宙のほぼ無限の資源を人類の経済的な領域に利用できる第一歩を踏み出したことになるだろう」と述べている。

READING COMPREHENSION 1:
それぞれの文を正しい選択肢を選んで，完成させなさい。

1. (B) 赤色矮星は，太陽より寿命が長く，太陽ほど高温でないと推測できる。
   (A) 太陽より寿命が長い
   (B) 太陽より明るい
   (C) 太陽ほど高温でない

2. (B) 「それが私たちの羅針盤が指し示す方向だ」と言うことによって，ダイアナ・アカーマンは，宇宙空間は私たちの運命であるということを暗示している。
   (A) NASAは私たちの援助を必要としている
   (B) 宇宙空間は私たちの運命である
   (C) 地球がこれからずっと長い間私たちのわが家であることはあり得ない

3. (A) エッセイの著者はステファン・ホーキンズ自身が生き延びていることで彼は人間の生存についても楽天的である。
   (A) ステファン・ホーキンズ自身が生き延びていることで彼は人間の生存についても楽天的である
   (B) ホーキンズは私たちが「目的を持った探検家」であるとは思っていない
   (C) ホーキンズは真の楽天家ではない

4. (C) 新会社「惑星資源」を設立した億万長者たちの重要な目標は主として経済志向である。
   (A) 自然探索
   (B) 活動範囲における環境保護
   (C) 経済志向

5. (C) 『ワイアード』誌は，宇宙空間の資源は誰のものかという質問は，億万長者たちの計画が実現するまで答えを待つべきだと結論づけている。

   (A) あまり重要でない
   (B) 決して最終的な答えが出ないだろう
   (C) 億万長者たちの計画が実現するまで答えを待つべきだ

READING COMPREHENSION 2:

音声で文を聞き，文が合っていればTに，合っていなければFに○をつけなさい。

1. F   2. T   3. F   4. F   5. T

Listening sentences

1. The HARPS spectrograph is a highly sophisticated telescope that scans the southern skies from its base at the Search for Extraterrestrial Intelligence Institute in Mountain View, California.

   HARPS分光写真機は，カリフォルニア州マウンテン・ビューにある地球外知的生命体探査研究所の基地から南の空を走査する高精度望遠鏡である。

2. Seth Shostak, one of the participants in the new research project, believes that the factors that may make the possibility of life on planets orbiting red dwarfs difficult should not keep us from continuing our search.

   新しい研究プロジェクトの参加者の1人であるセス・ショスタックは，赤色矮星の周囲を軌道を描いて回る惑星に生命体がいる可能性を少ないものにしている要因のために探査を続けるのをやめてはいけない，と述べている。

3. Hawking believes that we have less than 100 years to avoid disaster by finding ways to expand into and colonize space.

   宇宙に拡張し，植民地化する方法を見つけ出すことによって大惨事を避ければならないときまで100年も残されていない，とホーキングは信じている。

4. According to the author of the essay, robotic spacecraft and "droids" are already on their way to the nearest asteroids and will soon begin "scouring their surfaces" for precious minerals and metals.

エッセイの著者によると，無人宇宙船や「人造人間」がすでに最も近距離の小惑星に行く途中で，貴重な鉱物や金属を求めて「表面探査」を始めるだろう。

5. *Wired* magazine implies that space could eventually provide us with all the resources we would ever need.

『ワイアード』誌によると，宇宙はそのうちに私たちが必要な資源をずっと供給してくれるかもしれない。

READING COMPREHENSION 3:

ACTIVE READING の質問に戻って，できるだけ自分の言葉を使い，完全な文で答えなさい。

解答例

1. 赤色矮星の近くで生息可能な惑星を発見する上での 2 つの障害は何か？

   解答 One is that the habitable zone around red dwarfs would be very, very small, which means that it would be difficult to find a planet just the right distance from such a star or sun. The other is that the atmosphere or environment around these stars is very harsh, with high levels of radiation.

   1 つは赤色矮星の周りの生息可能地帯が極めて狭く，そのような恒星や太陽から適度な距離の惑星を発見することが難しくなること。もう 1 つはこれらの恒星の周りの大気や環境が，高レベルの放射能のためにとても厳しいこと。

2. ステファン・ホーキンズは人間にとっての「危険物」は何だと考えているか？

   解答 Hawking thinks that Earth is faced with the loss of its resources, a growing population, global warming, disease, nuclear war, or collision with an asteroid or meteor.

   ホーキンズは地球は，資源の減少，人口増加，地球温暖化，病気，核戦争，小惑星や流星との衝突に直面していると考えている。
   * be faced with A「A に直面している」

3. 宇宙条約は「宇宙空間」は本質的には誰のものかということに関して何といっているか？

   解答 The treaty essentially says that outer space is the property of all people of all nations.

   条約は本質的には宇宙空間はすべての人々，すべての国々の財産であるとしている。

Lesson 15　Education
教育

> **NOTES**
> Nineveh「ニネベ」紀元前 8 ～ 7 世紀ごろ首都となり栄えた古代アッシリアの都市で，その遺跡はイラク北部にある　AI「人工知能（=artificial intelligence）」　poverty-stricken「非常に貧乏な」　founding fathers「建国の父」憲法を起草しアメリカを興した男たち　project「研究課題」

● ● ● **READY TO READ** ● ● ●

下の練習問題はリーディングから最大限のものを得るのに役立ちます。

I. KEY VOCABULARY:

左の単語と右の定義／同義語を結びつけなさい。適切な下線に，a～j を書き入れなさい。

1. j　　学問的な＝学校や勉強に関係のある
2. i　　習得＝得ること；手に入れること
3. f　　評価＝判断；査定；テスト
4. h　　証明書＝資格；必要書類
5. g　　人を引きつける＝注目を集める；魅力的な
6. b　　～を徐々に衰えさせる＝～を徐々に減らしたりなくしたりする
7. d　　中間の＝平均の；標準の
8. e　　緊張＝ストレス；重圧；不安
9. c　　～にとって代わる＝～の代わりをする；～を引き継ぐ
10. a　　拷問＝痛み，苦しみを与えること，痛みを引き起こすこと

II. ACTIVE READING:

この課のエッセイを読んで，次の作業をしなさい。

(A) それぞれの番号のついたカッコから正しい語を選び，慣用表現を完成させなさい。

1. goes　　　go back to ~ 「～にさかのぼる」
2. draw　　　draw in ~ 「～を誘い込む」
3. setting　　setting up 「設置」
4. signed　　sign up for ~ 「～に参加の登録をする」
5. back　　　hold back from ~ 「～をためらう」

6. remains　　remain to be seen「まだわからない」
7. take　　take the place of ~「~の代わりをする」
8. stay　　be here to stay「定着している」

(B) これらの詳しい説明をさがしなさい。見つけたらそれぞれの説明に○をつけなさい。

1. 第1パラグラフで「利益を得るため売ること」を意味する単語

    解答　commercializing
    　　　営利化

2. エリ・ノームによると，将来，情報は何をするか

    解答　come to people [not the other way around]
    　　　人にやってくる［人が情報を求めるのではなく］

3. 現在のイラクにあった古代都市

    解答　Nineveh
    　　　ニネベ

4. デビット・ブルックスは少し前までオンラインコースは何だったと言ったか

    解答　interesting experiments
    　　　興味深い実験

5. ハーバード大学とMITのプロジェクトの費用とその名称

    解答　$60 million; "edX"
    　　　6,000万ドル；「edX」

6. スタンフォード大学の教師たちが開発したコースの名称

    解答　"Introduction to AI"
    　　　「Introduction to AI」

7. これまでスタンフォード大学のコースに登録した学生数

    解答　160,000 from 190 countries
    　　　190か国から16万人

    ＊ so far「今まで」

8. 大規模な大学建設プログラムが進行中の国名

　　解答　India
　　　　　インド

　　＊ under way「進行中で」

9. オンライン教育の有効性に関する研究を行った人たち

　　解答　the U.S. Department of Education
　　　　　アメリカ教育省

10. ジョン・アップダイクが学校をたとえたもの

　　解答　jails [equipped with torture]
　　　　　［拷問を備えた］刑務所

(C) これらの質問の答えをさがし，下線を引きなさい。
　　下の READING COMPREHENSION 3 を見なさい。

● ● ● ● READING ● ● ● ●

学ぶ冒険

[1] 1995年にさかのぼって，コロンビア大学，財政経済学の教授エレ・M・ノームは，「高等教育にとっての明るい脚本」からはほど遠いと彼が考える現状について講演（ついでながら，後に『サイエンス』誌に評論として発表され，インターネットでも閲覧できる）を行った。情報を「金儲けの手段とする」のではなく，オンラインで非営利的に情報を共有することは，あらゆる地域の人々にとって前向きな一歩であり，それによって研究が一段と強化されることは明らかだ，とノームは認めている。しかし，また，インターネットや他の通信技術手段が，高等学問機関としての大学の伝統的機能に「とって代わり」，その財政的基盤「を徐々に衰えさせ」，知的探求における大学の役割を低下させる可能性がますます高まるだろう，と彼は思っている。「以前は人が情報を求め，その情報は大学にあった。これからは，人がどこにいようと，情報が人にやってくる。そのとき，大学が果たす役割とは何なのか。大学は将来，科学系の実験室やフットボールチームのような残存する自然科学系機能の単なる寄せ集め以上の存在になれるのか。印刷技術が中世の大聖堂に及ぼした影響，すなわち，情報の転写における大聖堂の中心的役割に終止符を打たせた影響を，電子技術は大学にもたらすのだろうか。私たちは 2,500 年以上前のニネベにまでさかのぼる（図書館という）制度の終わりに達したのだろうか。私た

ちは大学を自己改革できるのか，それとも，最初に事態がもっと悪化するのは必然なのか」とノームは語っている。

[2] 世界中，特にイギリスとアメリカの大学は，ノームの心配事や警告に対して，最初は不安をもって反応したが，その後，ノームの「暗い脚本」を回避するために，この新しい技術を歓迎し適当させなければならない—いや，むしろ，その技術と共存することを学ばなければならないということを理解して反応してきた。そして今，大学はまさにそうした行動を実践している。デビット・ブルックスが最近の『ニューヨークタイムズ』紙のコラムに書いているように，「先導的なエリート大学インターネットを受け入れている。少し前は，オンラインコースは興味深い実験であった。今やオンライン活動はこれらの学校が描く未来図の核心にある。新聞や雑誌の業界に起こったことが高等教育にも起きようとしている。つまり，再び大慌てでウェブに集まっているのである。」

[3] ハーバード大学とMIT（マサチューセッツ工科大学）を例にとってみよう。この両校は—ともに世界の最も優れた大学トップ10にランクされている—6千万ドルの予算をかけ，「edX」と呼ばれる無料のオンラインコースを提供するプロジェクトを協同し，彼らは，これによって，世界中の数百万というネットユーザーの獲得を見込んでいる。両校の学者たちは，特別コースの開発を予定しており，他の主要大学もこのプロジェクトへ参加し，自分たちの目的に合わせてコースを採用・改変するよう誘われてきた（事実，この10年間，MITはすでに開講クラス中2,000以上からの教材を，無料でネット閲覧ができるようにしてきた）。インターネット教育の盛り上がりを示すもう1つの好例が，数人のスタンフォード大学の学者たちによってつくられた「Introduction to AI」という名称の無料オンラインコースの開設である。『ロンドン・オブザーバー』紙に寄稿したジョン・ノートンによると，190以上の国々から16万人の学生が，すでにオンラインコースに登録しており，「その平均年齢は約30歳」とのことだ。ノートンは，また新たな大きなチャンスが生まれようとしているとして，「現在まで大学は，オンラインコースに対して資格を認めてこなかった。しかし，この春からMITは，無料のオンラインコースを受講する学生に対して，ある評価に合格すれば，学業証明書を出す方針である」もちろん，この評価もオンラインで行われる，とノートンは述べている。

[4] これほど素晴らしいことはあるだろうか？今や世界中で何百万という人が，世界で最も優れた教師や偉大な学者にアクセスすることができる。例えば，インドは，最も貧乏な国民の多くが住んでいる国内の隅々にまで高等教育を普及させる計画を発表したばかりであり，ハーバード大学，スタンフォード大学，オックスフォード大学のオンラインコースをカリキュラムに組み入れた何百ものモデル大学をすでに建設中で，今まで大学に通う望みなどまったくなかった何百万という人たちとつながることができるのだ。素晴らしいことだ！しかし，この流行に疑問をいだく人もいて，あらゆる種類の重要な疑問が提起されているため，当然なことである。対面式の学習はどうなるのか？コンピューターの画面上で講義をじっと見るのと，直接自分で講義を聞き，他の学習者たちと経験を共有し，講義内容に関する熱い議論に参加するのとでは，両者に大きな違いはないのか？学問水準は維持されるのか？また，多くの人たちが恐れているように，最少公分母まで落ちてしまうのか？しかし，主な疑問は，オンライン教育には教室での学習と同じように効果的であるかということである。もちろん，まだわからないが，アメリカ教育省が

2009年に行ったある調査では,「オンラインで学習している学生の方が,対面式教育を受けている学生よりも成績がいい」という結論が下されている。伝統的な教室教育と違って,オンライン教育の本当の将来性は,「実践学習を強調し,個々の学生に合わせることできるために,より魅力的で役に立つ」学習体験を提供してくれる点にある,と同調査は述べている。

[5] アメリカの偉大な作家である故ジョン・アップダイクはかつて,「知恵ある建国の父たちは,子どもは親にとって異常な重圧であると考えた。そこで彼らは,教育と呼ばれる拷問を備えた学校という刑務所を用意した」と述べた。もちろん,誇張されてはいるが,あらゆるレベルでしばしば伝統的な教室型教育が決して魅力的ではないということを暗示している点で,アップダイクは正しかった。オンライン教育は,私たちが求めているものになれるのか。デビット・ブルックスは自らのコラムの中で,「e-education」(電子技術を用いて行う教育)は,生の学習の代わりは決してできないとほのめかしている。現在の努力目標は,「オンラインで得られる情報を,対面式の討議,個人指導,ディベート,コーチによる指導,ライティング,研究課題と融合させ」,それをブルックスが多くの要素から成る社会的心理的過程と呼んでいる真の学習に転換する方法を見つけることである。「私の推測では,まったく無防備なウェブ上では,より簡単にひどい大学をつくってしまう可能性もあるが,献身的な学校や学生が以前にも増して向上することも可能だと思う」とブルックスは結論づけている。言い換えれば,オンライン教育は定着しているのだ。だからこそ,オンライン教育を最大限に活用しようではないか。

READING COMPREHENSION 1:

それぞれの文を正しい選択肢を選んで,完成させなさい。

1. (A)　エリ・ノームは,無料のオンラインで情報を手に入れることは研究にとって都合がよいと認めている。
   (A) 研究にとって都合がよい
   (B) 自然科学の場としての大学の終わりを意味する
   (C) 大学が科学系の実験室とフットボールチームを処分しなければならなくなる
   * the end of the line「終わり」

2. (A)　ジョン・ノートンは,最近までほとんどの大学のオンラインコースでは正式な学位を得ることができなかったとほのめかしている。
   (A) 最近までほとんどの大学のオンラインコースでは正式な学位を得ることができなかった
   (B) オンラインコースは人気の限界に達した
   (C) 評価は決してオンライン学習の一部にはならないだろう

3. (C) インドの意欲的な大学建設計画に関して述べられていないのは，そのプロジェクトはどのようにその資金を集めたりお金を払ってもらうかということだ。
   (A) そのプロジェクトが誰をターゲットにしているか
   (B) そのカリキュラムがどんなコースを提供しているか
   (C) そのプロジェクトはどのようにその資金を集めたり，お金を払ってもらうか

4. (B) オンライン教育の基準が理想のものではないということを恐れている人たちもいるようだ。
   (A) 貧乏で恵まれない人たちしかオンラインで勉強できない
   (B) オンライン教育の基準が理想のものではない
   (C) 一流の教師が行うものではないので，オンライン講義は決して魅力的なものではない
   ＊ less than C「決して C ではない」

5. (C) デビット・ブルックスとこのエッセイの著者は一流大学がオンラインブームで向上するだろうと信じていると推論できる。
   (A) 対面教育はエリート大学に制限されている
   (B) オンライン教育はただの一時的な流行にすぎない
   (C) 一流大学がオンラインブームで向上するだろう
   ＊ be limited to A「A に制限されている」

READING COMPREHENSION 2:

音声で文を聞き，文が合っていれば T に，合っていなければ F に○をつけなさい。

1. T   2. T   3. F   4. F   5. T

Listening sentences

1. Universities around the world eventually took what Eli Noam had to say to heart and began "self-reforming" in response to the online information challenge.

   世界中の大学は最後にはエリ・ノームの意見を肝に銘じて，オンライン情報の挑戦に応じて「自己改革」を始めた。
   ＊ take A to heart「A を肝に銘じる」
   ＊ in response to A「A に応じて」

2. Many of the elite, pace-setting schools cannot now imagine their futures without taking online education into account.

   先導的なエリート校の多くは，オンライン教育を考慮に入れずに自分たちの将来を想像できない。
   ＊ take A into account「A を考慮に入れる」

3. MIT and Harvard are keeping their newly developed courses to themselves because competition for enrollment has become very intense, and the two schools do not want students signing up for courses at other universities.

   MITとハーバード大学は，登録者獲得競争が非常に激しくなり，両校とも学生たちに他の大学のコースに登録してもらいたくないために，新しく開発したコースを内緒にしている。

4. It has been found that watching a lecture online is essentially just as personal and face-to-face as sitting in a traditional classroom.

   オンラインで講義を見ることは，本質的には従来の教室に座っているのと同じくらい個人的で対面的であるということがわかった。

5. David Brooks thinks that a combination of online information gathering and on-campus instruction will make for a genuine learning experience.

   オンラインの情報収集とキャンパス内での教育の組み合わせが本物の学習体験に役立つ，とデビッド・ブルックスは考えている。

READING COMPREHENSION 3:

ACTIVE READINGの質問に戻って，できるだけ自分の言葉を使い，完全な文で答えなさい。

解答例

1. エリ・M・ノームが言った，無料のオンラインコースのために大学に起こる3つのことは何か？

    解答 First, universities' traditional functions might be taken over by communications technology tools. Second, universities could run out of money because of loss of tuition. And third, universities might not be as important as centers of the search for new ideas.

    1つ目は，大学の伝統的機能が通信技術手段に引き継がれるかもしれないこと。2つ目は，授業料がなくなるため，大学に資金がなくなってしまうこと。そして3つ目は，新しい考え方を探求する中心地だった大学がそれほど重要でなくなること。

2. デビッド・ブルックスが言った，高等教育以外に，インターネットの始まりによって変わるであろう伝統的な分野は何か？

   解答 He said that newspapers and magazines have also been forced to move some of their business online.

   新聞や雑誌もビジネスの一部をオンラインに移行しなくてはならない，と彼は言う。

3. オンライン教育と伝統的な教室教育を比較した研究の結論は何か？

   解答 It concluded that online learning was even better at educating pupils and students than traditional classroom teaching, mainly because online instruction can be adapted or tailored to fit the needs of individual students.

   研究は，主にオンライン教育は個々の学生のニーズに合わせて適合させ，細部を変えることができるという理由で，オンライン教育は生徒や学生を教育するには伝統的な教室での教育よりさらに優れている，と結論づけた。

MEMO

MEMO

MEMO

MEMO

MEMO